ENGAGING CHILDREN IN

FAMILY THERAPY

THE FAMILY THERAPY AND COUNSELING SERIES

Consulting Editor

Jon Carlson, Psy.D., Ed.D.

Ng

Global Perspectives in Family Therapy: Development, Practice, Trends

Erdman and Caffery

Attachment and Family Systems: Conceptual, Empirical, and Therapeutic Relatedness

Crenshaw

Treating Families and Children in the Child Protective System

Sperry

Assessment of Couples and Families: Contemporary and Cutting-Edge Strategies

Smith & Montilla

Counseling and Family Therapy with Latino Populations: Strategies that Work

Sori

Engaging Children in Family Therapy: Creative Approaches to Integrating Theory and Research in Clinical Practice

ENGAGING CHILDREN IN
FAMILY THERAPY

Creative Approaches to Integrating Theory and Research in Clinical Practice

EDITED BY CATHERINE FORD SORI

Routledge
Taylor & Francis Group
New York London

Routledge is an imprint of the
Taylor & Francis Group, an informa business

Routledge
Taylor & Francis Group
711 Third Avenue,
New York, NY 10017

Routledge
Taylor & Francis Group
2 Park Square,
Milton Park, Abingdon,
Oxfordshire OX14 4RN

First issued in paperback 2014

Routledge is an imprint of the Taylor and Francis Group, an informa business

ISBN 978-0-415-94981-1 (hbk)
ISBN 978-1-138-87279-0 (pbk)

Library of Congress Cataloging-in-Publication Data

Engaging children in family therapy : creative approaches to integrating theory and research in clinical practice / edited by Catherine Ford Sori.
p. cm. -- (The family therapy and counseling series)
Includes bibliographical references and index.
ISBN 978-0-415-94981-1 (hb : alk. paper)
1. Family psychotherapy. 2. Family psychotherapy--Practice. I. Sori, Catherine Ford. II. Series.

RC488.5.E64 2006
616.89'156--dc22 2005037158

Visit the Taylor & Francis Web site at
http://www.taylorandfrancis.com

and the Routledge Web site at
http://www.routledgementalhealth.com

When Moses' hands grew tired, they took a stone and put it under him and he sat on it. Aaron and Hur held his hands up—one on one side, one on the other—so that his hands remained steady til sunset.

—Exodus 17:12 (New International Version)

This book is dedicated to my father, Marvin L. Ford (my Aaron), and my husband, H. John Sori (my Hur), whose steadfast support made this book possible.

Also to my loving mother, Elnora Ford.

To our children, Jessica, Heather, Paul, Ann, Al, Marlene, and Marisa.

And to all our beautiful grandchildren with whom I love to play: Cameron, Alexis, Lyric, Lauryn, Marin, Diandra, Brendan, Elizabeth, Ethan, Annie, Johnny, Alfredo, Jr., Rachel, Jonathan, Victoria, Cassandra, Rick, Alec, and "Baby Paul" who is on the way!

Contents

The Editor

Catherine Ford Sori, Ph.D., is an associate professor of marriage and family counseling at Governors State University in University Park, Illinois, and associate faculty at the Chicago Center for Family Health. She has published numerous journal articles and book chapters, and frequently presents on children, families, illness, bereavement, and family play therapy. Her books include *The Therapist's Notebook for Children and Adolescents* (with Lorna L. Hecker, Ph.D.), *The Therapist's Notebook for Integrating Spirituality in Counseling*, Vols. I and II (with Karen Helmeke, Ph.D.), and *The Therapist's Notebook II* (with Lorna L. Hecker, Ph.D.).

Contributors

Nancee M. Biank, MSW, LCSW, is the director of Children and Family Services at Wellness House, Hinsdale, Illinois, a nonprofit organization that offers psychosocial support to cancer patients and their families, where she developed the groundbreaking Family Matters Program for children who have a parent with cancer. She has written numerous articles on children and illness, death, and divorce. Ms. Biank is also in private practice and is cofounder of Partners in Transition in Hinsdale, Illinois. She trained at the Institute for Psychoanalysis, Child and Adolescent Therapy Program, University of Illinois, Jane Adams College of Social Work in Chicago; and also with Judith Wallerstein. She lives with her husband, Vincent, in Hinsdale and enjoys spending time with her children and grandchildren.

Shannon Dermer, Ph.D., received her doctorate in 1998 from Kansas State University and her M.S. in 1994 in psychology. She is currently an assistant professor at Governors State University in the Marriage and Family Counseling Program (CACREP accredited) in the Division of Psychology and Counseling. Previously Dr. Dermer was program director of the master's and doctoral marriage and family counseling/therapy programs at the University of Akron. She has presented on solution-focused therapy, issues related to beginning therapists and supervision, and technology and training/therapy. Her publications include a feminist critique of solution-focused therapy, several book chapters related to children, issues related to sexual minorities, and technology and therapy.

Craig A. Everett, Ph.D., is codirector of the Arizona Institute for Family Therapy and in private practice in Tucson, Arizona. He is a past president of the American Association for Marriage and Family Therapy and a former faculty member and director of AAMFT-accredited graduate programs in marriage and family therapy at Florida State University and Auburn University. He has written numerous books and articles in the family therapy and divorce fields, and is editor of the *Journal of Divorce and Remarriage*.

Sandra Volgy Everett, Ph.D., is codirector of the Arizona Institute for Family Therapy and in private practice in Tucson, Arizona. She was chief psychologist at the Tucson Child Guidance Clinic and director of Child Advocacy Services for the Pima County Conciliation Court. She was also on the clinical faculty of the AAMFT-accredited doctoral program in marriage and family therapy at Florida State University.

Eliana Gil, Ph.D., has over 30 years' experience working in the field of child abuse prevention and treatment. She is a family therapist as well as a registered play therapy supervisor and a registered art therapist. Dr. Gil has a private practice at the Multicultural Clinical Center in Springfield, Virginia, and is developing a program, Children's Corner, to provide mental health services to young children. She is also director of Starbright Training Institute for Child and Family Play Therapy. Dr. Gil is the author of *Play in Family Therapy; The Healing Power of Play; Treating Abused Adolescents;* and coauthor of *Cultural Issues in Play Therapy.*

Lorna L. Hecker, Ph.D., is a professor of marriage and family therapy at Purdue University Calumet, Hammond, Indiana. She is the director of the Couple and Family Therapy Center, and the author (with Sharon Deacon) of *The Therapist's Notebook: Homework, Handouts, and Activities for Use in Psychotherapy*, as well as the coauthor (with Catherine Ford Sori) of *The Therapist's Notebook for Children and Adolescents: Homework, Handouts, and Activities for Use in Psychotherapy* and *The Therapist's Notebook II*. In addition, she edited (with Joseph Wetchler) an *Introduction to Marriage and Family Therapy*.

Salvador Minuchin, M.D., is a founding father of family therapy and the architect of one of the foremost theories in the field—structural family therapy. His classic book, *Families and Family Therapy* (1974), is fundamental in family therapy training. Another book that is rapidly becoming a classic, *Family Healing* (coauthored with Michael Nichols, 1993), has been hailed for its moving depictions of actual family sessions. Dr. Minuchin, a native of Argentina, studied with Nathan Ackerman and was the director of the Philadelphia Child Guidance Clinic, which he developed into a world-renowned center for family therapy training. Throughout his career, Minuchin has continued to be an advocate for children and families of the poor, and pioneered the work at the Minuchin Center for the Family on working with drug-abusing families and the multiple systems in which they are involved. Although officially "retired," Minuchin remains on the board of the Minuchin Center for the Family in

New York, travels with his wife, Patricia, who is an accomplished author and developmental psychologist, and speaks at numerous national and international conferences.

Don Olund, M.A., is a professional counselor specializing in marriage and family counseling. He is interested in helping families adjust to life cycle changes, particularly those involved in adult and adolescent transitions. Mr. Olund is a trained instructor in the Christian Prevention and Relationship Enhancement Program (CPREP), and also specializes in integrating spirituality and counseling. He is an ordained minister, with 20 years of experience in full-time ministry in the Chicago area, serving in various ministerial capacities including youth, associate, and senior pastor. His ministry includes extensive work with youth on a local and statewide level. Mr. Olund holds a master's degree in marriage and family counseling from Governors State University and is in practice at LifeWork Corporation, a Christian counseling center in Downers Grove, Illinois.

Lee Shilts, Ph.D., is a professor at Nova Southeastern University in the marriage and family therapy program. Dr. Shilts is a prominent practitioner in the field of brief solution-focused therapy, and has worked closely with Steve de Shazer and Insoo Kim Berg, the cofounders of this therapeutic specialty. Currently, he is engaged in a solution-focused school project involving research with Ms. Berg. His teaching interests include clinical practice, solution-focused theory and therapy, and the use of solution-focused therapy in school settings. Dr. Shilts has published often with students, primarily on the application of solution-focused therapy and training.

Rise VanFleet, Ph.D., is the founder and president of the Family Enhancement & Play Therapy Center, Inc., in Boiling Springs, Pennsylvania, an organization specializing in the training and supervision of child, family, and play therapy professionals as well as the provision of mental health services for children and families. A licensed psychologist, Dr. VanFleet is also a certified filial therapy therapist, supervisor, and instructor, and a registered play therapist–supervisor. She brings over 30 years of clinical, supervisory, and leadership experience to her workshops. Dr. VanFleet is the author of *Filial Therapy: Strengthening Parent-Child Relationships Through Play, A Parent's Handbook of Filial Play Therapy,* coeditor of *The Casebook of Filial Therapy,* and coauthor of *Play Therapy for Traumatic Events.*

Gene Wesolowski, A.M., LCSW, is the director of Oak Lawn Family Service, Oak Lawn, Illinois, and is a longtime adjunct professor in the Department of Psychology and Counseling at Governors State University, where he teaches courses in assessment, family counseling techniques, and live supervision. He specializes in both a family systems and psychoanalytic approach to working with children and families.

Series Editor's Foreword

What's done to children, they will do to society.

—Karl Menninger

Of all the challenges that cause partners to seek professional help, one of the most common is the battle over how to handle their offspring. If partners have dissimilar values or come from different backgrounds, disputes may arise from genuine concern over what is really best for the child. Although it would be ideal, it is unrealistic to expect two people always to agree on how to raise their children. When partners disagree over childrearing or other problems, children often get involved. Some children are impacted by being confused, while others are actually "triangulated" in the problem and begin to have problems that take the focus off the partner's problems.

These problems historically have been treated by directly working with the child via therapy or medication. Research consistently demonstrates that the treatment of choice for children and teens with many problems is family therapy. Even though this seems to be a fact, there are very few books that have been written on how to work with children in this context. Children seem to be willing to be involved with looking at problems within the family setting. This context provides a familiar setting for looking at difficult issues.

Family therapy with children makes it possible to work efficiently, effectively, and with a lower chance for relapse. Therapy that involves the entire system makes it possible for all family members to develop satisfying roles. When working with children, talk therapy is augmented by the use of play. Therapists also need to understand how to use play effectively in the family setting. This requires knowledge of the developmental issues of both children and families and to possess a theoretical orientation that allows for a clear understanding of children within the family context. This requires an understanding of how the family system works, as well as how to assess and treat children in this context.

Catherine Sori and her associates explore these issues and offer practical treatment guidelines related to working with children in a family context. The authors provide a comprehensive text that will benefit all who work with children or families. The incredible interviews with Salvador Minuchin, Eliana Gill, Rise VanFleet, and Lee Shilts add great substance to the text. The specialty chapters show the reader how to work with parents; ethical and legal considerations; divorce and stepfamily issues; children with ADHD; and serious illness and death of a family member.

The old African saying that "it takes a village to raise a child" seems to address the importance of working with the child in the village (i.e., family) context.

Jon Carlson, Psy.D., Ed.D.
Lake Geneva, Wisconsin

Preface

A study conducted a few years ago found that children overwhelmingly wanted to be involved in family counseling, even when they were not the focus of the problem (Stith, Rosen, McCollum, Coleman, & Herman, 1996). Yet other research indicated that despite their wishes, to a large degree children are being excluded from family sessions (Korner & Brown, 1990; Johnson & Thomas, 1999). Many clinicians who exclude children admitted that they are not comfortable with children, and that their training was not sufficient to prepare them to counsel children in a family context. Especially lacking was training in using play with children and families. Another study found that even when children were physically present in the counseling room, they were not actively engaged in the counseling process. The therapists were uncertain of just what role children play in family therapy (Cederborg, 1997).

How can the field of family therapy neglect the needs of the youngest members of families? How can we do family therapy without addressing the needs of individual family members, and how can we counsel individuals without addressing the needs of the family? What knowledge and skills do counselors need to know to be effective in child-focused family treatment? When should children be included, and under what circumstances should they be excluded from family sessions? How might play techniques be integrated in family counseling? Although little has been written on these issues, one recent study explored these ideas, and identified specific content areas and training methods to increase clinicians' comfort and skills in working with children and adult family members (Sori & Sprenkle, 2004).

The goal of this book is to interpolate the research findings of Sori and Sprenkle (2004) into both theory and clinical practice. Part I of this monograph begins in chapter 1 with a summary by Catherine Sori of the research by Sori and Sprenkle (2004) that addresses the above questions, while the topics covered in the remaining chapters of this book are based on some of the major recommendations of the panel of experts in this study. One of the unique features of this volume are the interviews with the experts, which provide readers with rare insight into the minds of some of the most creative clinicians of our time, all of whom specialize in different approaches to working playfully with children and families. Chapter 2 is the transcript of an interview with Salvador Minuchin, in which he reflects on the findings reported in chapter 1, and offers insight into the neglected topic of child-focused family training. As one of the founders in the field of family therapy and a leading champion of children, Minuchin discusses the importance of considering training videos as literature, articulates the differences between playfulness and play therapy, and differentiates between inductive and deductive training methods. In chapter 3, Shannon Dermer, Don Olund, and Catherine Sori (equal authorship) propose family play therapy as a meta-model that can be integrated with the major schools of both modern and postmodern family therapy, such as experiential, structural, solution-focused, and narrative approaches. They describe several creative and playful techniques that fit the therapeutic goals of these models, each of which is demonstrated with a case example.

Part II highlights three approaches to use in counseling children and families that are woven throughout the book: family play therapy, filial therapy, and solution-focused family therapy. These three models come alive through interviews with innovative experts in these approaches, and provide a rare window into the creative process of the art of applying these models in counseling children and families. Included are poignant case examples to illustrate the artistry of these gifted clinicians. Chapter 4 is an interview with Eliana Gil, the leading pioneer in the field of family play therapy. Gil explains the numerous benefits of integrating play in family therapy for children and adults, as well as clinicians. She introduces readers to several of her creative techniques, and explores topics such as intuition, using countertransference, and the symbolic meaning in play. An interview with Rise VanFleet on filial therapy is the focus of chapter 5. VanFleet, one of the foremost proponents of this method, describes the effectiveness of filial therapy, the steps used to train parents to be the change agents for their children using nondirective play, and emphasizes how this approach can be adapted across cultures. The final interview, in chapter 6, is with Lee Shilts, who describes his playful approach to treating children both in a school setting and in family therapy, by integrating strength-based, postmodern theories. Shilts also introduces readers to a research and training project he has developed with Insoo Kim Berg, which involves using the WOWW approach in a classroom setting. All of the chapters in this section include moving case studies that bring these diverse approaches to life.

Part III of this volume addresses specific topics related to child-focused counseling. In chapter 7, Catherine Sori, Shannon Dermer, and Gene

Wesolowski offer an in-depth examination of theoretical and practical issues related to how and when to involve children in family therapy, as well as when and how to engage parents in children's counseling. This chapter offers guidelines for making decisions on whom to see when, and recommends a multimodal approach which is illustrated through case examples. The authors also provide suggestions on talking to children, setting up a room that is child-friendly, selecting toys that are most useful for counseling children and parents, and for conducting the first and subsequent sessions. Chapter 8 fills a major gap in the literature on specific ethical topics related to counseling children and families. This chapter by Catherine Sori and Lorna Hecker has both breadth and depth in addressing critical ethical and legal issues, including privacy, privilege, confidentiality, reporting issues, parents' rights, responding to subpoenas, the use of touch, and special cultural considerations in child-inclusive family treatment.

The final section of this book, Part IV, examines four specific topics that affect children and families but have been largely neglected in the family therapy literature. These chapters address problems children and families face from changes in family configuration, from the biological disorder of ADHD, and from the untimely impact of illness and death. In chapter 9, Lorna Hecker and Catherine Sori present research on both divorced families and stepfamilies, and offer guidelines for assessing children, parents, and overall family functioning. Most clinicians lack specialized training in how to treat the unique issues often seen in these families. The authors describe several family and playful interventions designed to help both young and mature clients adjust to family reconfigurations, strengthen individual and family functioning, and promote healthy family relationships. Chapter 10 addresses the important topic of treating ADHD in a family context. Many clinicians become quickly overwhelmed by hyperactive children and the frustrations expressed by their parents, and are unsure how to proceed. This chapter, by specialists Craig Everett and Sandra Everett, summarizes diagnostic criteria and the numerous aspects of assessing these children and families, and provides an overview of their acclaimed systemic model.

While children with ADHD are often characterized as "externalizing," children whose families experience illness or death often "internalize." In chapter 11, Catherine Sori and Nancee Biank make visible many of the struggles that are often overlooked in families who are experiencing a serious illness in a child, teen, or parent. They highlight the importance of assessing the adaptability, cohesion, structure, and communication in families at various stages of an illness, from diagnosis to the terminal phase. Also discussed is the impact of an illness on individual children, parents, couples, grandparents, and overall family functioning at various stages of the life cycle. Sori and Biank offer several creative interventions for opening communication and promoting adaptability and cohesion throughout an illness experience. The final chapter (chapter 12) addresses the topic of how to promote coping in children when there has been a death in the family. Nancee Biank and Catherine Sori explain important factors in assessing children, how death impacts children and surviving siblings, and the importance of addressing spiritual issues. The authors provide concrete suggestions designed to help keep children on track developmentally, including the therapeutic use of play. The case vignettes in chapters 11 and 12 illustrate how children often internalize their reactions to illness and death, and the clinical interventions in these final chapters are designed to also be useful with children who have internalizing disorders, such as anxiety or depression.

Two themes that are woven throughout the book include integrating play in family therapy, and using a multimodal approach in counseling children and families. The techniques and playful therapeutic approaches described in these chapters can be applied to many other presenting problems in addition to those included in this book. Most chapters contain moving case vignettes of internalizing and/or externalizing problems, and they illustrate how the concepts and ideas presented translate into the real world of counseling hurting children and parents. (Note: Names and identifying information in the case examples have been changed to protect clients' confidentiality.) Several chapters also address specific considerations and suggestions in treating adolescents, as well as cultural issues.

One overarching goal of this book is to alert clinicians and educators to the importance of child-focused training in order to better prepare family therapists to work with children and families. Professionals are encouraged to use this book as a text and as a reference, with the hope that they will apply the knowledge and skills described in this volume to the treatment of these and other child-presenting problems, as well as to the many issues of parents that affect children.

REFERENCES

Cederborg, A. D. (1997). Young children's participation in family therapy talk. *American Journal of Family Therapy, 25*(1), 28–38.

Johnson, L., & Thomas, V. (1999). Influences on the inclusion of children in family Therapy. *Journal of Marital and Family Therapy, 25*(1), 117–123.

Korner, S., & Brown, G. (1990). Exclusion of children from family psychotherapy: Family therapists' beliefs and practices. *Journal of Family Psychology, 3*(4), 420–430.

Sori, C. F., & Sprenkle, D. H. (2004). Training family therapists to work with children and families: A modified Delphi study. *Journal of Marital and Family Therapy, 30*(4), 479–495.

Stith, S. M., Rosen, K. H., McCollum, E. E., Coleman, J. U., & Herman, S. A. (1996). The voices of children: Preadolescent children's experiences in family therapy. *Journal of Marital and Family Therapy, 22*(1), 69–86.

Acknowledgments

I wish to thank the many people who offered practical support and encouragement during this process. First, my father, Marvin Ford, who tirelessly volunteered to read and reread chapters in their various stages of development. Next, thanks to my mother, Elnora, for her love and patience, and to Albert; and to my daughters, Jessica and Heather, for lending a hand with research and proofreading (and cleaning!). The prayers and encouragement of my friend, Kathleen Hazlett, sustained me and are so greatly appreciated. Thanks also to Kathleen and to Mona Douglas for transcribing interviews, and to Lorna Hecker, Nancy Nickell, Anna Bower, Julia Yang, Pat Robey, Byron Waller, Lori McKinney, Rachel Berg, Shannon Dermer, and Judy Stiff for their humor, support, suggestions, collegiality, playfulness, and friendship.

I would especially like to acknowledge those who offered so freely of their time and expertise by contributing to this volume: Salvador Minuchin (and his wife, Patricia), Eliana Gil, Rise VanFleet, Lee Shilts, Lorna Hecker, Nancee Biank, Craig Everett and Sandra Everett, Shannon Dermer, Don Olund and Gene Wesolowski. It has been an honor to collaborate with all of you! And a huge thanks to Jon Carlson for his support for this project.

And for when I became too absorbed in this project, I thank Cameron, Alexis, and Lyric, who were often here to remind me to play, and read, and sing, and dance!

Above all, thanks from the bottom of my heart to my husband, John, who is and always will be the love of my life.

PART I

Issues Related to Working with Children

CHAPTER 1

On Counseling Children and Families

Recommendations from the Experts

CATHERINE FORD SORI, PH.D.

The field of family therapy was predicated on the concept of the family as an interdependent system made up of subsystems (Bateson, 1971; Bowen, 1978; Haley, 1976; Minuchin, 1974). Children are seen as vital family members, and many of the early founders in the field expressed strong opinions regarding the importance of including children in therapy (e.g., Ackerman, 1970; Keith & Whitaker, 1981; Minuchin, 1974; Montalvo & Haley, 1973; Satir, 1964). Yet in the field that purports to treat whole families, there is a paucity of research (Estrada & Pinsof, 1995; Sori & Sprenkle, 2004) and literature (Combrinck-Graham, 1991; Lund, Zimmerman, & Haddock, 2002) about treating children in the context of the family. Over the years, surprisingly little has been published on child-related training methods (S. Minuchin, personal communication, April 17, 2000). Although Lund et al. (2002) recently published a review of the literature on children in family therapy, the recent study by Sori (2000; Sori & Sprenkle, 2004) is the first to empirically identify specific issues related to child-inclusive family counseling. This chapter reports some of the major findings of this study and their application to practicing family therapists and training programs.

PERSPECTIVES OF CHILDREN IN FAMILY THERAPY

Children can offer clinicians a wealth of information about the relationships, structure, and communication among family members, and their participation was seen by many of the founders in the field as vital to the process of family therapy (Johnson, 1995). Ackerman (1970) commented on the central importance of children in family therapy when he stated: "Without engaging the children in a meaningful interchange across the generations, there can be no family therapy. Yet ... difficulties in mobilizing the participation of children are a common experience" (p. 403). Keith and Whitaker (1981) wrote that families need children to participate in therapy to stay alive. From the inception of his career, Salvador Minuchin has been committed to helping children within the context of both the family and larger systems. Montalvo and Haley (1973) point out the danger in "over-focusing on the couple and losing the child in the process" (p. 234). If the therapist does not engage the child who is the "regulator of speed of therapy, as moderator of the pace of change ... the child fails to change" (p. 234).

Wachtel (1991) recognizes that even when children are removed from the role of symptom-bearer, they still may be troubled. Too often, children who internalize try to falsely assure their parents that they are fine, when they may really be worried, anxious, or depressed. Young children often have a difficult time expressing their thoughts and feelings due to the limitations of their language development.

More recently, postmodernists have written about using narrative ideas (e.g., Freeman, Epston, & Lobovits, 1997; White, 1984) and applying solution-focus theory (e.g., Berg & Steiner, 2003; Selekman, 1997; see Sori, 2006c) in the treatment of children. These strength-based approaches offer many creative ideas for playfully engaging children in child-focused family treatment.

Other authors have suggested ideas on how to integrate play interventions within the context of family sessions, especially for child-related issues (e.g., Busby & Lufkin, 1992; Chasin & White, 1989; Gil, 1994; Gil & Sobol, 2000; Sori, 1995, 1998; Sori & Hecker, 2003; Zilbach, 1986). Without play it may be difficult to engage young children in family counseling. Play methods are a good "fit" with family counseling, in part because they offer developmentally appropriate methods to engage both children and adult family members. However, there is no consensus in the field as to when or how to integrate play in family counseling.

RECENT RESEARCH ON EXCLUDING CHILDREN

Recent studies have reported the alarming finding that, to a large degree, children are often excluded from family treatment, even when the presenting problems are child-related. Korner and Brown (1990) found that an amazing 40% of family therapists in their study *never* included children in therapy, while 31% invited children to be present without engaging them in the therapeutic process. In fact, 86.4% of respondents reported that they included children less than 25% of the time. This study found that those *therapists who excluded children were the least comfortable with children.*

A follow-up study by Johnson (1995) found that approximately one-half of the respondents reported that they made decisions to exclude children based on their personal comfort level with children; those who were more comfortable included children more often. Korner and Brown (1990) discussed that the tendency to exclude children was related to the amount of child-focused coursework, the quality of supervision, and how adequate therapists perceived their child-related training. Unfortunately, many respondents in these studies claimed that their training was inadequate to prepare them to work successfully with children and families (Johnson & Thomas, 1999; Korner & Brown, 1990). In fact, therapists' self-perceived competence predicted their inclusion practices (Johnson & Thomas, 1999). Johnson (1995) points out the lack of theoretical and practical guidelines in the field on how to make inclusion decisions. Although Lund, Zimmerman, and Haddock (2002) recently offered suggestions from a review of the literature on when to exclude children, no study before the one by Sori (2000; Sori & Sprenkle, 2004) empirically examined this issue, or identified specific "theories, content areas, readings, skills, and techniques" (Sori & Sprenkle, 2004, p. 479) necessary to effectively train therapists to work successfully with children.

One ethnographic study that explored children's views of family sessions found that although often excluded, children overwhelmingly wanted to participate in family sessions, even when they were not the focus of treatment (Stith, Rosen, McCollum, Coleman, & Herman, 1996). Children wished to be physically present in the counseling room, and found being left in the waiting room both boring and sometimes worrisome. The children in this study wanted to know more about what was happening in their family, to participate in the counseling process, and to be a part of the solution to the family's problems. Stith et al. concluded:

> … children need ways to participate in therapy that are different from the ways adults participate … Doing activities, not just talking, made many of the children we interviewed feel included. Especially for younger children, play more than words may be their medium of expression and interaction. (1996, p. 78)

So what exactly does occur in sessions when children *are* present? A study by Cederborg (1997) that analyzed videotapes of sessions indicated that just having children physically present in the counseling room does not mean that they are actively engaged in the therapy process. The Cederborg study found children spoke only 3.5% of the total words in sessions (most of which were attempts to gain parents' attention) and were not granted "full membership status" in family sessions. Cederborg found that young children appeared to have the status of nonpersons because they were "not talked to but rather talked about" (p. 37). Therapists in this study admitted that they were unclear of the exact role of children in family sessions. The individual needs of children may be lost if clinicians lack the special skills needed to connect with children and provide them with an opportunity to participate and to express their thoughts and feelings.

Lee Combrinck-Graham (1991) has raised the question of how there can *be* family therapy without including children. She warns that the field that is known for treating multigenerational families must exercise care to hear the voices of children and ensure that adult needs are not privileged over the needs of young family members.

This raises the question of just what types of therapist skills and attributes are essential for engaging young children, and counseling them and their parents. While there are no clear guidelines in the field, Hines (1996) points out that what first must be determined is exactly what knowledge areas and skills are necessary to produce competent clinicians. The Delphi study by Sori (2000), reported in Sori and Sprenkle (2004), examined these issues and is discussed in the remainder of this chapter.

OVERVIEW OF THE DELPHI STUDY ON TRAINING THERAPISTS TO TREAT CHILDREN AND FAMILIES

This study utilized a panel of 22 experts in treating children and families in order to gather a consensus of opinions in response to research questions related to child-focused training and treatment. Experts selected for this panel were widely published on this topic and had a great deal of experience in training clinicians to work with children in a family context. Panelists were invited from a wide range of theoretical backgrounds, as the goal of the Delphi study was to have panelists with diverse backgrounds reach consensus on items related to the topic under investigation. The Delphi methodology (see Stone Fish & Busby, 1996) utilized a series of questionnaires that allowed panelists to dialogue about issues while maintaining anonymity. Thus, panelists were freed to express their ideas with no pressure or fear of repercussion from other panelists.

The Delphi study consisted of four rounds of data collection: two questionnaires with a series of panelist interviews following each questionnaire.

Both quantitative and qualitative methods were used to collect and analyze the data. The first questionnaire asked panelists to respond to six opened-ended questions that addressed these topics: (1) what are the primary issues where children should *not* be included in family sessions; (2) what topics are important to cover in a child-focused graduate course in family therapy; (3) what readings should be included in this course; (4) which skills are most essential for therapists to successfully counsel children; (5) how should therapists be trained in ways that promote comfort and increase their skills in counseling children and their families; (6) specifically, what are the most helpful play interventions that can be utilized with various family therapy approaches (see Sori & Sprenkle, 2004).

Panelists' responses from these six questions in the first questionnaire generated a large amount of data, which was categorized, edited for redundancy and clarity, and used to construct the second questionnaire. Several panelists were interviewed to better understand some of their responses. Clarifying comments from these interviews were included in the second questionnaire, which asked panelists to use a 7-point Likert scale to rate how strongly they agreed or disagreed with each of the 277 items that were generated from the first questionnaire.

Responses to the second questionnaire were analyzed to find the medians and interquartile ranges. Items on which panelists reached consensus were those with high medians of at least 6.0 (items that were very highly rated) and low interquartile ranges (panelists reached a high degree of consensus). The final round of this study was another series of telephone interviews with select panelists to enrich the data, explore discrepancies in the findings, and allow them to offer possible interpretations of the results (Sori & Sprenkle, 2004). Thus, this study utilized both quantitative and qualitative analyses of the data.

Of the 277 items in the second questionnaire, 81 (29.24%) met the standards to be included in the final profile of this study. (Note: All of the original items generated in the first round of this study that were included in the Delphi Questionnaire II may be viewed at http://hometown.aol.com/katesori/delphi.)

FINDINGS

The results of this important study are summarized here. Readers are referred to Sori and Sprenkle (2004) for a more detailed discussion, including tables that report statistical findings.

Decision to Exclude Children

The first goal of the study was to identify specific times when children should *not* participate in family sessions. A strong finding was that these expert panelists believe that, in general, children should be included in family therapy sessions. They concurred with previous studies (e.g., Johnson & Thomas, 1999; Korner & Brown, 1990) that therapists often make indiscriminate decisions to exclude children in order to avoid them. Panelists recommended using a multimodal approach that combines family, couples, and individual child/adult sessions, depending on the needs of family members. They also concurred that children are central to the counseling process, that it is important to understand children's contributions to the family, and to recognize the reciprocal impact of the child on the family, and vice versa. These items underscore that children are vital family members whose participation is essential to understand overall family functioning. These are important findings, especially in light of Cederborg's (1997) study in which the clinicians were not exactly sure of the role children play in family counseling.

Panelists also emphasized that children are affected by adult problems and should be included at some point to determine how they are affected, and how well they are coping. According to these experts, there are only a few times when children should not be included in family sessions. Children should only be excluded when two topics are being discussed: individual or adult sexual issues (including affairs), or when parents are making decisions about how to share sensitive information with children regarding topics such as terminal illness, adoption, or terminating parental rights. However, once parents have decided what and how to tell children, the panel recommends that children should be included in sessions (see Sori & Sprenkle, 2004, p. 483).

Important Topics and Knowledge Needed

According to Lawrence and Kurpius (2000), psychotherapists cannot simply apply an understanding of adult issues to the treatment of children's problems. A second goal of the study was to identify specific topics and areas of knowledge that are essential for family counselors who work with children. These topics are discussed by category here.

Developmental issues. In response to the question about what content areas should be included in child-focused coursework, panelists in this Delphi study first highlighted developmental issues. This included not just stages of cognitive, emotional, and language development but also knowledge of children's interests and capacities at different stages, as well as issues that families face. They also emphasized the importance of understanding the intersection of adult and child development, and the needs of family members at various stages of the life cycle, as well as developmental shifts that can be challenging.

Theoretical knowledge. Panelists highlighted the importance of understanding that children have a central place in therapy. This supports the systemic position that there is a reciprocal influence among children and parents. This again is important in light of Cederborg's (1997) study where clinicians were uncertain of children's role in family sessions. Panelists also emphasized the importance of structural and boundary issues, including hierarchy and the rules and consequences. This suggests that structural family therapy (Minuchin, 1974) is an important theory to be taught in graduate level courses on treating children in the context of the family.

Therapists' knowledge. A key finding in this study was that graduate courses on treating children and families need to teach clinicians to engage children and families in practical ways, such as using art, games, or other creative techniques. Counselors need to be knowledgeable about ethical issues (such as reporting abuse and confidentiality). They need to appreciate and respect children, how they express themselves and make sense of things, and how they contribute to the family. It is important to know what age-appropriate and normal (as well as abnormal) roles are for children in families, and appropriate ways for parents and children to communicate. Clinicians must understand how parental and sibling relationships impact children. Coursework needs to teach clinicians to conduct family sessions that are intelligible and helpful to all family members.

Play. Play should be an important component in child-focused graduate coursework, according to panelists in this study, in two broad areas. First is to understand the role of play in child development and therapy. Specifically, coursework should teach that play has therapeutic benefits. Panelists recommend the inclusion of creative activities and play therapy methods in child-focused graduate coursework. Second is the use of play in family therapy. Courses should briefly cover histories of both play therapy and family therapy, how each profession has neglected different family members, as well as the logic for integrating both approaches. Demonstrations should be given for how family therapy theories and play therapy theories can be integrated (see Sori & Sprenkle, 2004, p. 484).

Child assessment and treatment. The experts in this study emphasize that coursework should include how to use family therapy methods to treat common disorders of children. Interestingly, the panel did not reach consensus for items that suggested specific family treatment approaches for particular child-focused problems. This is likely due to the diversity of panelists' theoretical backgrounds.

Family issues. According to the panelists in this study, trainees need to know how to treat specific family issues that are related to children. These include issues related to family organization, abuse, and trauma.

Counselors need to understand parenting and power issues that occur between children and parents. The effects of divorce and stepfamily dynamics and how children adapt are also important topics, as are issues related to attachment, such as foster care, parents who aren't nurturing, and how children are impacted by abuse and trauma. Family illness and death are other significant areas that should be addressed in child-focused coursework.

Contextual focus. Another strong finding was the emphasis panelists placed on contextual issues that impact children. Specific contextual topics include how children and families are impacted by the educational system, and how clinicians can collaborate with other professionals, such as physicians or school personnel. Courses need to cover current social issues (e.g., sex roles, gender issues, the role of peers, ethnic diversity, and the drug culture) (see Sori & Sprenkle, 2004, p. 484). It is important to understand how cultural issues impact children and parenting practices. Counselors need to know how to help children in multicrisis families: those who are on welfare or live in poverty, are in foster care, and the homeless. These findings reflect the current emphasis of multiculturalism in the field of psychotherapy.

Recommended Readings for Child-Focused Graduate Coursework

A third goal of this study was to generate a list of the most highly recommended readings to be included in graduate courses to train family therapists. Although panelists initially recommended hundreds of readings, surprisingly, consensus was reached on only one reference. This was a chapter by Chasin and White (1989), "The Child in Family Therapy: Guidelines for Active Engagement across the Age Span," which was a chapter in a book by Lee Combrinck-Graham. This chapter offers an excellent overview of issues related to child-inclusive family counseling, with numerous ideas on playful methods to engage both children and adults in the process of therapy.

The panel in this study was purposely comprised of experts from diverse backgrounds, but an effort was made to explore why consensus wasn't reached for more of the readings. Panelists were dichotomized into two groups according to their stated theoretical orientation, and the data were then reanalyzed. The first group listed their first-choice theoretical orientation as either psychodynamic, child therapy, or object relations, while the second group contained panelists from all other theoretical choices (e.g., structural, strategic, narrative, solution-focused family therapy theories). In the post-hoc analysis, a significant difference was found between the groups; there was a relationship between theoretical orientation and items that reached consensus. Ten additional items reached consensus for the first, more psychodynamic group (which were Bloch, 1976; Chasin, 1981; Combrinck-Graham, 1989, 1991; Gil, 1994; Johnson & Thomas, 1999; Keith & Whitaker, 1981; O'Connor & Schaefer, 1994; Schaefer & Carey, 1994; and Wallerstein, 1991). Interestingly, in the post-hoc analysis, the Chasin and White (1989) chapter did not reach consensus for the second group. However, Combrinck-Graham's (1989) book that contains that chapter did reach consensus, as did one additional reading: Johnson and Thomas (1999) (see Sori & Sprenkle, p. 487). It should be noted that the Johnson and Thomas article was the inspiration for this study.

THERAPIST ATTRIBUTES AND SKILLS

One of the research questions in the study was to determine what skills are most important for therapists to develop to facilitate successful therapeutic work with children and families. Panelists reached consensus on many items in this portion of the study.

Attributes. One of the strongest findings was that panelists reached consensus for all the items in only one category, and that was therapist attributes that are important in child inclusive counseling. Panelists agreed that those who counsel children should genuinely like children, and be honest and caring, since children recognize insincerity. Therapists need to nurture their own curiosity and playfulness, and utilize a sense of humor that children respond to by using, for example, children's riddles or jokes, or by engaging children through the use of puppets. It is important to note that the item that reads, "respect and appreciate children and their ways of being" received the highest score possible from all panelists (Sori & Sprenkle, 2004, p. 488).

One of the purposes of this study was to find ways to increase therapists' comfort with children, and help them develop skills that will promote the inclusion of children in counseling. Panelists agreed that psychotherapists should be a "non-anxious presence" (Sori & Sprenkle, 2004, p. 488), and be flexible and comfortable with the ambiguity that is often inherent when working with children. Being spontaneous and comfortable with informality, and developing a tolerance for messes and imperfections are also important attributes, as is being comfortable with small children, who are the most likely to be excluded from therapy sessions. This study supports earlier research on the importance of being comfortable with children, and identifies specific areas in which counselors need to increase their comfort.

Relational skills. Another important finding in this study is how essential relational skills are when counseling children and families. The therapist's ability to join, build rapport, and emotionally engage both children and adults was another item that received the highest possible score (see Sori & Sprenkle, 2004, p. 488). These findings support the research on common factors across theories, that relationship factors are the most important contributors to change in therapy (Lambert & Bergin, 1994). Those who have looked at common factors have focused primarily on therapy with adults (see Blow & Sprenkle, 2001); however, Sori and Sprenkle (2004) believe that relationship factors are even more essential when working with young children, who are often more difficult to engage (see Sori, Dermer, & Wesolowski [2006] on how to engage children and adults in psychotherapy).

Other important relational skills include how to empathically join and validate children, while also being able to challenge children's roles in dysfunctional family interactions. The panel also suggested measuring the amount of closeness and how much contact a child can tolerate, avoiding too much direct eye contact, and picking up on children's cues (see Sori & Sprenkle, 2004, p. 488).

Therapeutic skills. Another area of exploration in this study was what therapeutic skills are needed to successfully engage children. Panelists emphasized that counselors need to know how to ensure that children's thoughts and needs are vocalized, and how to communicate with children in child-friendly ways, such as through the use of puppets or therapeutic stories. They should know how to talk to children of all ages with an understanding of developmental and cultural issues. Parents need to be respected, and counselors should work collaboratively, taking time to hear their stories, and to avoid pathologizing or blaming them for their child's behavior. Another key skill is being able to discuss family members while others listen, without them feeling embarrassed or ganged up on. Counselors also need to be innovative to promote positive exchanges among family members, being careful not to intrude in the conversations. Finally, another finding was the importance of clinicians using their own creative selves in the counseling process (see Sori & Sprenkle, 2004, p. 488).

Play therapy versus playfulness. While play therapy was highly endorsed as an important component in child-focused coursework, panelists did not reach high consensus on any item that listed play therapy as an important skill. This may reflect the diversity of panelists, some of whom were trained in play therapy and some who were not. However, the panel did endorse several skill items related to *playfulness*. They emphasized the importance of the therapists' own playfulness and of developing a childlike sense of humor.

When asked to comment on possible reasons why play therapy was endorsed as a topic to be covered in coursework, but not as an important skill, one panelist who was interviewed commented:

> And the fact that they need to get in touch with their playing selves is crucially important. And your results suggest that most therapists haven't. Because they don't really understand *how* to play or *why* to play. (Sori & Sprenkle, 2004, p. 487)

The topic of play was explored in more depth in another component of this study, which is discussed later.

Conceptual skills. Numerous conceptual skills that are vital when counseling children and families reached consensus in this study. One important finding that reflects panelists' belief in systems thinking was the need to understand the reciprocal impact of children's behavior on family members, as well as how family interactions affect children. Panelists endorsed the idea of clinicians developing an integrative approach, from which interventions can be chosen that would best address the specific issues of the child and family. Other conceptual skills include having a knowledge of parent management training, having an awareness of models related to attachment, trauma, and stress, and being able to use interventions with both individual children and families. Counselors are also encouraged to maintain realistic expectations and work with parents who have committed despicable acts, while avoiding the urge to rescue children from these adults (see Sori & Sprenkle, 2004, p. 488).

Executive skills. Only two items in this category reached high consensus. First, panelists believe it is important for therapists to know when to be nondirective and when to be directive with children. A second vital executive skill is knowing how to set limits in a session and deal with children who try to take over the session.

Training and Supervision

One important goal of this study was to identify training methods to increase therapists' comfort in working with children, as prior studies had linked lack of comfort to the exclusion of children from family sessions (Johnson, 1995; Korner & Brown, 1990). Panelists were asked to identify training methods that would increase trainees' comfort level and skills in counseling children and families.

Experience increases comfort. According to the expert panelists, counselors gain comfort through experience, and that experience should be in counseling families with children of various ages and stages of development, and who have a wide range of child-focused problems. Surprisingly, panelists did not agree on training items related to individual play therapy or play in family therapy, even though they did endorse both of these as topics to be included in child-focused coursework (see earlier).

Attitude toward children and parents. Although play therapy was not highly endorsed as a training method by this panel, therapist *playfulness* was. Panelists believe it is important to "teach therapists to touch inside themselves their playful, spontaneous, forgiving, trusting, and creative parts" (Sori & Sprenkle, 2004, p. 489). This implies that children are likely to relate to clinicians who have childlike and playful qualities. These findings suggest that panelists are making a distinction between being playful and play therapy (see Sori, 2006b).

Some panelists were invited to reflect on the discrepancy that although play therapy was recommended as a theory that should be taught in child-focused coursework, and playfulness was an important skill, no specific play therapy skill items reached consensus, nor did items related to play therapy in the question on training methods to increase comfort and skills in working with children. One panelist questioned if people were not really sure how to define play or being playful, and compared trying to teach individuals to play to trying to teach them to be spontaneous. While it is likely that some people may be naturally more playful and comfortable with children than others, these characteristics can be fostered with good training and supervision as people gain experience working with many different types of children and families (Sori & Sprenkle, 2004).

Vital skills and training issues. Therapist playfulness was a common thread that ran throughout this study. Panelists suggested that it is helpful to observe family play therapy sessions, and then have trainees try the skills themselves. Trainees are also encouraged to help parents to reconnect to their playful parts, and then coach parents and children to have playful interactions. This suggests an experiential, hands-on approach to training.

Training methods. Specific training recommendations were made to increase therapist comfort with children and families. These specific steps were to be followed sequentially: (a) lecture (in order to provide a rationale, theory, or research); (b) live or videotape demonstration; (c) practice using role play; (d) practice with actual children; and (e) feedback on individual skills (see Sori & Sprenkle, 2004, p. 489). Of interest is the fact that these are the steps used to train parents in filial therapy (VanFleet, 1994; see Sori, 2006a); however, the panel did not highly endorse filial therapy, probably due to the diversity in their backgrounds.

Supervision. In addition to the training steps outlined earlier, the panel also emphasized the importance of supervision in training. They highly endorsed the use of live supervision with a one-way mirror. In addition, supervisors are encouraged to use video- or audiotape supervision, and to stop the tapes at pertinent spots to elicit questions about alternative possibilities.

It is important for supervisors to be able to model specific skills for trainees. First is modeling how to handle children who act out in a session and parents who act powerless to intervene. Second is being able to demonstrate empathy and sensitivity for a child, while modeling how to confront and set limits.

Play Interventions

This final area of inquiry was to determine what play techniques are most useful to integrate in the treatment of children and families. In the first phase of the study, panelists generated 43 items related to play techniques. Surprisingly, panelists reached consensus for only two items: "Using nonverbal therapeutic art techniques allows family members to express themselves without talking, or allows them to talk later about their drawings" and "Mural drawing—a family projective experience that provides information about family structure and authority, boundary management, and acceptability of expressiveness" (Sori & Sprenkle, 2004, p. 490).

One possible explanation for the lack of consensus on items may be that play was not defined nor differentiated from play therapy in the original open-ended question. The words play, playfulness, and play therapy may have different meanings to panelists. In fact, in the final interviews one panelist commented on this issue: "I think play is kind of an attitude … that having that playful kind of attitude is different than having the skill of how to do play therapy with children" (Sori & Sprenkle, 2004, p. 492). While many panelists advocated for some type of play in family sessions, not all believed that play therapy is helpful. This panel was selected based on their expertise in working with children and their diverse theoretical orientations, and perhaps the lack of consensus reflects the larger attitude in the field regarding the use of play in family therapy.

Other panelists reflected on the question of why panelists endorsed play therapy and how it can be integrated in family therapy in child-focused coursework, but only reached consensus on two specific play-related items. One commented:

> There are a lot of articles on the importance of incorporating children and play therapy ideas into family therapy, but there's very little on *how to do it* … Is it just a reflection of the fact that people aren't trained in it, and there's nonspecific ideas on how to go about doing it? As family therapists we don't receive training in working with children in general, and certainly not in play therapy. (Sori & Sprenkle, 2004, p. 492)

To determine if the lack of consensus for items relating to play interventions reflected differences in panelists' theoretical orientation, the panel was once again dichotomized according to how they listed their primary theoretical orientation, and these items related to play were reanalyzed. In the post-hoc analysis for the first group, whose primary orientation was more psychodynamic, 10 items reached high consensus. The second group, which was comprised of more mainstream family therapy theorists (e.g., structural, solution-focused), only reached consensus on three items in the post-hoc analysis.

Both the more psychodynamic groups and the more mainstream family therapy group agreed that the two items discussed earlier (nonverbal art and family mural drawings) are useful to integrate in family therapy. Only the more mainstream group of panelists reached consensus on an additional item that suggested that being playful in ways that both children and parents find exciting provides the best therapeutic experience. Counselors should observe how children respond to different techniques and use those to promote connections among family members.

By contrast, the more psychodynamic group reached consensus on eight additional items: (1) teaching play therapy techniques and approaches that have been found to be effective, such as the child-centered approaches of Rogers and Axline; (2) be aware of the primary senses children use to process information (visually, tactilely, auditorally, or kinesthetically); (3) therapists tell or collaborate with clients to create therapeutic stories; (4) before learning filial therapy, teach nondirective, child-centered play therapy; (5) use directive play interventions with children individually or with families; (6) clinicians direct activities using objects such as drawing materials, puppets, or a dollhouse; (7) sandtray helps children express sensitive issues symbolically, as they and family members make their world in the sand; and (8) have children and families use art techniques, such as drawing themselves doing something, or before and after a divorce (see Sori & Sprenkle, 2004, p. 491).

It is important to note that of the eight additional items that reached consensus for the psychodynamic group in the post-hoc analysis, most had the highest median score possible. This group of expert panelists suggests both individual directive and nondirective play therapy techniques, as well as playful interventions to use with children and parents. The item that suggests learning nondirective, child-centered play therapy before filial therapy implies an endorsement of filial therapy (see Sori, 2006a). All of the play ideas from both groups of panelists discussed earlier would be useful for any psychotherapist who is interested in incorporating play in counseling children and families.

LIMITATIONS AND STRENGTHS OF THE STUDY

The findings of this study reflect the consensus of opinions of those particular expert panelists. Another panel may have found different results. However, this panel was chosen because of their reputation, knowledge, and expertise, and was comprised of many of the best thinkers on this topic in the field. While the Delphi method calls for the selection of a diverse panel, obviously the more diverse the members the more difficult it is for them to reach a consensus of opinion. But this means that these findings cross theories and can be applied in general to child-focused training and treatment, regardless of one's theoretical orientation. Although the Delphi method has been criticized by some for emphasizing consensus over diverse opinions (Stone Fish & Busby, 1996), an attempt to address this issue was made by including some of the comments from the interviews in reporting these findings.

CONCLUSION

There are several important implications from these findings. The first is that those who work with children need theoretical training that emphasizes the reciprocal impact of parents on children, and of children on their parents. Parents are affected by child problems (and need to be part of the treatment), and children are impacted by parental problems. Although children may not attend every session, when not included they at least need to be assessed to ascertain how they are being affected by problems their parents or siblings are experiencing. Children are central figures in the process of family therapy. In general, children should be included in family sessions unless sexually explicit or other sensitive issues are being discussed. Comfort with children will only increase with much experience meeting with children of different ages with different presenting problems, and with good supervision.

Counselors need training that is both theoretical and practical. Coursework should include topics related to development, life-cycle issues, ethics, the assessment and treatment of specific child disorders and family problems (e.g., trauma, divorce and remarriage) and contextual issues, including illness, poverty, how to work with other systems (e.g., schools) and children in multicrisis families (see Sori, 2006b). Marriage and family therapists also need to be competent to use multiple treatment modalities, based on the needs of children and family members.

While only the chapter by Chasin and White (1989) was endorsed by this panel, additional references that reached consensus in the post-hoc analysis are recommended. Also, several newer books address the application of family therapy theories to treat specific problems encountered by children and families (e.g., Bailey, 2000; Berg & Steiner, 2003; Sori & Hecker, 2003). These volumes also suggest playful techniques to engage and treat children and adults. In addition, many of the recommendations of this study are addressed in the remaining chapters in this volume.

Practical skills, such as how to talk and listen to children, how to engage children and adults simultaneously, and how to facilitate helpful family interactions, are essential (see Sori, Dermer, & Wesolowski, 2006). Relationship skills, such as joining with kids and adults, being genuine, caring, and empathic, should be woven throughout training. Training methods should include both inductive (e.g., training videos, observation, and live supervision) and deductive (lecture, demonstration, trying out skills) methods.

While some family play techniques were endorsed, this panel emphasized therapist creativity and playfulness. Playful language and playful ways (e.g., talking through puppets or family drawings) are important tools to engage young and old alike, and can promote healthy family communication.

FUTURE DIRECTIONS IN THE FIELD

There has been increasing evidence of the effectiveness of family treatment that includes children (Sprenkle, 2002). However, much more research needs to be done related to issues regarding the inclusion/exclusion of children in family sessions. Research to determine effective training methods to prepare family therapists to work with children and families is a new and significant focus for the field (Sori & Sprenkle, 2004).

It is alarming that so many professionals feel their child-focused training was inadequate, and are uncomfortable working with children. Hopefully, the concrete suggestions offered in this study and in the remainder of this volume will begin to restore the long tradition in the field of allowing children's voices to be heard (Sori & Sprenkle, 2004).

REFERENCES

Ackerman, N. (1970). Child participation in family therapy. *Family Process, 9,* 403–410.

Bailey, C. E. (Ed.). (2000). *Children in therapy: Using the family as a resource.* New York: W. W. Norton.

Bateson, G. (1971). *Steps to an ecology of mind.* New York: Balantine.

Berg, I. K., & Steiner, T. (2003). *Children's solution work.* New York: Norton.

Bloch, D. (1976). Including the children in family therapy. In P. Guerin (Ed.), *Family therapy: Theory and practice* (pp. 168–181). New York: Gardner.

Blow, A. J., & Sprenkle, D. H. (2001). Common factors across theories of marriage and family therapy: A modified Delphi study. *Journal of Marital and Family Therapy, 27*(3), 385–402.

Bowen, M. (1978). *Family therapy in clinical practice.* New York: Jason Aronson.

Busby, D. M., & Lufkin, A. C. (1992). Tigers are something else: A case for family play. *Contemporary Family Therapy, 14*(6), 437–453.

Cederborg, A. D. (1997). Young children's participation in family therapy talk. *American Journal of Family Therapy, 25*(1), 28–38.

Chasin, R. (1981). Involving latency and preschool children in family therapy. In A. Gurman (Ed.), *Questions and answers in the practice of family therapy* (pp. 32–35). New York: Brunner/Mazel.

Chasin, R., & White, T. B. (1989). The child in family therapy: Guidelines for active engagement across the age span. In L. Combrinck-Graham (Ed.), *Children in family contexts: Perspectives on treatment* (pp. 5–25). New York: Guilford Press.

Combrinck-Graham, L. (Ed.). (1989). *Children in family contexts: Perspectives on treatment.* New York: Guilford Press.

Combrinck-Graham, L. (1991). On technique with children in family therapy: How calculated should it be? *Journal of Marital and Family Therapy, 17*(4), 373–377.

Estrada, A. U., & Pinsof, W. M. (1995). The effectiveness of family therapies for selected behavioral disorders of childhood. *Journal of Marital and Family Therapy, 21*(4), 403–440.

Freeman, J., Epston, D., & Lobovits, D. (1997). *Playful approaches to serious problems: Narrative therapy with children and their families.* New York: W. W. Norton.

Gil, E. (1994). *Play in family therapy.* New York: Guilford Press.

Gil, E., & Sobol, B. (2000). Engaging families in therapeutic play. In C. E. Bailey (Ed.), *Children in therapy: Using the family as a resource* (pp. 341–382). New York: W. W. Norton.

Haley, J. (1976). *Problem-solving therapy.* San Francisco: Jossey-Bass.

Hines, M. (1996). Follow-up survey of graduates from accredited degree-granting marriage and family therapy training programs. *Journal of Marital and Family Therapy, 22*(2), 181–194.

Johnson, L. M. (1995). *The inclusion of children in the process of family therapy.* Unpublished doctoral dissertation, Purdue University.

Johnson, L., & Thomas, V. (1999). Influences on the inclusion of children in family therapy. *Journal of Marital and Family Therapy, 25*(1), 117–123.

Keith, D. V., & Whitaker, C. A. (1981). Play therapy: A paradigm for work with families. *Journal of Marital and Family Therapy, 7*(3), 243–254.

Korner, S., & Brown, G. (1990). Exclusion of children from family psychotherapy: Family therapists' beliefs and practices. *Journal of Family Psychology, 3*(4), 420–430.

Lambert, M. J., & Bergin, A. E. (1994). The effectiveness of psychotherapy. In A. E. Bergin & S. L. Garfield (Eds.) *Handbook of psychotherapy and behavioral change* (4th ed.) (pp. 143–189). New York: Wiley.

Lawrence, G., & Kurpius, S. E. R. (2000). Legal and ethical issues involved when counseling minors in nonschool settings. *Journal of Counseling & Development, 78*(2), 130–136.

Lund, L. K., Zimmerman, T. S., & Haddock, S. A. (2002). The theory, structure, and techniques for the inclusion of children in family therapy: A literature review. *Journal of Marital and Family Therapy, 28*(4), 445–454.

Minuchin, S. (1974). *Families and family therapy.* Cambridge, MA: Harvard University Press.

Montalvo, B., & Haley, J. (1973). In defense of child therapy. *Family Process, 12,* 227–244.

O'Connor, K. J., & Schaefer, C. E. (Eds.) (1994). *Handbook of play therapy: Advances and innovations* (Vol. II). New York: Wiley.

Satir, V. (1964). *Conjoint family therapy.* Palo Alto, CA: Science and Behavior Books.

Schaefer, C. E., & Carey, L. (Eds.) (1994). *Family play therapy.* Northvale, NJ: Jason Aronson.

Selekman, M. D. (1997). *Solution-focused therapy with children: Harnessing family strengths for systemic change.* New York: Guilford Press.

Sori, C. E. F. (1995). The "art" of restructuring: Integrating art with structural family therapy. *Journal of Family Psychotherapy, 6*(2), 13–31.

Sori, C. E. F. (1998). Involving children in family therapy: Making family movies. In L. Hecker & S. Deacon (Eds.), *The therapist's notebook: Homework, handouts, and activities for use in psychotherapy* (pp. 281–287). Binghamton, NY: Haworth.

Sori, C. F. (2000). *Training family therapists to work with children and families: A modified Delphi study.* Unpublished doctoral dissertation, Purdue University.

Sori, C. F. (2006a). Filial therapy: An interview with Rise VanFleet, chap. 5 in this volume.

Sori, C. F. (2006b). Reflections on children in family therapy: An interview with Salvador Minuchin, chap. 2 in this volume.

Sori, C. F. (2006c). A playful postmodern approach to counseling children and families: An interview with Lee Shilts, chap. 6 in this volume.

Sori, C. F., Dermer, S., & Wesolowski, G. (2006). Involving children in family counseling and involving parents in children's counseling: Theoretical and practical guidelines, chap. 7 in this volume.

Sori, C. F., Hecker, L., & Associates (2003). *The therapist's notebook for children and adolescents: Homework, handouts, and activities for use in psychotherapy.* Binghamton, NY: Haworth.

Sori, C. F., & Sprenkle, D. H. (2004). Training family therapists to work with children and families: A modified Delphi study. *Journal of Marital and Family Therapy* 30(4), 479–495.

Sprenkle, D. H. (Ed.). (2002). *Effectiveness research in marriage and family therapy.* Washington, DC: American Association for Marriage and Family Therapy.

Stith, S. M., Rosen, K. H., McCollum, E. E., Coleman, J. U., & Herman, S. A. (1996). The voices of children: Preadolescent children's experiences in family therapy. *Journal of Marital and Family Therapy, 22*(1), 69–86.

Stone Fish, L. S., & Busby, D. (1996). The Delphi method. In D. H. Sprenkle & S. M. Moon (Eds.), *Research methods in family therapy* (pp. 469–484). New York: Guilford Press.

VanFleet, R. (1994). *Filial therapy: Strengthening parent-child relationships through play*. Sarasota, FL: Professional Resources Press.

Wachtel, E. F. (1991). How to listen to kids. *Family Therapy Networker, 4*, 46–47.

Wallerstein, J. S. (1991). The long-term effects of divorce on children: A review. *Journal of the American Academy of Child and Adolescent Psychiatry, 30*(3), 349–360.

White, M. (1984). Pseudo-encopresis: From avalanche to victory, from vicious to virtuous cycles. *Family Systems Medicine, 2*(2), 150–160.

Zilbach, J. J. (1986). *Young children in family therapy*. Northvale, NJ: Jason Aronson.

CHAPTER 2

Reflections on Children in Family Therapy

An Interview with Salvador Minuchin

CATHERINE FORD SORI, PH.D.

> You know, if you know the answer, but you don't know the question you are in a bad way. But if you have questions, you will find answers.
>
> **—Salvador Minuchin, 2000**

As one of the founders in the field of family therapy, Salvador Minuchin's early research on psychosomatic families led to the concepts that formed the basis of his structural family therapy model. Minuchin and his colleagues discovered that problematic families were often characterized as being either enmeshed, with boundaries that were too diffuse; or disengaged, where boundaries were too rigid. Structural family therapy offers clinicians a way to make sense of family interactions by providing them with a map to recognize how families are organized in ways that keep them stuck and prevent them from solving their own problems.

Minuchin was born and lived in Argentina before immigrating to the United States. He has long amazed therapists with his dazzling ability to simultaneously charm, confront, challenge, and cajole even the most reluctant clients into changing. Many have tried to adopt his style and emulate his flair, but he is truly a great artist who possesses skills to which most of us aspire.

Minuchin was in Palo Alto with Jay Haley in the early 1960s, and later became the director of the Philadelphia Child Guidance Clinic, which he developed into an internationally renowned training program for paraprofessionals working with urban minorities. He has written many of the classic texts in the field of family therapy that are still widely read and form the foundation of many training programs. Minuchin founded the Minuchin Center for the Family in New York, where, although officially retired, he remains on the board. He still travels widely and teaches with his wife and fellow scholar, Dr. Patricia Minuchin.

Since the inception of his career, Salvador Minuchin has been a leading proponent of helping children in the context of their families and the institutions that impact their lives. He graciously offered to give this interview at the conclusion of the study on "Training Family Therapists to Work with Children and Families: A Modified Delphi Study" (Sori, 2000). This study explored the thoughts and beliefs of leading experts in treating children in a family context on issues related to child-focused training. A summary of the findings was sent to Minuchin before the interview, and the following are excerpts from the interview that followed the conclusion of the study. Minuchin discusses his reactions to the results, and offers his own thoughts on elements that are important to prepare counselors to treat children and families. (The results of this study may be found in Sori, 2000, 2006; and in Sori & Sprenkle, 2004.)

* * *

In the first part of the interview, Minuchin reflected on the founding of the field of family therapy, and emphasized that at its inception the focus was on interviewing children and parents. Next, he responded to the finding that expert panelists in the Sori study reached consensus for only one reference to recommend for courses on child-focused training: a reading by Chasin and White (1989).

Sori: Dr. Minuchin, first I would like to get your reaction to the issue of how children are not being included in family therapy, and your perception on how well training programs are preparing marriage and family therapists to work with children. Then would you share your reactions to this study (Sori, 2000), and offer any general advice that you have to the field on how we can better meet the needs of children and families?

Minuchin: OK ... You know, clearly, children are not very much part of family therapy, neither in training or in practice, and that is due to many things. One of the things is that family therapy in general is, at this point, under great stress. HMOs are very much challenging all kinds of therapy that takes more than eight sessions. So we have the generic umbrella issue of what's happening to all the talking therapies in the United States. That, and the inclusion of children in family therapy is, and has always been, an area that has not been very much focused on. Most therapists at this point work with couples. Even psychoanalysts and people who had always worked with individuals, they have expanded and include couples.

Children is not an area that therapists have included, and that's interesting because really, originally, Ackerman and myself were two of the pioneers of family therapy that were child therapists. And family therapy started in New York with Nathan Ackerman, who was the first director of the Child Development Center, and then worked in the Jewish Family Services. What he developed was a therapy in which the emphasis was on children, and so did I in the Child Guidance Clinic. Actually, there are tapes of Ackerman doing interviews with parents and children.

And one of my major areas of question in this study [Sori, 2000] was the fact that while people responded to literature that is written, there is a large literature of tapes that are tremendously useful for training and that were not included. I don't know if people did not understand that this is also literature, or they felt that literature is only what is written. But I think that would be an interesting project that could be a wonderful Ph.D. thesis for some bright social worker or psychology student to collect—to have a library of tapes of family therapies that include children. I have here some starters for the people that would like to do that.

First, there are a number of tapes in the AAMFT and *Networker* libraries that include children. There are some tapes, I think in the *Networker*, of Olga Silverstein from the Ackerman Institute for the Family working with children. And Jay Haley has a number of tapes of strategic family therapy working with children. One is called "Never on Sunday," that is the tape of a 10-year-old masturbating, in which Haley prescribes the symptoms. And it's very, very nice. There is one that Jay did a number of years ago called, I think, the "Study of Little Hans," or just "Little Hans," like Freud. There are tapes that I had done at the Psychiatric Hospital at Staten Island, one of working with the family with a young schizophrenic, a 16-year-old adolescent, a family with adolescent and young children. There are tapes of anorexia that I had done, one in Staten Island, and they are distributed all over. There is a tape that I have done recently called "Hearing Voices," which includes one 16-year-old girl, and is essentially about an adult with symptoms. Then there is one called "The Caretaker," in which the mother is a drug-addicted woman with issues of foster care, and two young children, one aged 5, and one aged 3. There is the work of Duke Stanton working with drug-addicted adolescents. But the literature is full. I am calling the videotapes "literature," and I'm doing that purposefully because I want to move the focus away from the written articles and books and say that there is something that can be extremely useful for any school that is teaching family therapy—to have a library of tapes that includes all the models. For example, Michael White has this old tape of externalization of the Poopy Monster.

In general, one of the issues that I felt about the questionnaire [which asked expert panelists to recommend "the most important books, chapters, and/or articles that should be included as required readings in a graduate course on children in family therapy" (Sori & Sprenkle, 2004, p. 481)] is that by focusing on certain areas maybe the respondents shrank away from spontaneous remembering that there is a lot of literature that is not specifically labeled "children." For instance, you have the work of Gillian Walker at the Ackerman Institute for the Family, who worked with hyperactive children in DHS, and I think it is specifically related to children. She has done, I think, a book on hyperactive children. Then there is Marsha Sheinberg's work on incest. She is also at the Ackerman Institute.

What I am saying is that it's not specifically about children, because as the field has moved toward looking at and responding to specific areas, then the literature has adopted the name of the areas in which people are working. So the work on incest is certainly work about children. The work on psychosomatic families that I did with diabetic children and anorexia does not figure in the literature of children, but it is on psychosomatic families. The work is about anorexia and about brittle diabetics. There is a work on drug addiction that was written by Thomas Todd and Duke Stanton a number of years ago.

What I'm saying is the focus here is not labeled "children," it is labeled "symptom." But since the symptom is child-related, then the literature and the way in which people work with drug addiction, the techniques of working with drug addictions, are techniques that could be useful. At some point in the training of working with children, trainees would need to begin to think that the way in which the patients come is not under the generic rubric of children but under the diagnosis.

Jay Haley has a tape of a young adult who is deaf, and they work with deaf children and their parents, helping the children to teach parents to understand sign language. One of the things that used to happen with deaf children is that in the schools they were taught to sign, and the parents were not taught to sign, so that the children were really caught in a situation in which at home their communication with their parents was a communication across languages that neither one of them spoke. And we had a project in which Sam Scott, who was a therapist whose parents had been deaf, used to teach the children to teach the parents how to sign.

I am sure that if you look at the work of John Rolland you will see the way in which he includes families in the work of pediatric illness, and then there is all the work with autistic children. But this seems to be under the generic rubric that looks at symptomotology, that is children's symptomotology, and ways in which family therapists have responded to this area of needs, and in which they have developed techniques to work with them. Maybe when people responded to the literature question in the study [Sori, 2000] and reached consensus only on the article by Chasin and White, they just did not think about these other things. For example, there is work that has been done by Cloe Madanes and Jim Keim on oppositional children.

Sori: I'm familiar with Keim's work on oppositional children.

Minuchin: So what I am saying is that maybe something about the responses is that they were looking at specific articles that were generic, where what I am talking about is looking at—not the diagnosis, because I don't care about the diagnosis—but about areas in which children manifest problems. And look at what has happened with the work that people have done—certainly the work on incest, and all the techniques of working with incest that the Ackerman Institute for the Family has available. And also in England, I think that one of the people who has worked with incest there is Ben Tobin.

But these are specific techniques that involve working with children that includes working with individual children, working with groups of children, working with subsystems of parents and children, mother and child. The work of the Ackerman Institute is interesting because it is multiple responses in multiple modalities. So I don't know if that's useful to you.

Sori: It's very useful. The panel did recommend using training videos in general, but there were no specific recommendations like you're suggesting. I've had the opportunity to see some of the ones you've mentioned, and they were very beneficial. So I think that's an excellent suggestion.

Dr. Minuchin then addressed another research question in the Sori (2000) study, which explored what content areas should be included in coursework on children in family therapy. He then addressed the two items that reached consensus for expert panelists under the category of "Application of Theories." These were having a "Theoretical understanding of the central place of children in therapy," and "Structural/boundary issues: Family rules, consequences, hierarchies" (Sori & Sprenkle, 2004, p. 484).

Minuchin: I had been looking at your tables, and for instance, "Application of Theories," Table 2 [see Sori & Sprenkle, 2004, p. 484]. It says … "Structural/boundary issues: Family rules" … and so on and so forth. But there is, in almost all of the different schools of family therapy, techniques that have been very specifically child-related. Externalization is one of them. Circular questioning, that is, children gossiping about parents, is a technique of the Milano School. Jay Haley prescribing the symptoms is one of the techniques specifically related to the strategic theory that is children related. I think I told you that Jay has a tape called "Never on Sunday," and that is about prescribing the symptom, that Monday, Wednesday, Friday, etc.

And another thing that could be looked at is that Europe has produced some useful family therapists that, maybe, American family therapists are not in contact with. Among them, the English people are Alan Cooklin, Ben Tobin, John Bing-Hall, and Jill Gorrel Barnes, who are people who had worked on theory and techniques. Jill Gorrel Barnes has worked a lot in issues of policy for children. She is Alan Cooklin's wife, but she has a literature of her own and she is a very political person who has worked a lot on issues of policy in England. The English people have been much more advanced than the Americans on issues of policy. There have been papers about how to treat children in which the English family therapists have been very involved in the reform of some of the judicial children's courts, and so on. That, I'm sure is not related to your question, but I just mentioned it.

Sori: Excellent point, though.

Minuchin: In Italy, I think Andolfi has done some work with children, and so did some of the Milano people, Boscolo and Cecchin. And there is all the work of Mara Selvini Palazzoli during the period in which she worked with the invariant prescription, which was kind of radical and lasted for only a couple of years. But Mara was very much involved in issues related to children. Her first book was a book on the work of families with anorectic children. So, as you see, you asked me a question, and I went all over the place.

Sori: That's wonderful!

At this point Minuchin moved on to address another aspect of the Sori (2000) study, which was related to making decisions on when to exclude children from family sessions.

Minuchin: Now, in Table 1 [see Sori & Sprenkle, 2004, p. 483], you have "Criteria for decision making: Include if there is a reason and they are central to the process," including children, and so on. Now, one of the things that is important is to understand that when children are in a session, the adults behave differently. So, let's say you have a couple that comes for therapy and the couple is involved in conflict. You bring in an infant, and at the point in which you include the infant in the session you introduce nurturance. You change from the symmetry of conflict to the complementarity of parents, and all the ways in which the parents involve the child in the conflict.

So I include children even when the issue is not the child's issue, but it is the parents' issue. Because then you move the parents to deal with the conflict and see in what way they involve the child; the issue of triangulating the child. The issues of, "Be loyal to me and not loyal to the spouse." That's one of the issues, but also the issue of the fact that, at the point at which you have children in the room, then the spouses' transactions change in nature, by having the children as witnesses. Actually, putting children as witnesses is a technique of the inclusion of children in the family, you know. This is the work of not only Michael White, but some of the narrativists here in the United States, like Jill Freedman and Gene Combs.

Sori: Are you talking about children as witnesses, where the therapist would be talking to a family member while the other family members are watching?

Minuchin: Yes, and that's a technique of involving children.

Next, Minuchin reflected on another important aspect of the study, as he discussed the distinction between therapeutic playfulness and play therapy with children in family therapy.

Minuchin: Now, in terms of play, here there is something that many family therapists would question; the way in which play is seen. You see, play is a technique that evolved in individual child development—in individual therapy with children. I used to do it when I was a child psychiatrist, and it has a particular purpose, that is to deal with some of the internal voices and fantasies of the child. But if you look at the work of Alan Cooklin, for instance, or my work, what we do is to put the children in contact with the parents, or we talk with the children around family issues, so that the play is not separated from the narrative of the family, from the issues of the family.

In my work with young children, for instance, in which I ask ... let's say the parents do not exert parental authority or parental responsibility, or there is enmeshment with the children and so on, I do things in which I say to the child, "Stand up. Are you taller than your father? Are you younger" ... I ask the child to stand on a chair and measure with the father. I ask the mother to hold the child. This is play. Or I ask the mother and the father to sit on the floor and play with the child. But this is not play therapy. This is the utilization of language with younger children. It's concrete language, but it is language. It is the language of movement. It is the language of tall and short. If I say to a child, "Are you older or younger than your mother, because when you are criticizing your mother, you become the grandmother of your mother," or saying to the parents, "Do you think your child is six, two, or eighteen?" These are playful techniques. They are not play therapy. These are playful techniques of working with children around the issues of their relationship with parents.

When I work with adolescents, then I am asking, "Are your parents fair or unfair? What are the rules that you think your parents should change?" Here I engage adolescents in issues of justice, issues of fairness. I also ask the children, "Do you think your parents know your age? Do you think they are related?"

These are issues in which children are involved in playful ways in issues of how they interact with their parents, and what is the parents' relation to them? Something similar goes on in the Milano school when they ask the child, "Who is the one who responds more to you or less to you?" or "Who is the one who talks more with you?" These are playful techniques of involving the child.

And when I work with the parents of children, then I always talk about the issue of the rights of the parents and the rights of the children. The parents need to be responsible, but they also need to request respect from the children. So that kind of involvement with the children is playful, but it's not play therapy. It is involved.

So that when panelists say, the "Brief history of family therapy, integration of family therapy theories and play therapy theories, demonstrating how the two orientations can be combined" [Sori & Sprenkle, 2004, p. 484], I think that's a mistake. Because I think that when you train the young trainees to techniques, if you are teaching and you teach trainees props, you give them props—and in the beginning we always do teach some kind of map so that they navigate without drowning. But I am concerned that if it is too specific then they get wedded to the technique instead of responding to the stimuli that the family and the children send. So you have sometimes young, inexperienced trainees like I have worked with, who come and present the writing of the genogram. And it becomes not a way of knowing the family, but it becomes a rigid writing of the genogram. Or they have play techniques, and that becomes then something of teaching parents how to play. I have seen a lot of narrowness given by the half-knowledge of techniques.

Now I think that techniques of play therapy can be perfectly good for experienced therapists, once you know. But if your study is involved in trying to help people to develop curriculum for training, I think that this needs to come later in the training, when the people are so comfortable with interviewing families with children that then they can include some techniques without that wagging the dog. That's my feeling, OK?

Sori: I like what you said about that. I think it's a good summary about not focusing so much on technique that you're losing the theory, or focus of what you're trying to do, is that correct?

Minuchin: Yes. Yesterday I was reading in the *New York Times,* an article actually on medicine, in which it said that one of the famous early physicians used to say that a good doctor treats the illness, but a great doctor treats the patient. Today with all the pills that we have, most doctors treat the illness and not the patient. Now I think that's the issue about how to help family therapists to treat the child in the family, instead of narrowly following any techniques. Now, I also think that it is useful.

At this point, Minuchin moved on to another finding, where the panel in this study emphasized the importance of contextual issues when treating children and families.

Minuchin (continued): OK, "Contextual Issues" …

Sori: I was going to ask you your reflection on that.

Minuchin: Yes. Well, family therapy today is growing, if it's growing at all, in the area of poverty. The Department of Welfare, the Department of Mental Health, since HMOs, have kind of put a rein on therapy for the private patients. And family therapy, like all the therapies, has been suffering. At the same time, in the area of working with poor families, the Department of Mental Health provides home-based therapy for symptomatic children that have a diagnosis. So that I think that the subject of contextual issues becomes an important area, certainly if people are going to develop training programs for a family therapy, social work, or a psychology course. How to work with families of the poor becomes an area where manpower is needed. Certainly, all training needs to include economic issues. That means, do we have a job. In the area of welfare and poverty there are jobs, so it is important to think about programs like home-based programs that are family-centered, but family-centered in the home-based approach. Actually, the wife of Steve de Shazer, Insoo Kim Berg, has done a book on home-based therapy, with families in poverty in the area of strength-based and solution-focused therapy.

Returning to the issue of "Application of Theories" as a content area in child-focused coursework, Minuchin suggested expanding the findings to include solution-focused theory. He then continued to discuss contextual issues.

Minuchin (continued): But also, in terms of the "Application of Theories," I think that not to include de Shazer's solution-focused theory is a mistake, because his orientation toward small changes and toward strength is significant, if you are going to work with families and children.

So what I think is that maybe your respondents narrowed their responses and thought specifically about children. While if I am thinking about the application of theories, I'm thinking, OK, de Shazer doesn't talk specifically about children, but his orientation toward strength instead of pathology is a very significant theoretical response to working with children. And so I would put that.

And Insoo Kim Berg had done some work in home-based therapy that I think is significant. And certainly the book of Patricia (Minuchin), of working with families of the poor, which includes three or four different areas of working with families of the poor: home-based, working with foster-care children, working with children in psychiatric hospitals, working with children in residential places. Again, this is context. Residential placement is context. The question is, who are put in residential places? Children. And how do residential places work with families? Very little.

Sori: You are right.

Minuchin: How can we begin to infiltrate, to train students to go to work in residential places where there are jobs with an orientation toward the inclusion of families?

Certainly, in the drug addiction area where you put mothers in residential places, and a fence is put between them and their families. And we have been doing some work in which we are training people that are working in residential places for drug addiction, drug-addicted adults. This is at the Minuchin Center in New York, in which the idea is to help therapists in these residential places for adult drug-addicted mothers to work with these families.

So you see, it seemed to me that at the point at which you are talking about working with children in families, instead I took the position of thinking of working with children in issues in which the *parents* are sick. Certainly, the work of John Rolland, and other people who have been working with medical illness, such as working with children with families in which an adult has cancer. So here it is, the inclusion of children and the benefits of including children not only in areas where the child is the identified patient, but in areas where the parents are the identified patient.

OK. Now there are some people who have been working in the area of stepparents. I'm thinking about Emily and John Visher, who have worked with stepfamilies. You see they are not family therapists, but nonetheless, their work is work that should include family therapy techniques.

Sori: One final question would be if you have any other recommendations or general advice to the field? And how do you think this study will be received? I see it hopefully as a wake-up call that more needs to be done to train therapists to even look at the issues of children and families.

Minuchin turned his attention next to debate items that suggested specific steps in the training process and had reached consensus among panelists in this study. Using a historical backdrop, he then presented his views on the benefits of an inductive versus a deductive approach to training.

Minuchin: OK. You remind me of the area of training. I was interested in the way in which training was responded to here. Let me see, "Training Methods," Table 5 (Sori & Sprenkle, 2004, p. 489). The way in which training is described here is going from theory to the practice. It starts with lecture, followed by demonstration, followed by practice, and role-play, followed by actual practice with children, followed by individual skill feedback. The way in which we used to do training was from inductive to deductive. This goes from deductive to inductive.

When we started training many years ago, Jay Haley wrote about working with paraprofessionals. I think it's in one of his books, a guideline for the first interview, with four stages. It's very broad and I think it is useful for people, a kind of a map of how to start the first interview. Then with this map of how to navigate and survive in the first interview, we trained paraprofessionals. And actually, students in family therapy are in some way paraprofessionals.

We used to have them do a session with the family that was live supervised. Live supervision was, for me, the most active and economical way of training people to see children and families. That means that it's not the use of demonstrations, live or video demonstration. Clearly that is very useful. But, to have live and videotaped supervision of the students because then, instead of engaging the students' intellect, or left brain, into thinking about the process of therapy, you engage the student's right brain in terms of how to interact, how to respond to the situations in therapy.

Sori: Yes. What you are saying is in agreement with the panel's consensus that trainees should receive live supervision with a one-way mirror.

Minuchin: Now I want to address the differences in training that moves from theory to practice, to training that goes from practice to theory. These are two different methodologies. And actually both are useful and important. The question is what is the ratio? How do you integrate? At which point? How do they interface? In the responses it is as if the emphasis is—and I can see how when you are teaching at the university, then the emphasis on going from theory to practice seems relevant. I would still like to say in your interview comment that there should be much early involvement of practice. Then the items ["actual practice with children"; "followed by individual skill feedback"; "the use of training videos to demonstrate methods"; "use an apprenticeship model"; "supervisor models how to be in the room with disruptive children ..."; "supervisor models how to balance sensitivity with challenge"; "live supervision"; "video/audio tape supervision" (Sori & Sprenkle, 2004, p. 489)] should enter much earlier, or should interface with theory and practice—should be interpolated, so that theory comes from practice in the same way that practice comes from theory. That was the last point I wanted to make.

Sori: That's excellent.

In conclusion, Minuchin addressed the question of the relevance of this study.

Minuchin: Now, clearly this is an arena that is nonfocused. And so your study is an important call to the need to be looking at that and the development of training in working with children.

I think it's very important to know child development and the way in which children respond at different stages of development. But that in itself is not sufficient, it's not enough. You can be an extremely competent child developmentalist, and that is the area in which I was trained, and still not be a good child therapist. I think also if you're focusing very much on children you may lose the focus that is so necessary in looking at the transactions between parents and children, and the effect of children on parents, and the effect of parents on children. And the effects on siblings. The first book that I wrote, *Families of the Slums*, was on the fact that the siblings of the delinquent children were tremendously significant in the socializing processes of children. So to me that is a very important area of exploration, and it has not been explored enough because all the emphasis is on parents as socializing agents, and in effect we have children as socializing agents.

So your question about it being an important study? Yes, absolutely. No question that it's necessary. How to do it … how to train people, it's still a big question mark. Because I think that the people who had been doing that, and we did a lot of this training in the Philadelphia Child Development Clinic. Ackerman originally did a lot of this training, and we had not written about how to train people to work with children. It is not an area which people had written about. Ron Taffel worked at the Ackerman Institute with children and adolescents, and writes a lot now about working with children. His work is usually in the *Networker.* He's done some interesting work. What I'm impressed with is that the responders didn't put that in the literature.

Sori: Certainly I've ended up with more questions than I started with.

Minuchin: That's wonderful! That's always wonderful. You know, if you know the answer, but you don't know the question you are in a bad way. But if you have questions, you will find answers.

Sori: That's wonderful. I can't tell you how much I value this.

Minuchin: Thank you very much!

Sori: I appreciate you giving this time and hope that the field will make really good use of this information.

Minuchin: OK! Thank you very much.

REFERENCES

Ackerman, N. (1970). Child participation in family therapy. *Family Process, 9,* 403–410.

Berg, I. K. (1993). *Family based services: A solution-focused approach.* New York: W. W. Norton.

Bing-Hall, J. (1995). *Rewriting family scripts: Improvisation and systems change.* New York: Guilford.

Boscolo, L., Cecchin, G., Hoffman, L., & Penn, P. (1987). *Milan systemic family therapy: Conversations in theory and practice.* New York: Basic Books.

Chasin, R., & White, T. B. (1989). The child in family therapy: Guidelines for active engagement across the age span. In L. Combrinck-Graham (Ed.), *Children in family contexts: Perspectives on treatment* (pp. 5–25). New York: Guilford.

de Shazer, S. (1988). *Clues: Investigating solutions in brief therapy.* New York: W. W. Norton.

Freedman, J., & Combs, G. (1996). *Narrative therapy: The social construction of preferred realities.* New York: Norton.

Haley, J. (1987). ***Problem-solving therapy*** (2nd ed.) San Francisco: Jossey-Bass.
Keim, J. P. (2000). Oppositional behavior in children. In C. E. Bailey (Ed.) ***Children in therapy: Using the family as a resource*** (pp. 278–307). New York: W. W. Norton.
Minuchin, P., Colapinto, J., & Minuchin, S. (1998). ***Working with families of the poor.*** New York: Guilford.
Minuchin, S. (1974). ***Families and family therapy.*** Cambridge, MA: Harvard University Press.
Minuchin, S., Montalvo, B., Guerney, G., Rosman, B., & Schumer, F. (1967). ***Families of the slums: An exploration of their structure and treatment.*** New York: Basic Books.
Minuchin, S., Rosman, B. L., & Baker, L. (1978). ***Psychosomatic families: Anorexia nervosa in context.*** Cambridge, MA: Harvard University Press.
Rolland, J. S. (1994). ***Families, illness, & disability: An integrative treatment model.*** New York: Basic Books.
Sheinberg, M., & Fraenkel, P. (2000). ***The relational trauma of incest: A family-based approach to treatment.*** New York: Guilford.
Sori, C. F. (2000). ***Training family therapists to work with children and families: A modified Delphi study.*** Unpublished doctoral dissertation, Purdue University.
Sori, C. F. (2006). On counseling children and families: Recommendations from the experts, chap. 1 in this volume.
Sori, C. F., & Sprenkle, D. S. (2004). Training family therapists to work with children and families: A modified Delphi study. ***Journal of Marital and Family Therapy, 30***(4), 479–495.
Taffel, R. (1991). How to talk with kids. ***Family Therapy Networker, 4,*** 39–69.
Todd, T. C., & Stanton, M. D. (Eds.) (1991). ***Family therapy approaches with adolescent substance abusers.*** Boston: Allyn and Bacon.
Visher, J. S. & Visher, E. B. (1988) ***Old loyalties, new ties: Therapeutic strategies with stepfamilies.*** New York: Brunner/Mazel.
White, M. (1997). Pseudo-encopresis: From avalanche to victory, from vicious to virtuous cycles. In M. White & D. Epston, ***Retracing the past: Selected papers and collected papers revisited.*** Adelaide, Australia: Dulwich Centre Publications.

CHAPTER 3

Integrating Play in Family Therapy Theories

SHANNON DERMER, PH.D., DON OLUND, M.A.,
AND CATHERINE FORD SORI, PH.D.*

We don't stop playing because we grow old;
We grow old because we stop playing.

—Rose

The Adventures of Peter Pan, a novel written by J. M. Barrie (1911), is the story of a young boy who travels to Neverland with his friend Wendy Darling, to engage in enchanting adventures highlighted by battles with Captain James Hook and his band of pirates. The movie *Hook* (1991) revisits Peter Pan as a grown-up Peter Banning, a detached husband and father with misaligned priorities. When his two children are kidnapped by Captain Hook and brought to Neverland, he embarks on a mission to rescue them, only to discover that first he must become the young boy he left behind when he decided to grow

* The authors contributed equally to this chapter.

up. Once he remembers he's "the Pan," he defeats Hook, retrieves his children, and returns home a changed person.

In family therapy that integrates play, clinicians help families get in touch with their "inner Pan." They enter a child's sphere and bring the parents along for the journey. They do not limit themselves to the "rational," verbal style adults tend to use. They incorporate storytelling and the nonverbal code (e.g., facial expressions, body movements, silly noises, and playful gestures) children often use to express themselves. Through the magic of make-believe, children can be simultaneously both self (5-year-old girl) and "someone else" (e.g., a princess) (Ariel, Carel, & Tyano, 1985). In short, play provides a metaphorical channel whereby children can communicate their thoughts and feelings, beliefs and ideas, including their perception of themselves—often by projecting them onto an object. The symbolical language of play reveals children's experiences and reactions, their wishes, wants, and needs (Gil & Sobol, 2000).

Expert panelists in a study by Sori (2000; 2006c; Sori & Sprenkle, 2004) recommended that child-focused graduate coursework include practical suggestions on how to integrate family therapy with play therapy. Nevertheless, many family therapists find they are at a loss for how to do this. In this chapter, we present ways to use family play therapy as a "meta-model" for use with various family therapy approaches. A brief description of family play therapy will be followed by a review of four family therapy models and how play therapy can be congruent with the concepts, goals, and interventions of each model.

FAMILY PLAY THERAPY: A META-MODEL

Family play offers therapists a clear vantage point to observe family dynamics at work. During play, clinicians observe family structure, communication, emotional connectedness, and level of cohesion. Gil, who has spearheaded the integration of play in family therapy, described the use of play as a window for therapists to observe process and content within family interactions (Gil & Sobol, 2000). Process information concerns how the family interacts, the verbal and nonverbal expressions, and stylistic idiosyncrasies. Content information centers on what is being said, including the symbolical meaning conveyed through the play metaphor. It also includes the actual product created by the family (see Sori, 2006b). The information obtained from these interventions helps therapists formulate a working hypothesis and treatment plan.

Another goal in family play therapy is to create an experience for families that encourages them to work together to create solutions. Family play therapy helps families address the problems they face in a nonthreatening manner. Family interactions in the context of play offer them a different view of their problems and each other (Gil & Sobol, 2000). Often families enjoy the novelty of playing together, which cultivates a new emotional climate and promotes cohesion among the members.

Finally, family play therapy is useful when therapists are stuck isomorphically with families. Play stirs things up, gets families (and therapists) out of their ruts, and opens new channels of communication. Furthermore, play therapy helps analytical families (and therapists!) trapped in their left brains to use the creative, spontaneous, and playful aspects of their right brains (Gil & Sobol, 2000). Therapists must be just as capable at play and creativity as they would like their clients to be.

In order to engage families in play therapy, clinicians must be comfortable entering into and participating in the world of play. They set the tone by being enthusiastic, expressive, and active in play. In various scenarios, such as make-believe play, therapists may assume the role of an audience, director, actor, commentator, reporter, critic, or observer (Ariel, Carel, & Tyano, 1985).

Therapists may work with the metaphor evoked in play therapy to employ a wide range of interventions, from restructuring relationships to increasing emotional expression in the family. The material derived from family play is used to engage families in a dialogue about their experiences, feelings, and hope for change.

Interventions should be selected to fit the particular family, the child, and the goal of the session. Most family play interventions can be integrated to fit the tenets of major family therapy models, and are useful to both assess and to intervene. There are many family play interventions (e.g., Gil, 1994; 2003; Gil & Sobol, 2000, Sori & Hecker, 2003) that offer creative methods to observe families interacting, assess their dynamics and intervene, according to one's therapeutic model and the goals of therapy. Playfulness and the use of creative play techniques help families (and therapists) to feel more fully alive. It is essential that clinicians *do* these activities themselves first, and process them with a peer or supervisor. The most important thing is being there with the family—allowing oneself to be playful and becoming immersed in the metaphor, rather than trying to cognitively analyze the activity. Being aware of one's own emotional reaction to a family and to their activity are key elements to being a successful family play therapist (see Sori, 2006b).

EXPERIENTIAL FAMILY THERAPY

Experiential family therapy is an approach that easily accommodates family play therapy. Experiential therapy is rooted in existential-humanistic belief about the inherent goodness of humans and their need for self-expression. Healthy families create an atmosphere that fosters individual expression and family cohesiveness. These families balance individual expression with family cohesion. Parents should encourage and value the expression of feelings from all family members. As children are listened to and affirmed, they are liberated to express a broad spectrum of emotions. These shared experiences enhance family cohesion. Virginia Satir, a leading figure in the experiential family therapy movement, added the idea of encouraging higher levels of self-esteem to the experiential approach (Nichols & Schwartz, 2004).

If emotional expression, balancing individual and family needs, and increasing self-esteem are the hallmarks of health, then the opposite processes are likely to result in symptoms. Experientialists view emotional suppression as the root of family problems. The process of suppression begins in early childrearing practices. Parents regulate children's behavior by placing restrictions on the expression of emotion. For example, comments such as "You shouldn't feel that way" or "Don't act like that" establish rules of conduct in the system. In order to adapt and meet parental expectations, children suppress emotions they deem as unacceptable to their parents, resulting in children who appear unsure of themselves, and who subsequently may have difficulty expressing their feelings.

Goals and Focus of Change

To encourage individual expression and generate family harmony, experiential family therapists attempt to defuse defensiveness and encourage emotional expression. A primary goal in therapy is to create here-and-now experiences that elicit atypical emotional responses among family members. According to Keith and Whitaker (1981), these experiences are central to effective therapy. They stated, "Our goal in family therapy has always been to have an experience with the family, not simply to induce understanding" (p. 244).

In the experiential model, the therapist serves as an activating agent, who, on the one hand, alleviates defensiveness, and on the other hand agitates the system enough to awaken passive emotions. The family moves closer toward one another as they move away from predictable patterns of interaction. This frees family members to share their feelings, creating genuine intimacy.

The process begins in initial sessions as the therapist joins with every member of the family. For Satir, the joining phase establishes three primary goals: the value of every individual, the freedom of every person to speak honestly, and allowances in the family for individuals to be different (Nichols & Schwartz, 2004). Her active engagement with each member of the family modeled for them how they should behave toward one another.

Integrating Play in Experiential Family Therapy

Experientialists tend to utilize playful interventions in order to break old patterns of interaction and create new meanings. Family art therapy is a typical form of intervention experiential therapists use to help families more openly express themselves (Nichols & Schwartz, 2004, p. 218). In a conjoint family drawing, a therapist instructs a family to "draw a picture as you see yourself in your family." Once the drawing is complete the therapist goes around to each member and has them talk about how they experience their family, while exploring the emotions that were evoked in this exercise. Family members listen quietly to gain insight into one another's experience. The dialogue that ensues provides opportunities for family members to feel empathy toward each other, resulting in greater cohesion.

Another intervention that works well with children and their parents is a role-reversal technique that requires them to switch generations. In this approach, the therapist instructs the parents to act like children and the children to act like parents. A parent's annoying childish behavior may give the child acting the role of the parent a feeling of frustration similar to the parent (see Sori, 1998). Or the child might be asked to give advice to parents who have adopted the angry position of a child. Playfully enacting a problem, such as a temper tantrum, has a make-believe quality that changes the emotional context in which the problem is embedded. The family will never experience that problem in the same way again (Ariel, Carel, & Tyano, 1985; Sori, 1998).

Family sculpture, developed by David Kantor and Fred Duhl, and popularized by Virginia Satir (1988), is a form of psychodrama that allows family members to gain deeper understanding of one another through reenactments of conflicts. The purpose of this intervention is to provide a fun, nonthreatening activity for children to express their hidden feelings about issues going on in the home. Furthermore, it helps parents see conflicts from their children's perspective, so they change harmful patterns and provide emotional care (see Sori, 2003, for a practical explanation of how to use this technique with children and families).

Case Example of Integrating Play with Experiential Family Therapy: The "Art" of Family Sculpting

Tom and Brenda Smith had been married for 15 years and had two children, a daughter, Danielle (13), and a son, Jason (11). The couple had experienced problems in their relationship throughout their marriage. They entered counseling as a "last-ditch effort" before they decided to divorce. When Tom called the therapist to set up the first appointment, he was instructed to bring the entire family.

In the first session, the therapist joined with everyone, and asked questions about things they enjoy such as music, movies, sports, video games, and fashion. After some friendly discussion, the therapist asked the family to engage in a discussion about the problems that brought them in. Each person was encouraged to share his or her view.

While discussing this, the parents engaged in a heated argument. The therapist, seeking to interrupt what seemed like a typical pattern, turned to Danielle and Jason, and asked, "Is this one of those looping arguments that gets played over and over like the *Christmas Story* movie during the holidays?" They sheepishly grinned and nodded their heads in agreement. The therapist stated that because this argument is a familiar story, she would like them to work together to draw a mural of this scene on a large roll of paper that was taped to the wall. After some brief discussion the family began, but they worked quietly and independently, each absorbed with his or her own creative process.

In the mural drawing Dad drew himself in the kitchen with his hands on his hips and his face filled with disappointment. Mom was drawn with her back toward her husband, on the phone with a smile on her face. Jason depicted himself sitting on the floor with his headphones on, and he was the furthest away from the family. His expression was a blank stare. Danielle drew herself between her parents with a look of exasperation on her face.

The therapist then asked the family members to assume the positions and expressions they had drawn for themselves in the family mural. While in this frozen position, the therapist asked each of them to express how they really feel in the conflict. Tom began by sharing feelings of defeat and failure because his family life was such a mess. He stated that he didn't feel appreciated for his hard work and how he provides for his family. Brenda shared that she feels unimportant and rejected by her husband because he is more dedicated to his work than to his family. She said, "While I may appear happy and smiling on the telephone, on the inside I'm lonely and sad." She also admitted to feelings of guilt and failure because she neglected responsibilities at home as a way to express her resentment.

Jason discussed how his parents' arguments frightened him, and shared his fear that they might divorce. He said, "I may look disinterested in the fight, but actually I'm overwhelmed and don't know what to do. So I act like I don't care." Danielle added that she felt stuck in the middle between two parents who were "acting like kids." She stated that she was getting tired of being the referee and wanted out of the family. Danielle burst into tears.

The therapist used this time to help the family process the scene and begin to open up to each other about their feelings. She was careful to encourage expressiveness, but did not allow family members to criticize or make judgments about statements or feelings expressed.

The therapist then asked Danielle to sculpt how the scene usually ends. Danielle had the family members moving away from each other in opposite directions, with herself remaining in the middle, slightly bent with her hands on her stomach, and a look of agony on her face. During the processing phase where the family discussed their reactions to this sculpture, Danielle shared how hopeless she felt about her family, to the point where it was affecting her physically with a stomachache.

Finally, Danielle was instructed to create an ideal ending. Danielle positioned the parents facing each other with open palms. Jason was "wireless" (no iPod) and stood looking at his parents with his mouth open and finger pointing in the air. Danielle placed herself on the floor seated in a restful position reading a book. In this preferred scene, the parents talked about how they need to be open to hear each other and communicate more. Jason told his parents that though he is the youngest in the family, he has something to say. Danielle wanted to go back to being a teenager and effectively fired herself from being her parent's referee.

Summary

From this example, we see how experiential family play therapy can help families experience their emotions on a deeper level, and how communication among family members becomes more open. Families are no longer hiding behind masks but are more able to be themselves and to experience life and one another more fully. Family mural drawings and family sculpting are just two of many in-session interventions that experientialists may utilize in order to help families become more expressive and spontaneous. Activities that children often do (e.g., pretending, drawing, acting, dancing, or singing) are creative endeavors that typically enhance expressiveness and spontaneity, so the experiential family therapist adapts these for therapeutic purposes. Most family play techniques meet the goals of experiential therapy as they free family members to be more spontaneous and expressive, to enjoy one another and to feel more fully alive.

STRUCTURAL FAMILY THERAPY

Structural family therapy describes family structure in terms of family boundaries, hierarchy, and roles that govern how members interact (Minuchin, 1974). In this model, therapists observe and modify existing structures so families can function more cohesively. Structural therapists believe problems occur when families fail to adapt to life-cycle changes and stressful situations.

Salvador Minuchin, who founded structural family therapy in the early 1970s, described four sources of stress: stressful contact of one member with extrafamilial forces, stressful contact of the whole family with extrafamilial forces, transitional points in the family's evolution, and idiosyncratic problems (Minuchin, 1974). In a therapeutic setting, clinicians observe family transactions, identify faults in the structure, and make necessary modifications.

Goals and Focus of Change

According to Nichols and Schwartz (2004), a major goal in structural therapy is to modify the existing structure and activate successful, latent structures families can use to solve their problems. In the assessment phase, therapists observe family interactions to test the integrity of the existing structure. Here, clinicians examine hierarchical structure, boundaries, subsystems, and coalitions in order to form a hypothesis about the family. A structural map emerges that depicts hierarchy, patterns of communication, and types of boundaries in the system. With a working hypothesis and clearly delineated structural map, therapists can set treatment goals for the family. Afterward, interventions are carefully chosen to match treatment goals.

Role of the Therapist and Major Interventions Used

In the assessment phase, structural therapists build an alliance with the family by joining with all the members, including the children. Here, therapists enter the system by accommodating to the family structure. This process is a matter of accepting the family and blending in with them in order to experience their transactional patterns (Minuchin, 1974). Becoming syntonic with families gains access into the system and begins the process of restructuring.

Beginning in the assessment phase and throughout treatment, therapists use interventions to restructure the system. A key therapeutic tool used for both assessment and intervention is enactments, in which counselors direct two family members to have a conversation about an issue, or perhaps to plan an outing together. As they observe interactions, therapists create in-session enactments involving two or more individuals to activate a dormant structure (Nichols & Schwartz, 2004).

Integrating Play in Structural Family Therapy

Minuchin differentiates between being playful and using play therapy when working with children and families (see Sori, 2006d). He cautions that too much concentration on props or play techniques may be distracting, and novice therapists may miss important family interactions. Until therapists are experienced and comfortable working with many different types of families and presenting problems, Minuchin suggests the playful use of language, such as metaphors, to engage children and adolescents, and to challenge the roles and boundaries of children and parents.

In structural family therapy involving children, more experienced therapists can integrate play interventions to use for assessment and intervention purposes, keeping in mind the goals of this approach. Play activities can be effective assessment tools to formulate a systemic hypothesis as therapists carefully observe family interactions. For example, two family members may be asked to select puppets to use to enact a problem. From this enactment the therapist might hypothesize that there is a coalition between the mother's momma bear puppet and her son's little bear puppet, and that the father's fox puppet seems distant from the others. A structural intervention might be to have the fox and little bear puppet plan an activity together (such as a trip to a Cubs or Bears game), while momma bear gets to spend the whole day hibernating or looking for honey (at the mall) with a friend. Or perhaps momma bear and papa fox need to put their heads together to decide how to keep little bear from getting into so much trouble.

Other techniques, such as play genograms (Gil, 2003), family puppet interview, family sandtray, and family aquarium (Gil & Sobol, 2000) are excellent tools structural therapists can use to observe family interactions, and the product the family produces to assess family structure. Sori (1995) described the "art" of restructuring families using family drawing techniques for structural assessment and intervention purposes. Family art can be used for process observations, and the content or product is often a metaphoric depiction of the family structure. Family art enactments give therapists a window to observe structural patterns such as hierarchy, boundaries, roles, and coalitions. Furthermore, family art activities are useful for unbalancing the system, restructuring boundaries and hierarchy, and empowering members to take on new roles. For example, assigning a parent the task of leading a drawing of the family doing something, and supporting the parent when he or she is faced with children who try to take over the project, unbalances the system, and reinforces the parent's hierarchical position in the executive subsystem. Thus, with the support of the therapist, the parent is empowered to assume this role in further interactions. In addition, poor boundaries may be evident in a family drawing where members draw over each other's figures, when one child's drawing encroaches into a sibling's space or is disproportionately large and looms over other figures. Family drawings can be playful, less confrontational ways to help parents set limits for their children, while reinforcing parental hierarchy.

Case Example of Integrating Play with Structural Family Therapy: Play as Metaphor and Playful Enactments

Anna, a 35-year-old Hispanic-American, requested counseling for her 9-year-old son, Juan Jr., who was exhibiting disruptive behavior at home and at school. His school counselor made the referral following numerous episodes of Juan's unruly behavior and physical aggression toward classmates. Anna scheduled an appointment with a family therapist, and at his request she also brought the remaining members of her household: oldest daughter Carlita, age 15, and Maria, age 7. Anna and her husband, Juan Sr., had been separated for the past 9 months, and his visits with the children were irregular.

When they arrived, Maria was clinging to her mother's waist and proceeded to sit on her lap. Carlita sat next to her mother and kept a watchful eye on Juan Jr., who positioned himself furthest away, slumped in his chair, with his arms folded across his chest. Carlita snapped at her brother to sit up straight. Meanwhile, Maria hugged and kissed Mom in an attention-seeking manner.

The therapist's initial goal was to join with each family member. Beginning with Anna, they talked about her dual role as mother and provider for the family. He validated Anna's feelings and remarked on how impressed he was that she was successful in getting the whole family to the session. His objective here was twofold: to accommodate to the structure, and to elevate Anna's status in the family hierarchy.

The therapist next joined with Carlita by asking her questions about school and things she enjoyed in life as a teenager. As they interacted, Juan Jr. made sotto voce insulting comments to Carlita. Predictably, Carlita unleashed a verbal counterattack, leaving her with a disgusted look and Juan Jr. with a devilish grin. The therapist noted this interaction, asked Mom if this was how the children typically behaved at home—playfully suggesting that they sounded like two sparring lion cubs, and engaged Mom in a brief conversation about what she does when her "cubs" tangle with one another.

Afterwards, the therapist asked Juan what he enjoyed doing when he's not in school. With a cocky grin, Juan said he likes to make money by stealing candy and selling it to friends. The therapist commented on his youthful ambition and wondered aloud if Juan used the money to help his family. He asked Juan if he'd ever been caught stealing. Juan, who had been lying about his career in crime, replied "No." The therapist then inquired, "What will you do if you get caught? Will you remain in this career or look for another way to make money?" Juan shrugged his shoulders, not knowing how to keep the charade going. The therapist related how he used to have a paper route when he was Juan's age because he, too, enjoyed having money in his pocket. At that point, Juan seemed to decide to give up on the game and pay more attention.

When the therapist attempted to engage Maria, she seemed more eager to talk to Mom than to him. Anna encouraged her to talk directly to the therapist; however, Maria clung to her mother and whispered her answers so that Anna had to convey them. The therapist playfully remarked that they reminded him of a ventriloquist and puppet. He asked Anna, "Mom, does the puppet ever speak on her own, or only through you? Does she speak directly to Carlita? How about to Juan Jr.?" Everyone laughed at this playful activity except Maria, who loudly protested, "I can speak to anyone I want!" "So you have a voice, don't you?" remarked the therapist. Everyone, including Maria, had a good laugh.

Next, the therapist asked each of them their own view of the problem. Anna commented on how hard it was on everyone since their father left home, and had minimal contact with the family. Carlita stated the problem was Juan's attitude and behavior. She remarked that he was disrespectful to everyone, especially Mom. Maria said the problem in the family was her brother acting mean all the time. The therapist spread the symptom by asking each of them what they did when they were angry. As the conversation moved along it became clear that there were more problems in the family than just Juan's anger, and this led Juan Jr. to sit up in his chair and pay more attention.

From his early observations, the therapist formulated a hypothesis about the family, including a structural map that depicted a cross-generational hierarchy involving the mother, Anna, and her 15-year-old daughter, Carlita. In a parentified role, Carlita viewed her main job as supervising the behavior of her brother, Juan Jr. This arrangement served to block Mom's interactions from her son and compromised her matriarchal position in the executive subsystem. Mom's feelings of inadequacy at parenting her son were avoided by her overinvolvement with Maria, who assumed a dependency role.

To test his hypothesis and further assess the family, the therapist created an enactment involving family play. He instructed Anna to lead her family in constructing a mural of their family on a large poster board. Giving Anna the task of taking charge of the activity elevated her status and established a hierarchical boundary over the sibling subsystem.

First, Anna drew a picture of herself and then she asked Carlita to come to the board to draw next. Meanwhile, Maria ran to the board, begging Mom to let her be next. "I want to draw myself next to you, mommy!" she declared. Mom directed Maria back to her seat. Although Maria whined, Mom remained firm with her. The therapist commented, "Good job Mom!" to shape her competency.

As Carlita was finishing her picture, Juan ran up to the board. Carlita told him to sit down because he wasn't called yet. The therapist interjected, "Mom, tell Carlita you'll handle Juan." Anna instructed Juan to sit back down and wait until she called him. After Juan finished his picture, Maria, who was seated quietly, was invited by her mom to draw her picture.

The family picture supported the therapist's hypothesis about the family. Mom was depicted in light, translucent colors with an exasperated look, pulling her hair out. Maria drew herself at her mother's side with her hands extended up as if she wanted to be picked up. Juan Jr. drew himself towering above everyone else, but was positioned farthest away. Carlita drew herself as a two-headed, split-in-half body—half dressed like a teenager and half dressed like a worn-out mother. The mother side of the head had an angry face while the teenager side of the head was crying.

The therapist reentered the system, asking each family member to describe how the picture reflected his/her experience of family life. Carlita expressed sadness and anger because she felt torn between two worlds: that of a fun-loving teenager and of a responsible adult, attempting to fill the gap left by her absent dad. Anna described feeling powerlessness in managing a household and working a full-time job. She also felt guilty and responsible for the problems Juan Jr. had, due to her lack of involvement. Juan surprisingly admitted that he acted mean because he was mad at his father for leaving home and not spending much time with him. In a soft voice Maria said she clings to Mom because she's scared and lonely. As each one shared, the other family members were encouraged to listen, ask questions, and try to understand one another. The tone of the conversation was noticeably more open and caring.

In subsequent sessions, the therapist continued to work on restructuring the hierarchy by having Anna and Carlita discuss her role under her mother. This intervention placed Mom in the primary leadership role, giving Carlita limited authority, thus freeing her to enjoy being a teenager again. Mom decided to handle disciplinary matters in the family and have Carlita supervise the siblings' chores only when she was working. Mom led an enactment to negotiate responsibilities for family chores among the children. Additionally, Mom agreed to teach Maria age-appropriate ways to soothe herself.

In one session that included only Mom and Juan Jr., they made two worlds together in the sand—one of their world when Dad was living with them, and one of their current world. The first sandtray was full and showed much life and activity, was organized and had fences to depict boundaries around the family. The second, of their world without Dad, was chaotic and had symbols of danger, such as pirates and wild animals. When discussing these two worlds, Juan shared the hard time he was having adapting, and how he wanted things like they were before. He was able to express the sadness he felt that was under his anger, how he blamed himself for Dad leaving, and how much he worried about his mother and how they'd get along. Mom reassured Juan that they would be OK and he was not responsible for the separation, and she validated his feelings. She then told Juan and the therapist that her husband had become so intrigued with the changes in the family that he wanted to come to sessions! This session ended with an enactment between Mom and Juan, where they planned a fun activity together.

Juan Sr. did come to the next session and began participating in family sessions. Enactments with father and son helped Juan Sr. become more active in a parental role. In one session the family did a family puppet interview (Gil, 1994), where they were to select puppets and make up a story with a beginning, middle, and an end (but it had to be an original story), and then act out the story with puppets. Mom selected a bear puppet, Dad a wolf puppet, Juan a skunk, Carlita a lion, and Maria a kitten. Their story consisted of the bear trying to round up the skunk, lion, and kitten to go on a car trip to Disney World. The skunk and lion kept arguing over who would sit in the front seat, while the kitten mewed in the back and kept sneaking up next to the bear. The bear quietly growled for all three to sit in the backseat or there would be no trip! They did so, and were on their way, but soon they had a flat tire. The skunk got out to begin changing the tire, when along came the wolf, who offered to help the skunk. After they finished, the wolf asked where they were going, and inquired if he might accompany them to Disney World. The animals all jumped up and down, squealing an excited, "Yes!" The wolf climbed into the front seat with the bear, and off they went! The story ended with everyone happy to be going on a trip together. In processing the story the therapist asked if anything about the story reminded them of their lives. Dad immediately saw a similarity, as his wife and children seemed to be moving forward, and he wanted to be part of the journey. The family remarked at how much they enjoyed the puppet story and the other play activities, saying that they hadn't laughed or enjoyed playing together in a long time. This led to a commitment to plan fun family times together on a regular basis.

As Mom became a stronger parent and Dad was more involved with the children, Juan Jr.'s behavior gradually improved at both school and home. Carlita objected at first to giving up her position of power, but with the therapist's support Anna and Juan worked to relieve Carlita of her role as a parentified child so she could enjoy her adolescence to a greater degree. As Mom grew stronger and more confident she mentioned that she felt less anxious, and, interestingly, Maria's clingy behavior also diminished.

With the success of initial modifications to the structure and the infusion of playfulness in the family, Juan Sr. and Anna began to address their marital problems. They agreed to enter couples counseling to work toward a possible reconciliation.

Summary

Structural family therapists believe families have problems because they are stuck in a structure that limits the resources they have to solve problems. Similar to experiential family therapy, which attempts to get families to experience new interactions by unblocking emotional resources, structural therapists create new possibilities by restructuring the system. This is accomplished by identifying unhealthy structural patterns in hierarchy, boundaries, subsystems, and coalitions.

By accommodating the family, therapists are free to assess the system and look for ways to restructure it. Enactments are the primary means to assess and restructure families. Play therapy is a useful tool to reorganize hierarchy, set boundaries, and break coalitions that cause family dysfunction. As therapists balance their involvement by active and inactive measures, they can restructure family interactions so that they are empowered to solve their problems without the help of the therapist.

SOLUTION-FOCUSED

A solution-focused approach to working with families is a systemic, strengths-based, collaborative, future-oriented model. There are several assumptions underlying solution-focused therapy: (a) change is constant; (b) one should highlight solutions, positives, and possibilities facilitating change; (c) there are always exceptions to problems; (d) families are competent and are experts in their choices of goals and solutions; (e) solutions evolve through conversation (social reality is co-created through language); (f) there is no one right way to view things, because different views may be equally valid and fit the facts equally well; and (g) one need not know a lot about a problem in order to solve it (de Shazer, 1985; O'Hanlon & Weiner-Davis, 1989; Selekman, 1993). Therapists endeavor to reframe situations in workable, solvable terms within the context of client strengths (Dermer, Hemesath, & Russell, 1998).

Goals and Focus of Change

The objective is to assist people in moving toward their stated solutions, not to hypothesize about the family structure, hierarchy, rules, or patterns and then change them. The goals are established by the family, and whatever means are dictated by that goal are then used to reach the goal. The therapist elicits family observations, expertise, and fantasies to assist them in recognizing what parts of their goals they have already achieved, and what parts of their behavior they want to change or keep the same.

Role of Therapist

Therapists should take a stance of curiosity. Therapists need to inquire about things that are working well during nonproblem times, what has worked for the family in the past, and what their general strengths and talents are (Selekman, 1997). All of this information is used to help the family construct potential solutions to reach their goals. Therapists should take a collaborative, nonexpert, encouraging role with their clients. They need to negotiate the careful balance between empathizing with the painful past and problems people have with the role of being a realistic encourager, a motivator, and collaborator. Entering a truly collaborative relationship means that therapists need to utilize the language of clients (rather than expecting them to adapt to "expert" language) and be "real" with their clients. The therapist should be able to be, when called for, serious, empathetic, humorous, and playful.

Each conversation with someone provides an opportunity to see something differently and to *do* something differently. In addition, our language tends to influence what we do and how we feel; language cannot be separated from action. The solution-focused therapist's ability to use language in order to tap into the imagination and creativity of clients is the clinician's most effective tool.

Integrating Play in Solution-Focused Therapy

Berg and Steiner (2003) offer a plethora of playful ways to engage and treat children within a solution focus framework. For example, asking the child to select a puppet and then interviewing the puppet about his interests and what he does well is a delightful way to engage children and parents in a discussion of the child's strengths. Children might pick two puppets to help them build on exceptions to the problem—when solutions are already occurring.

For example, a rabbit puppet might caution a child when it is not safe to speak up, while an owl might offer wisdom on when it is good to talk, and how to overcome shyness. The characteristics that children assign to the puppets help them find ways to solve their own problems and build on exceptions that are already occurring (see Berg & Steiner, 2003). These metaphors create a context in which children feel safe by talking *through* a puppet, instead of directly talking to the clinician about themselves. Selekman (2000) offers other playful solution-oriented interventions, including asking children and parents to draw a picture of their family when the problem is solved.

One of the most famous questions in solution-focused therapy is the miracle question (de Shazer, 1985). This question basically posits that a miracle has occurred such that while the clients were sleeping all of their problems were solved. The clients are then asked a series of questions relating to how they would recognize that their problems were gone and how it would affect each of them.

One of the problems with the miracle question is that it may be too ambiguous for children or they may not understand what a miracle is. There are more concrete ways to ask the question. For example, the therapist could hand the child a stick, ask the child to pretend it is a magic wand, and ask what the child might wish to change with the magic wand. A fairy godmother or wizard puppet also could be used to wave a magic wand and ask the child what the miracle would be (Berg & Steiner, 2003). Also, many children have seen the movie *Aladdin* (1992), and the child could be asked what his or her three wishes would be. Multiple variations can be used, but the main point is to have people fantasize about a different future in order to help them set goals and identify solutions. Storytelling (see Berg & Steiner, 2003), in which the therapist makes up a story where a hero overcomes a problem that is similar to the child's, also helps create new possibilities for solutions.

Another particularly important type of question is the *scaling question*. Solution-focused therapists ask clients to rate themselves on a scale from 0 to 10 with 10 as usually the most desirable outcome. Depending on the age of children involved they may or may not understand scaling questions. Instead, counselors can ask them draw three pictures: the first picture depicts life when their problems are really bad; the second picture is when life is "normal" or "pretty good"; the third picture is when there are no problems at all. Each week the therapist can lay the pictures side-by-side and ask the family which picture they seem closest to that week. An alternative would be to utilize "visual scaling," by having a child stand on a chair and stretch to indicate the maximum size of the problem. Each week the child could show how much smaller the problem has gotten, and the clinician could discuss how the family has moved toward their goal (see Sori, 2006a; Shilts & Duncan, 2003).

Case Example of Integrating Play with Solution-Focused Family Therapy: Visualizing Solutions

Mr. and Mrs. Orsen sought therapy for their son Brian's anxiety. Brian was an 11-year-old boy in the fourth grade. In the first meeting, he was quiet and shy. His parents explained that Brian tended to like to be on his own, would get easily irritated with his bother and sister, and had several learning disabilities. Brian was in a special education class and had trouble with short-term memory, reading, and auditory learning. He was far behind where his learning should be for a typical 11-year-old.

When asked what they had already done to help the situation before coming to therapy, Mrs. Orsen rather nervously responded that she had met with Brian's teachers to find out what she could do at home to help with his learning, and she volunteered to be a helper in Brian's class. She felt that much of his frustration and anxiety related to his learning problems. Mr. Orsen stated that he wasn't at home as much as his wife to help with homework and learning strategies, but that he made an effort to make sure the kids did their chores, and tried to spend fun time with the kids. Although Brian was sometimes reluctant to join in family activities, once Mr. Orsen convinced him to participate he almost always had fun. Brian seemed to especially enjoy certain outdoor activities, playing board games, and anything that related to mechanics. Brian's father repaired heating and air conditioning units for a living.

The parents were asked what they admired about their son and what he was good at. They focused on his lovingness and his fascination with mechanical things. Sometimes Brian would accompany his father on jobs where he would be happy for hours just watching his father work on air conditioners. In fact, even though Brian had trouble reading, he would borrow his father's manuals and struggle for hours to read them. He would frequently ask his father questions about what different words meant and about the diagrams in the manual. In addition to his keen interest and perseverance in trying to understand mechanics, they admired Brian's ability to ride his dirt bike. Brian was an excellent rider and patiently taught his younger sister and brother the basics of riding. The therapist remarked how proud the parents are of their remarkable son.

When the therapist asked Brian what he was good at (see Berg & Steiner, 2003) Brian stated that he was good at fixing things and drawing. He also said that he loved motorcycles. Someday he wanted to be a motorcycle mechanic or work with his father. When asked what he'd like to have happen in coming to counseling, Brian said he didn't want to get so angry, and he wanted to do better in school.

Using a magic wand the therapist asked Brian and his parents if they would pretend for a few minutes, and then she asked them the miracle question (de Shazer, 1985; Berg & Steiner, 2003):

> If after you leave here you go home, have supper, and go to bed, and while you are sleeping a miracle happens, and the reasons that brought you for counseling are suddenly gone, what would be the first thing you'd notice in the morning that would let you know that this miracle had occurred?

Brian stated that the first thing he'd notice is that he wouldn't get so annoyed with his brother and sister in the morning because they wouldn't start arguing and making a ruckus. When asked what would be happening instead, Brian said they would all be sitting together eating breakfast, and Mom would be singing and making pancakes. The therapist asked what else would let him know that the miracle had taken place, and Brian said that he wouldn't be anxious about going to school, so his stomach wouldn't hurt. Instead he would be thinking about recess and playing with friends. When asked who would notice first that things were different he said Mom, because he'd eat his breakfast and not complain about his stomach or about going to school. At school, his teacher would know the miracle had occurred because he'd be smiling and would raise his hand to answer questions. In the evening, Brian would not get angry at his siblings when they were noisy, and would do his homework without complaining. A short discussion followed regarding how all these changes would affect Mom and Dad, his parent's relationship, as well as his siblings.

Brian was then asked to draw pictures of the miracle. In his first picture, instead of being angry, Brian, his father, and his siblings were playing a board game, and his mother was bringing them a plate of freshly baked cookies. In his second picture, Brian drew himself at his desk with his hand raised to answer a question asked by his teacher. These pictures offered very concrete images that the therapist could address later in helping Brian and his parents explore steps to take to begin to reach these goals.

The family had difficulty describing what Brian's anxiety looked like or how those outside the family would recognize his anxiety. The best they could do was say that when he became anxious he would yell at people. The therapist suggested that the whole family watch the movie *Parenthood* (1998) and enjoy it as a family activity, but also to think about how the young character in the movie who struggled with anxiety was similar to or different from Brian.

In the next session, the family reported that they had watched the movie together and enjoyed it. Brian saw some similarities with the character with anxiety in the movie, but he didn't think he was as bad off as that kid. His parents agreed with him. They stated that Brian was quick to yell at his brother and sister when things seemed chaotic or they would not listen to him, and that he sometimes cried, like the character, when he got upset. However, they didn't think that Brian got as upset as often, and he was easier to calm down.

Interestingly, Mrs. Orsen commented that she really identified with the parents in the movie. She hadn't realized that she had been blaming herself for Brian's anxiety and that maybe she was too sensitive to making sure that he never got upset, and was somewhat overprotective of him because of his school problems. She felt Brian was smart, but he had a hard time with academic things because of his learning disabilities. She worried at times that others would not recognize all his wonderful qualities. She also admitted that she'd been an anxious child, so she easily identified with Brian.

When asked to rate the character's anxiety on a scale from 0 to 10 (with 0 being no anxiety and 10 being anxiety at its worst) the family rated the character at a 7. When asked how they would rate Brian they rated him at a 5. Next, Brian was given 10 large cardboard blocks and asked to make a pile that depicted how high his anxiety got. He piled up six blocks. When asked if this was the highest his anxiety had ever been, Brian said it had been a 7 before the beginning of the school year. The therapist enthusiastically pointed out that somehow Brian had already figured out how to lower his anxiety one whole point on the scale! When asked how he did that, Brian said, "I just kept telling myself it wouldn't be so bad, and to think about going to work with Dad on weekends."

In discussing goals, Brian's parents said they would be happy if his anxiety were at a 3 and Brian stated that he would be happy if his anxiety were at a 2 or 3. Brian was then asked to note any days in the next week that his anxiety fell lower than six blocks.

The family also reported that one part of the miracle had already occurred! On Friday night Dad had played board games with the children while Mom baked chocolate chip cookies. When his siblings got excited and rather loud, Brian had remained calm. Everyone had a wonderful time, and Brian brought a cookie in for the therapist.

The therapist commended Brian and the family for already noticing times when anxiety wasn't present and when happy times were in evidence instead! She then asked Brian and his parents to each draw a picture of other exceptions to the problem—to draw other situations where Brian was not showing anxious behavior. He considered himself a "good drawer" and sometimes when he was upset he drew to feel better. In Mom's picture he was drawing at the kitchen table while she was cooking spaghetti and singing "You Are My Sunshine." Dad's picture showed Brian and him sledding, whereas Brian's picture showed him and Dad bending over a car, working together on a motor.

Subsequent sessions. Each week Brian was given the blocks (see Berg & Steiner, 2003) and asked to stack them to show how anxious he'd been that week. In the third week Brian had reduced his stack to five blocks. When asked what made a difference, Brian commented that Dad had started helping him with homework, and that they sometimes played math games, so he was feeling less anxious about school. One week his stack was down to three, and he excitedly reported that he had been the only kid in the class to raise his hand with the answer to a tough math story problem question.

In a subsequent session the family was introduced to a visualization and relaxation exercise activity (see Sori & Biank, 2003). Following the breathing and muscle relaxation portion of the activity, the therapist led them in a visualization that helped them picture in their minds the most relaxing thing they could think of. Following this they were asked to draw what they had visualized. Mrs. Orsen drew an island paradise, Mr. Orsen drew a cabin, and Brian drew himself coasting down the road on his dirt bike, his face to the wind, wearing his White Sox cap with a big smile on his face. Each family member shared his or her drawing and described why they thought it was relaxing. They discussed when they were able to relax currently and what they could do in the future to recreate the relaxed feelings represented by their pictures. They enthusiastically agreed to practice the relaxation and visualization together at home using a tape of the therapist's voice.

Over time some of the *doing* and some of the *viewing* of the situation changed for the family. Brian started to recognize some of his strengths and would focus on his breathing, relax, and picture himself riding on his dirt bike when he started to feel stressed out, or imagine he was working on an engine with Dad. He was less angry at home and his teacher reported that he was participating more in class. By the last session his pile of blocks had been only three high for four consecutive weeks, and he reported feeling less anxious, and said that he looked forward to spending time with Dad, even when they were only doing homework.

Mr. and Mrs. Orsen began to recognize that many of Brian's behaviors were typical of a boy his age, but their concerns had been compounded by their worry for his future because of his learning difficulties. They wanted Brian to be happy and to be a mechanic, but knew that he would have to struggle to be able to gain a reading level that would make it possible for him to become a mechanic and at least obtain a high school degree. However, they were pleased that he was happier, less anxious, and seemed to feel better about himself. In fact, they all reported feeling less anxious and closer to one another.

Summary

The focus of change in solution-focused therapy is to help clients reach their stated goal. This is accomplished by checking on behavior and reactions that occur between sessions, complimenting and highlighting change, and asking future-oriented questions (Dermer, Hemesath, & Russell, 1998). The focus on the expertise of each person in the family and his or her goal makes it a flexible, respectful approach easily utilized with both children and adults. Integrating play is a natural fit with the goals and key interventions of solution-focused therapy.

NARRATIVE

Most of us have heard fairy tales as children. These stories represent some dilemma in life and are meant to teach us a lesson. Hopefully, none of us have been threatened to be eaten by a wolf or stuffed in an oven by a witch; nevertheless, we all have our personal stories about ourselves and the people in our lives. The difference between our favorite bedtime stories and our personal stories (narratives) is that, according to narrative therapists, these stories don't reflect life—they create it. In trying to make sense of their experiences, people create a self-narrative of their own life and the world around them (White & Epston, 1990). People tend to become the stories they hear and tell about themselves and their experience. Storying our experiences makes life meaningful and provides a context for understanding ourselves and the world (White & Epston, 1990).

Individual, couple, and family narratives are created within the context of larger societal narratives. These stories tend to become internalized truths within all people in a society so that people come to judge their bodies, achievements, and personalities on the basis of standards set by society's people in power (Nichols & Schwartz, 2004). Subjugated knowledge/stories are anything that does not fit within the dominant story. Narrative therapists explore subjugated knowledge for alternative meaning when dominant knowledge restricts a person's view of oneself and does not adequately account for a person's lived reality.

Because narrative therapy is based on social constructionism, language and its influence on the perception of reality has an exalted position within the theory. The language of children is play. How we communicate about experiences influences how we process and assign meaning to those experiences. How we assign meaning isn't usually based on just one experience, but how that experience fits in with our life story. One cannot just reframe that one moment—the narrative that leads that person to that interpretation has to be reconstructed.

In defining health, narrative therapists try not to make judgments about what is "normal." People typically need to be liberated from society's concept of normal rather than indoctrinated into it. Nevertheless, several basic assumptions guide narrative therapists: (1) people are good and don't need or want their problems; (2) people tend to internalize societal discourses; (3) people are separate from their problems; (4) once people become aware of their stories and can separate themselves from them, they can develop alternative, empowering stories (Nichols & Schwartz, 2004).

Therapist Role and Goal of Therapy

The goal of narrative therapy and the role of the therapist are closely connected. The therapist takes a collaborative, empathetic, exploratory role with clients. Therapists are encouraged to constantly monitor their own internalized discourses for signs of privilege and unhelpful assumptions and encourage clients to correct therapists if they mistakenly make assumptions that do not fit the clients' narrative. Overall, the goal is to help people reconstruct more productive narratives. This is done through first deconstructing narratives, externalizing problems, looking for alternative subplots, opening room for new stories, and then reconstructing the narrative. Meaning is the focus, rather than behavior.

Interventions

The first, and one of the most important, steps is to truly listen to a person's story. Narrative therapists start by listening to clients' stories in order to empathize with the client, understand the client's view of self and world, and begin to understand what led them to seek assistance (Freedman & Combs, 1996). This kind listening requires taking a position of not-knowing, rather than listening with the "ear of an expert." Listening and asking questions from a position of not-knowing means we ask questions without having a particular answer in mind when asking the question (Freedman & Combs, 1996).

As therapy progresses, narrative therapists identify messages people have internalized about themselves that lead them to think they are bad, abnormal, powerless, worthless, and so on. Narrative therapists work to externalize these internal discourses so that they can be deconstructed. Rather than being seen as something inherent in the person, externalizing internal discourses allows the *messages* to be combated, rather than the person. Problems occur because people become indoctrinated into limiting, self-defeating views of themselves and their possibilities. Externalization places the problem outside of the person and as something that influences people—clients can then choose to alter that influence.

As problems are externalized the therapist listens for exceptions to the problem's influence and for subjugated stories that may provide sources of strength for clients. Clients may be helped to own stories that may have been oppressed by larger society, to consider alternative stories that clients may not have been aware of, and to look for times when the problem didn't exist or when clients were able to resist the problem. All of this is done so that clients can be freed from negative internalized dialogues, subjective stories can be valued, and new stories can be integrated into a new, reconstructed narrative.

Integrating Play in Narrative Therapy

At first, narrative therapy may sound like a highly cognitive approach that would only appeal to adults. To the contrary, narrative approaches are well suited to children (Freeman, Epston, & Lobovits, 1997; Simons & Freedman, 2000). Children may not be able to sit down and have conversations about their beliefs, but their narratives are easily expressed through play and fantasy. It is the therapist's job to enter the client's worldview and find ways to understand their narratives. Using play, drawings, storytelling, externalizing, and utilizing one's imagination to combat the influence of the problem are all congruent with children's forms of communication. Rather than asking children to enter the adult world, adults are asked to tap into their playfulness and the creativity that characterize children.

The younger the child, the less he or she has internalized dominant stories of "how to be" and the more they are willing to consider alternative stories. Both children and adults are encouraged to name or externalize problems and find creative ways to outsmart them. Problems are personified through naming, which gives people something concrete around which to unify. This puts parents and the child together to team up against a common enemy (see Sori, 2006a). For example, children may be asked to draw a picture of "Anger Monster," use the wall to indicate his size when he is the most distracting, and then parents and children can be asked to notice times when they are able to "cut him down in size." Children may be asked to select a puppet or Furby to act as a "consultant" to offer advice on how to overcome the monster (see Sholtes, 2003). The use of therapeutic letters to young people (Pare & Rombach, 2003) and certificates (Simons & Freedman, 2000) are playful, creative ways to celebrate and thicken a child's new narrative that has replaced his or her old, dominant stories. There are many other excellent examples of how to utilize narrative therapy with both children and adults (see Freedman & Combs, 1996; Freeman, Epston, & Lobovits, 1997; Selekman, 1997; White & Epston, 1990).

Case Example of Integrating Play with Narrative Family Therapy: Dezapping the Distraction Monster

A therapist who worked in a medical family practice setting received a referral to see 7-year-old Sammy and his parents, Molly and Fred Dunston. Sammy, a gifted only child, had recently been diagnosed with attention deficit hyperactivity disorder, and was on a low dose trial of a medication. Although he was showing some improvement in school, his parents were frustrated with their attempts to help him organize and manage his homework and daily tasks. The physician thought that family counseling might help the parents and Sammy to learn to adapt to the demands of this diagnosis.

In the first session, Sammy was bright and talkative, with a vocabulary that far exceeded his second-grade level. The Dunstons seemed warm and supportive, and very proud of Sammy's accomplishments. When asked what he was good at and liked to do, Sammy replied that he was on the chess team, and played violin in both the school and inner-city orchestra. He also loved to do magic tricks, and write stories and illustrate them. The therapist remarked that all these activities took tremendous concentration.

When asked what everyone would like to have happen in coming to counseling so that they would feel it was worthwhile, Sammy said he wanted to be able to pay attention better and not forget things or loose things so easily. His parents agreed with these goals, and his mother explained that although Sammy was doing better in school since starting on the medication, mornings were still especially frustrating. Often Sammy seemed not to hear her constant reminders to get out of bed, brush his teeth and get dressed, come to breakfast, pack his school bag, find his shoes, coat, and gloves, and get out the door in time to catch the bus. Frequently Mom resorted to yelling as the minutes ticked away, and all too often the last-minute searches for homework or school books resulted in Sammy missing the bus. When asked his view of this, Dad replied that he was usually gone shortly after Mom first started trying to rouse Sammy.

The therapist summarized the goals as Sammy wanting to pay better attention, and being better at remembering things that he was supposed to do or where he had put things. Everyone agreed with these goals. Next, the therapist began to externalize the problem by asking if Sammy could give a name to this problem; what he would call this thing that was causing him trouble. Sammy promptly replied, "The Distraction Monster!" The therapist asked Sammy if he knew what Distraction Monster looked like. When Sammy replied yes, he was asked to draw a picture of the monster. While he drew, the therapist gathered some additional information from the parents, and discussed some parenting tips, such as giving one directive at a time and checking to see that Sammy had followed through, and then offering positive feedback.

Sammy's drawing depicted a monster with a large head and what appeared to be an enormous eye on a coiled spring in the middle of the monster's forehead. When asked about the picture and how Distraction Monster affected him, Sammy enthusiastically relayed the following:

> Distraction Monster tricks me! He hides, and when I walk in a room suddenly, "Boiing"—this eye springs out and zaps me on the forehead! Then I go (Sammy assumed a wide-eyed, dazed expression), and I just stare off into space! I'm a goner, and just can't pay any attention at all!

Next the therapist asked detailed questions about when, where, and how Distraction Monster has the most influence on Sammy. He learned that Distraction Monster bothered Sammy most often in the mornings (before the medication) and in the evenings. However, sometimes the monster still appeared at school. He tricked Sammy by distracting him with daydreams or thoughts of stories he might write. The therapist explored how Distraction Monster affected Sammy's parents and got Sammy in trouble. The session ended with the homework assignment for Sammy and his parents to be "detectives" and to observe times when Distraction Monster is not around, or when he tries to trick Sammy, but Sammy is able to outsmart him.

The second session began with the therapist exploring the homework assignment of finding unique outcomes to the problem. He learned from Sammy that Distraction Monster was appearing less often at school. His parents had noticed that he still tried to distract Sammy before school, but that Sammy had managed to defeat his influence and to catch the bus on time four days that week—a record!

The therapist asked if he could interview Distraction Monster (see Morgan, 2000; Sholtes & Sori, 2004). Sammy agreed, and holding his picture from the previous session, he answered the therapist's questions. Speaking as Distraction Monster, Sammy told the therapist he'd been at this job of distracting Sammy since before he started school, but that he'd gotten really good at it in second grade, as Sammy gets easily bored with the school work. Some of his best tricks to distract Sammy included putting the sound of orchestra music in his head and making his fingers move along an imaginary violin fingerboard, or distracting him with images of drawings he could do for his stories. When asked what the most difficult part of his job was, Distraction Monster said it was when Sammy was practicing violin, playing in the orchestra, writing, drawing, or reading. Those were times when Sammy just plain ignored him! When asked what part of his distracting work he was most proud of, Distraction Monster said it was when he succeeded in getting Sammy in trouble for missing the bus! When asked if he ever took a vacation, Distraction Monster said yes, when Sammy went to summer music camp.

After this interview the therapist presented Sammy with numerous animal puppets and asked him to choose one that might be a good consultant (see Sholtes, 2003) to help him know when he should focus on something he should be doing. Sammy selected the owl, saying that owls were wise and had sharp eyes to see what they were supposed to be doing (even at night), and sharp ears to hear things around them (even the sounds of mice in the woods). The therapist then interviewed the owl puppet, asking what he was good at (music and art!), and inquiring as to whether he would agree to watch Sammy this week and help advise him when to pay attention to something or someone, and when it was safe to notice other things. Sammy, talking through the owl puppet, agreed. Mom and Dad were encouraged to watch for more exceptions and times when Sammy was heeding the advice of the owl. The therapist took pictures of the owl puppet for Sammy to take home as a concrete reminder of his advisor.

In subsequent sessions, Sammy reported that his advisor had been helpful on several occasions. For example, the owl picture next to his bed reminded him to listen to mom and pack his school bag at night, and in the morning the owl helped him remember to get dressed quickly and eat, and that if he was ready early he could draw or practice violin before school! His parents also noticed that Sammy was becoming an expert at defeating Distraction Monster. When asked how he did this, Sammy responded:

> When I hear him sneaking up on me I surprise him—I jump around and give him a karate chop and his eye springs right back in his head! (He demonstrated this chop.) He can't get me then! The owl helps me listen for when he's trying to sneak up on me. Sometimes owl even helps me drag him into a closet where I lock him up! Other times I put on my magic cape and take my wand and say, "Monster be gone! Monster no more!" Then he just disappears! Sometimes when he tries to sneak up on me at school, I say "Wise old owl to the rescue!" And then I just listen hard to the teacher or stare hard at my math sheets. Owl reminds me that after I get my work done I can imagine in my mind, so I hurry up to finish.

The therapist commented on how brave and wise Sammy was (like the owl!) in finding so many ways to defeat Distraction Monster. Sammy, his parents, and the therapist made a list of all the ways Sammy had learned, with the help of owl, to diminish the influence of Distraction Monster. In addition, Sammy's parents decided to follow the therapist's suggestion and ask that he be tested for a new gifted program at his school.

As Sammy and his parents continued to team up to defeat Distraction Monster and his parents implemented some new parenting ideas (such as having him pack his bag and place it by the door the night before, and checking to be sure his homework was inside), he continued to improve. The teacher also noticed a difference in his ability to concentrate in school, and he did qualify for gifted classes, which he found quite interesting. Sammy's parents were happy with their progress, and his doctor was glad that he was doing well and did not need a higher dose of medication.

At their last session, the therapist asked Sammy to again draw a picture of Distraction Monster. This time the monster was quite diminished in size and rather withered and decrepit looking, and he leaned heavily on a cane. His zapping eye hung uncoiled, trailing on the ground, rather useless looking. Sammy wrote a letter to Distraction Monster (see Sori & Biank, 2006), in which he gleefully informed the monster that his power had been broken, and Sammy felt victorious. The therapist gave Sammy a certificate for "Bravery in Dezapping the Distraction Monster," and the certificate listed all the ways Sammy had learned to avoid the tricks and traps that had previously gotten him into trouble.

Summary

As stated earlier, one of the crucial aspects of narrative therapy is to listen to client stories. Listening, though, doesn't just have to be the recounting of memories and ideas. Stories can also be told through drawing, role-playing, sandtray, letter writing, interviewing the problem, and other forms of play. Fantasy play elicits feelings of mastery and control that can be internalized, enabling children to find ways to triumph over real-life difficulties.

APPLYING PLAYFUL INTERVENTIONS TO VARIOUS FAMILY THERAPY APPROACHES

The active nature of play makes it especially well suited for children and for family therapy—multiple people can easily be engaged at the same time. Play therapy ideas and interventions can be adapted to meet the theoretical assumptions of various family therapy models. For example, by observing the family process during play therapists can see who holds the power in the family, who appears distant, and how the members make decisions.

In the ***family puppet interview*** (Gil, 1994; Gil & Sobol, 2000; Irwin & Malloy, 1994) each family member selects a puppet and the family is instructed to make up a story with a beginning, middle, and end, but not a story with which they are familiar. They are to rehearse the story and then act it out, talking through the puppets. Sometimes the enactment is a different story than what they rehearsed. Therapists observe the family process as well as the content of the story. Clinicians can identify family structure, roles, the emotional climate, and how the family communicates.

In addition to being adapted to the tenets of structural therapy, this same intervention can also be used in narrative therapy or solution-focused therapy. Family members often project their thoughts and feelings onto the puppets, which can be used to externalize their feelings. From a solution-focused perspective, families also can be asked to create a new story, using the same puppets, about what will be happening when they have solved their problem.

Another example of a play technique that is easily adaptable to multiple models is ***family sandtray.*** With the family sandtray (Carey, 1994; Gil, 1994; Gil & Sobol, 2000; McWay & Ruble, 2003) the family might be invited to use miniatures to create their world in the sand. As family members work together the counselor is able to observe their interactions, how they negotiate the task, and their level of enjoyment (Gil & Sobol, 2000). In families with diffuse boundaries the tray may be divided, and each family member can construct their own scene. Another variation from a solution focus approach is to have the family build two worlds: one depicting how they see their family now and the other describing how they would like their family to be, if a miracle occurred. This could open space to discuss parts of the ideal world that are already occurring or have occurred in the past (exceptions). A picture could be taken of the ideal world, and sandtrays could be done every few weeks to measure the family's progress toward their goal (i.e., scaling questions). As in the family puppet interview, therapists observe family process and use their metaphor to create interventions. The content of the tray often represents the emotional climate and themes that the family is experiencing. There are numerous other family play techniques that can be adapted to fit the goals of various family therapy models.

CONCLUSION

Family therapists need not forsake family therapy models in order to utilize play activities. In fact, play can greatly enhance whatever therapy model one is already using. Therapists would do well to create a "therapeutic Neverland," where, through the wonder and magic of fantasy play, families can not only work through their problems but also can create better ways of relating together. Hopefully, when they leave Neverland, they will take the magic of play with them and become happier, healthier families.

REFERENCES

Ariel, S., Carel, C. A., & Tyano, S. (1985). Uses of children's make-believe play in family therapy: Theory and clinical examples. *Journal of Marital and Family Therapy, 11*, 47–60.

Barrie, J. M. (1911). *The adventures of Peter Pan*. Public domain.

Berg, I. K., & Steiner, T. (2003). *Children's solution work*. New York: Norton.

Carey, L. (1994). Family sandplay therapy. In C. Schaefer & L. Carey (Eds.), *Family play therapy* (pp. 205–219). Northvale, NJ: Jason Aronson.

Clements, R., & Musker, J. (Producers & Directors). (1992). Aladdin [Motion picture]. United States: Disney.

Dermer, S. B., Hemesath, C. W., Russell, C. S. (1998). A feminist critique of solution-focused therapy. *American Journal of Family Therapy, 26*(3), 239–250.

de Shazer, S. (1985). *Keys to solution in brief therapy*. New York: Norton.

Freedman, J., & Combs, G. (1996). *Narrative therapy: The social construction of preferred realities*. New York: W. W. Norton & Company.

Freeman, J., Epston, D., & Lobovits, D. (1997). *Playful approaches to serious problems: Narrative therapy with children and their families*. New York: W. W. Norton & Company.

Gil, E. (1994). *Play in family therapy*. New York: Guilford.

Gil, E. (2003). Play genograms. In C. F. Sori, L. L. Hecker, & Associates, *The therapist's notebook for children and adolescents: Homework, handouts, and activities for use in psychotherapy* (pp. 49–56). Binghamton, NY: Haworth.

Gil, E., & Sobol, B. (2000). Engaging families in therapeutic play. In C. E. Bailey (Ed.), *Children in therapy: Using the family as a resource* (pp. 341–382). New York: W. W. Norton.

Grazer, B. (Producer), & Howard, R. (Director). (1998). *Parenthood* [Motion picture]. United States: Universal Pictures.

Irwin, E. C., & Malloy, E. S. (1994). Family puppet interview. In C. Schaefer & L. Carey (Eds.), *Family play therapy* (pp. 21–34). Northvale, NJ: Aronson.

Keith, D. V., & Whitaker, C. A. (1981). Play therapy: A paradigm for work with families. *Journal of Marital and Family Therapy, 7,* 243–254.

Marshall, F., & Molen, G. R. (Producers), & Spielberg, S. (Director). (1991). *Hook* [Motion picture]. United States: Tri-Star Pictures.

McWay, L., & Ruble, N. (2003). Family sandplay: Strengthening the parent-child bond. In C. F. Sori, L. L. Hecker, & Associates, *The therapist's notebook for children and adolescents: Homework, handouts, and activities for use in psychotherapy* (pp. 79–82). Binghamton, NY: Haworth.

Minuchin, S. (1974). *Families and family therapy.* Cambridge, MA: Harvard University Press.

Morgan, A. (2000). *What is narrative therapy?: An easy to read introduction.* Adelaide, Australia: Gecko, Dulwich Centre Publications.

Nichols, M. P., & Schwartz, R. C. (2004). *Family therapy: Concepts and methods* (6th ed.). New York: Allyn & Bacon.

O'Hanlon, W. H., & Weiner-Davis, M. (1989). *In search of solutions.* New York: W. W. Norton.

Pare, D., & Rombach, M. A. M. (2003). Therapeutic letters to young persons. In C. F. Sori, & L. L. Hecker, & Associates, *The therapist's notebook for children and adolescents: Homework, handouts, and activities for use in psychotherapy* (pp. 199–203). Binghamton, NY: Haworth.

Satir, V. (1988). *The new peoplemaking.* Palo Alto, CA: Science and Behavior Books.

Selekman, M. D., (1993). *Pathways to change: Brief therapy solutions for working with difficult adolescents.* New York: Guilford.

Selekman, M. D. (1997). *Solution-focused therapy with children: Harnessing family strengths for systemic change.* New York: Guilford.

Selekman, M. D. (2000). Solution-oriented brief family therapy with children. In C. E. Bailey (Ed.), *Children in therapy: Using the family as a resource.* New York: Norton.

Shilts, L., & Duncan, B. L. (2003). Integrating externalization and scaling questions: Using visual scaling to amplify children's voices. In C. F. Sori, L. L. Hecker, & Associates, *The therapist's notebook for children and adolescents: Homework, handouts, and activities for use in psychotherapy* (pp. 230–236). Binghamton, NY: Haworth.

Sholtes, S. K. (2003). The use of consultants in play therapy: Narrative practices with young children. In C. F. Sori, L. L. Hecker, & Associates, *The therapist's notebook for children and adolescents: Homework, handouts, and activities for use in psychotherapy* (pp. 225–229). Binghamton, NY: Haworth.

Sholtes, S. K., & Sori, C. F. (2004, May). *Strength-based work with chronically ill children and their families in school settings.* Presentation at the Chicago Center for Family Health: Family and School Partnership Program, Chicago, IL.

Simons, V. A., & Freedman, J. (2000). Witnessing bravery: Narrative ideas for working with children and families. In C. E. Bailey (Ed.), *Children in therapy: Using the family as a resource* (pp. 20–45). New York: Norton.

Sori (1995). The "art" of restructuring. *Journal of Family Psychotherapy, 6*(2), 13–31.

Sori, C. (1998). Involving children in family therapy: Making family movies. In L. Hecker and S. Deacon (Eds.), *Therapist's notebook of homework, handouts, and activities* (pp. 281–284). Binghamton, NY: Haworth.

Sori, C. (2000). *Training family therapists to work with children in family therapy: A modified Delphi study*. Unpublished doctoral dissertation, Purdue University, Lafayette, IN.

Sori, C. F. (2006a). A playful postmodern approach to counseling children and families: An interview with Lee Shilts, chap. 6 in this volume.

Sori, C. F. (2006b). Family play therapy: An interview with Eliana Gil, chap. 4 in this volume.

Sori, C. F. (2006c). On counseling children and families: Recommendations from the experts, chap. 1 in this volume.

Sori, C. F. (2006d). Reflections on children in family therapy: An interview with Salvador Minuchin, chap. 2 in this volume.

Sori, C. F., & Biank, N. (2003). Soaring above stress: Using relaxation and visualization with anxious children. In C. F. Sori, L. L. Hecker, & Associates, *The therapist's notebook for children and adolescents: Homework, handouts, and activities for use in psychotherapy* (p. 25–39). Binghamton, NY: Haworth.

Sori, C. F., & Biank, N. (2006). Counseling children and families experiencing serious illness, chap. 11 in this volume.

Sori, C. F., Hecker, L. L., & Associates (2003). *The therapist's notebook for children and adolescents: Homework, handouts, and activities for use in psychotherapy*. Binghamton, NY: Haworth.

Sori, C. F., & Sprenkle, D. (2004). Training family therapists to work with children in family therapy: A modified Delphi study. *Journal of Marital and Family Therapy, 30*(4), 479–495.

White, M., & Epston, D. (1990). *Narrative means to therapeutic ends*. New York: Norton.

PART II

Models for Working with Children and Families

Interviews with the Experts

CHAPTER 4

Family Play Therapy

An Interview with Eliana Gil

CATHERINE FORD SORI, PH.D.

> Injecting play into the family interaction enhances opportunities for them to connect. Laughing together creates opportunities for attachment. It creates contacts that are really important, it helps people see each other in different lights ... Because now they've had an opportunity to see something that maybe they haven't seen before.
>
> **—Eliana Gil, 2005**

Dr. Eliana Gil is the director of the Starbright Training Institute for Child and Family Play Therapy, which offers comprehensive clinical training programs on the assessment and treatment of child abuse and neglect, and the application of play therapy in the treatment of children and families. For seven years, she was the director at the Anova Keller Center, where she developed a program using play therapy to treat abuse and trauma. Dr. Gil is also in private practice at the Multicultural Clinical Center in Springfield, Virginia, and she is currently developing a program called Children's Corner, which will provide mental health services to young children. She is a registered play therapy supervisor, a registered art therapist, and a licensed marriage and family therapist, having received her Ph.D. in family therapy from the California Graduate School of Family Psychology. She has served on the boards of directors of the American Professional Society on the Abuse of Children and the National Resource Center on Child Sexual Abuse, and is the past president of the Association for Play Therapy. Eliana Gil is an adjunct faculty member at Virginia Tech and George Washington Universities, where she teaches both family therapy and play courses. She has authored numerous books and articles on family play therapy and treating children who have experienced abuse or trauma. She recently finished a new book, called *Moving Mountains*, which outlines her integrative approach to treating abuse and trauma.

* * *

In the first part of this interview Eliana Gil, the leading proponent of family play therapy, discussed her background in family therapy and play therapy, and how she became interested in integrating play in family therapy. She then reflected on early family therapy theorists who emphasized playful, creative work that included children.

Sori: I'd like to start by asking you something about your background. Many counselors see the fields of family therapy and play therapy as diametrically opposed, and yet you have built a bridge between these two fields. Can you talk a bit about your background and how you came to be a family play therapist?

Gil: Well, I got a doctorate in family therapy in a program in California and I noticed that most of the family therapists enjoyed and encouraged the participation of older kids. As soon as the children got younger it was almost like an *aversion*—some kind of hesitation, that was really visible. It really sparked my interest in why that was so. What became clear was a *lack of preparation to work with children* and an acute level of discomfort—that if the kids couldn't engage in verbal conversation clinicians felt uncomfortable. It was almost—fear is a strong word, but there was some kind of hesitation, that kids say what's on their minds, or might call them on something. Some colleagues told me, "They push my buttons and I'm just not patient with them."

At the same time I started pursuing training in play therapy because I worked with abused children who often have barriers to speaking verbally. I was getting referrals of younger and younger kids, and all of the training that I'd had about having these therapeutic dialogues was wonderful, except that many little kids didn't have language skills available to them. And even when the kids did have language, these issues were difficult to discuss verbally.

In those days, around 1978, in terms of play therapy, there was very little available other than trying to find workshops. I was doing kind of a parallel process—I was into the family therapy program and then I was taking these additional trainings and pursuing as much as I could regarding this whole notion of trying to find avenues for making contact with kids. Really these are the seeds, and from there bloomed this interest in trying to integrate the two fields [family therapy and play therapy] because I just felt that it was so sad that so many family therapists seemed to be reluctant to invite and integrate kids into the sessions, and I felt that without the children, we were losing real opportunities to be of greater assistance to families.

Once we were watching through a one-way mirror, and this particular little boy was given paper and pencil—it was a domestic violence situation. After the session everyone went to clean up and all this kid's drawings went into the trash. I took them out and looked at them, and oh my gosh! They had symbols of caves and a child who was cowered in a corner, and there was a fist on top. All these images that, if we had looked at what the child was drawing, would have given us a better idea of how to intervene, and that safety was the primary issue in that particular family. So I said to myself, I really have to get more education, more training in the areas of expressive therapies and play therapy in particular.

There have been people who tried [to integrate play in family therapy] and have written about it and had some great ideas. But they don't seem to ignite the kind of interest that people run with, and so even though people are aware of it, it doesn't seem to be something that they are particularly drawn to.

Sori: Who are some of the early theorists who have written a bit about being playful or using play in family therapy?

Gil: Well, one was Carl Whitaker. Again, being in the family therapy program we would always be exposed to his videotapes, so I remember that he had a very playful quality. I saw some video tapes of him actually bringing toys into the room, sitting on the floor, and I thought that he in particular had a greater ease with children.

There have been other people since then, but Whitaker really struck me. Peggy Papp taught about family sculpting. I thought she was trying to get the family to utilize an energy—a sort of physical energy that was different than doing the question/

answer dialogue. Those were the people that I remember earlier on. Of course others include Minuchin and Combrinck-Graham. Family therapists are so creative as a group—they are always coming up with these really innovative theories and activities, and yet when it comes to kids, it just seems that something happens.

Gil then commented on the current state of family therapy regarding the integration of play, and the dichotomy between family therapy and play therapy that still exists today in the field of psychotherapy. She also discussed some of the resistance to play therapy, research issues, and the importance of the therapeutic relationship.

Sori: Do you think it has changed much in the last 30 years, or do you think the family therapy field is still kind of there where they were in terms of understanding the importance of play?

Gil: I'll tell you. I think I have greater luck convincing play therapists about family play therapy than I have convincing family therapists about integrating play. I don't know if it's as a whole, family therapists tend to be more analytical and intellectual, and you know, seem to like to debate theories, and are very focused on language and therapeutic dialogues.

Michael White, for example, has amazing creativity in working with families and children. Yet most of the time what he's asked to present on isn't highlighting that aspect of his work. But he's got some really creative things that he's done with kids and I really was hopeful that some of that would catch on a little more. I come back to this notion that people don't do things they don't feel competent doing, and if they don't have the training in play therapy …

Also, play therapy continues to have a credibility problem. Those of us that do it are very invested in it and recognize how useful it is. But other fields are very dismissive. Right now, mental health practitioners are very focused on evidence-based treatment. Play therapy has research, but probably not the type and level of research that could really sway opinion. Play therapy continues to have these problems in terms of how valuable people think it may be. I also think because it has all the toys, it sometimes gives the impression of being light, of being something more recreational than therapeutic. There is still much that needs to get done so that people understand the elements behind play therapy that can produce therapeutic change in the same way that other therapies might.

Sori: Do you think that there hasn't been more research on play therapy because it is just harder to do—it is harder to measure outcome research on children?

Gil: Well, that's what I think. The most well-researched area, at least in the treatment of sexual abuse, is cognitive behavioral treatment, and when I look at that, the research, there's a curriculum, there's a structured program, it takes this long, you do and say these things, so it is much more easy to measure. Whereas, when you are talking about play therapy you are talking about things that you may not be able to connect together and you may not see immediate results. I should say it's much harder to define it, plus I think that most good play therapy occurs in the context of a therapy relationship.

Sori: Exactly. And the therapeutic relationship is so important.

Gil: Which again is very difficult to measure, especially if you are trying to measure the child's response to it. At least with adults, when you ask adults what is it about the therapy that is helpful, they are able to tell you that it is all relationship based. But I think with kids it just gets a lot more complicated.

But that's where the field of play therapy has to grow. The APT [Association for Play Therapy] is working with a task force to look at what research we need to do to increase our value and visibility and credibility. So efforts are under way.

Next, Gil described her training work at Starbright Training Institute for Child and Family Play Therapy and the Multicultural Family Institute with Monica McGoldrick. She offered insight into the conception of the family play genogram (Gil, 2003), which sprang from her supervision of students who were presenting genograms at the Multicultural Family Institute.

Sori: That is fascinating. Would you touch on your work at Starbright Child and Family Play Therapy Institute, and at the Multicultural Family Institute, too? I know you work with Monica McGoldrick, and one of my favorite interventions you developed is the family play genogram. I can't tell you how many clients and trainees are so moved by that. Could you talk about how you developed that?

Gil: Yes. I started Starbright Training Institute probably 12 years ago. I was in Pennsylvania doing a training and there were 600 people in the audience. I remember saying to myself, I will never do this again, because I couldn't make any contact with anyone. I said, "I want to do something where I can have fewer than 20 people at a time, where I can actually build relationships with people. Where we have the ability to exchange ideas, and people can actually do experiential work." Without that component, you cannot move further than someone's vague understanding of why something might be helpful.

In Starbright Institute Training the idea was to provide all those opportunities in small groups and try to have a more personal kind of contact with people.

Sori: Well, I can personally attest to how wonderful it is!

Gil: In terms of Multicultural Family Institute, my relationship with Monica McGoldrick goes back probably a good 10 to 12 years. We met at an AFTA (American Family Therapy Academy) conference, and I was struck because she is so humble and so personal and congruent with her theories. She is just, "What you see is what you get!" I mean she is wonderful. Her friendships are really important to her. I met her and she invited me to come to New Jersey. Initially we were doing family puppet stories and family artwork, and one day a light went on and she just said, "I want to have this program incorporate play therapy!" So we went about trying to develop some kind of curriculum.

Probably eight years ago, the students at Monica's were presenting these huge genograms with lots of generations, symbols, and signs. It's exciting because they are immersed in Bowenian theory. They would bring families in and then I would demonstrate family play therapy, and we would sit around and process the sessions. One day this family was presented to me, and by then Monica had miniatures all over the building. Now every room has puppets and sandtrays, and it is wonderful to see how play therapy really "took"! She has this incredible respect for family play therapy. It's been great—a very collaborative process. Anyway, we were talking about what we should do with this family and I said, "I would like us to lay out a genogram on an easel and then I think we should ask them [family members] to pick miniatures that most represent that person and put them down on the genogram, and see what happens from there." And that was it—the birth of the family play genogram! It's been refined and expanded some from that time.

Sori: So the idea sprang from your work with Monica McGoldrick and her student's work with that particular family!

Gil next began to describe the value of play therapy, the benefits of nonverbal work, and using objects such as miniatures that can serve as metaphors to express both conscious and unconscious meaning.

Gil: It was so interesting. We spent about three hours after that, talking about everything that had come up and how the family had manipulated the figures. When you ask people to do the miniature work, the verbal process, the cognitive process, in some ways all that is set aside and it's a much more raw and honest language. These miniatures speak to the person. Suddenly there's layers of meaning and associations that may be made, but it is a process that lowers the defenses in some way and allows access to the emotional life of the client.

Probably it is not just the miniature, but that it can go into a fantasy, it can expand its own possibility because the person is interacting with it so much (projecting, observing, reacting, expanding with the metaphor). That is probably the proudest moment that I've had. I don't know where it came from. There was probably something about that family that just elicited the response.

Sori: When you talk about the relationship that people get with an object, with a puppet or a miniature, I think of two things. I think of Gestalt—an empty chair where they are in dialogue with something or in a relationship, or it is like externalizing, and the object becomes that. It takes on a life of its own.

Gil: I think that's true. Again, I think there's a "feeding off"—it's like a circularity because then the person observes the object and the object is endowed with other qualities or possibilities. It is a circular process with the potential to grow. Once you've got a miniature you can then put it in different settings in your imagination. It's a very interesting thing to do.

Sori: Sometimes a student or intern will give me a gift, and often it's a puppet. I always wondered why they chose a particular puppet and what that means.

Gil: It's not accidental. There is nothing accidental. There's the conscious meaning of "I picked this because of THIS," but there's layers of unconscious meaning as well. You're picking up on some kind of other level of contact, and it's really fascinating work to do.

Sori: How interesting! So that was the play genogram.

Next, Gil explained how the selection and use of play objects facilitates externalization and projection. She also described the importance of containers in children's play.

Gil: When you reduce it to its more basic elements, I think that play allows for externalization of something that can really not be verbalized, or sometimes cannot even be perceived accurately. Kids in particular have a lot of events in their lives that often are overwhelming. They may have been overstimulated and can't really give you narratives of what happened to them, how they felt about it, what they did about it and what other people did. The most important and valuable thing is that once things are externalized, they have the potential to be understood by someone else.

The other important point is that when kids select things to play with, there's some reason for their interest in those objects. The potential is for those things to represent other things and for projection to occur. Once the projection has occurred, you know it is not just a squirrel, it's an *angry* squirrel or it's a *scared* squirrel or whatever it may be. There is the potential for working that through and doing it in a safe enough way, which means with the distance that the child needs to be able to begin to look at and address that particular thing.

Another aspect of externalization is that most of the time in play, certainly it's true in sand or in art; there's a container that occurs. The therapist can be part of the container, the room can be part of the container, but sometimes it's the ability to miniaturize things onto a page, a box, an area, that becomes a container. Once externalized and contained, the child can go from a passive victim stance to a management response in some kind of physical, energetic way. This movement may make children feel a little bit less like victims, and a little more active in terms of having personal control and power.

So this describes some of the value and benefits of play therapy. It is also more user-friendly for kids and it is their natural medium. We sit across from them and expect them to answer a whole bunch of questions, but play is really what they do best. For us it is a shift because we have to get comfortable with their language, and for some people there is a much broader gap to cross.

In the following segment, Gil emphasized the importance of treating children in the context of the family, and how vital relationships are to children. She discussed theory and her decision-making process in choosing therapy approaches. Finally, she elaborated more on the benefits of play, and explained some of the basic premises that guide her work.

Gil (continued): In family therapy the family is always in a context; you are never dealing with anything in a vacuum. There are many different parts to any problem that are connected to whether they grow, stay small, or stay the same, depending on how people are responding to the child. Problems expand or constrict based on whether needs are being met, whether direction is being given, whether important limits are being provided, and whether boundaries are appropriate. The child in the context of the family, or whatever system they are in, needs to be constantly invited into therapy, or clinicians miss a huge part that could be the hidden problem.

Reconnection is also critical to kids. It is not enough that they have a therapy relationship with someone. They've also got to be able to have some kind of connection to the world. Trying to find adults who are invested in children and encouraging substantive contact is critical.

Sori: That's it! I see so many elements in your work of psychodynamic and experiential theories, and I think of Satir and also Minuchin and structural issues. You've written a lot about working with boundaries and hierarchies and narratives and externalization. Can you comment on what key theories have guided your work?

Gil: You know it's a really interesting thing. The question around "What is your theory?" keeps coming up. People ask, "What kind of play therapy do you do?" I will answer this second question but I'll go back to the first one as well.

In terms of what kind of play therapy I do, it is going to be different with each child that I meet. It is meeting the child that determines what I think might be the most helpful approach for that child, which could be Gestalt play therapy, or it could be Jungian, and it could be cognitive behavioral play therapy. I do different kinds of therapy with different people because they are all so different in terms of their styles of communication, of contact, of approaching problems, of negotiating problems—everything is different. So, I try to respond based on what I think they most are pulling for or need in any particular juncture.

Now, having said all that, I have this incredible belief in the value of play. I think play is good for people. Most of the time people relax around it, benefit from it, experience each other in different ways, and there's a great possibility that some changes will occur based on those therapy sessions. And of course I'm most informed by how people react to it. I've had people cry and say, I can't tell you what it was like for us to sit here and be with each other and have these experiences of playing and laughing together for the first time in years and years.

Sori: Then you respond to that and you do more …

Gil: Absolutely! I follow some basic premises. One is relationship. I'm much less interested in technique. I'm much more interested in making contact with people and sitting down and listening and making sure that they feel heard and seen. I'm very relationship oriented. I also believe in resiliency. Most of the time people have all kinds of resources within them that may be obstructed at that moment, that they may not feel comfortable accessing, or they may not even know that they are there. I think creativity is one of them. I think laughter is another one, as well as imagination. Sometimes I try to take these guided explorations to uncover where their strengths might be.

Gil then discussed postmodern family therapy theories and her belief in a collaborative approach, cultural issues, and being able to integrate models.

Gil (continued): I love to read professional books and learn others' approaches. I love narrative therapy. I think it's wonderful. I like solution-focused therapy. I think of those as invitations that you make to people to see if it is something they are interested in or if it works well with them. If you get into the type of treatment where you expect that everyone is going to follow a particular agenda that you have, that's less useful than really having a collaborative approach to looking at what is the problem as you see it, and in what way can I best help you with that particular problem.

Sori: So you would recommend diverse training so that therapists can pull on a lot of different theories. And technique … to be able to work with people and what they bring in, and who they are.

Gil: I would. And this is particularly true if you are working across cultures, because that is when you really get into the fact that traditional verbal psychotherapy is a Western tradition that all cultures don't really acknowledge, or think of as a particularly helpful thing to do. Some cultures are very hesitant about therapy because they associate it with mental illness, so I think that you really have to look at what some other options might be. In the old days having lots of theoretical approaches used to be called eclectic. Eclectic got a bad name because it sounded like it was someone who was loosey goosey or was flying by the seat of their pants. But the reality is that to be eclectic, you have to have *more* training than a purist. People can be so structured and rigid that they don't go outside their own theory. If you have a real commitment to a particular theory and you think it applies to everyone, that is, one way of thinking about it. For me, I have some things I really truly believe in—like play therapy—*that* would be my guiding force. You treat people within the context of their systems—their various systems—and that's another sort of guiding principle, and beyond that it's kind of like wait and see. I need to meet people. I really need to meet them.

In the following portion of the interview, Gil emphasized the importance of intuition and countertransference, and the use of play techniques for clinicians to explore these issues in themselves.

Gil (continued): It's funny, when I do consultations, I'm meeting the person through the eyes of the therapist who is talking about them, but what I try to let myself do is to *listen for the person,* not the case, but to really listen for the person. If I'm really listening for that person then things start coming into my mind. I have developed an intuition that really seems to respond to individual clients, the consultation question per se. I don't know if that makes sense or not.

Sori: It does. In fact, I wanted to ask about intuition. Can you say more about that? The value you see in the power of intuition?

Gil: Yes. I guess traditionally it's called the gut reaction that you have to people. I've been doing some more work on countertransference, trying to really accept it better and trying to work with it. Larry Rubin and I just finished an article on the use of countertransference using play. That's been a very interesting project to do. You know, those "Gee I want to whisper when that person leaves the room" or "I find myself really feeling sad right now" or whatever it may be. I had a group supervisor once—this will all connect in a minute—and he had us sit and listen to the case and then he'd say, "I'd like all of you to tell me what you are feeling right now." He was really trying to pull our countertransference responses. Once he heard it, like we were sad or depressed or hopeless, he'd say, "Now you know what that person feels. Now you know what the client feels." That was very useful for me. The reality is that all those emotions don't happen in a vacuum and they really do inform you about that particular client.

So play countertransference is the kind of thing where you have a session with someone and you go and do a sandtray or you go and you make a piece of art. Or you go and you do a collage, or whatever it may be, and then you allow yourself to be informed by that process. Countertransference is a form of intuition, a form of gut reaction, a series of thoughts, feelings and reactions that occur in response to this person in front of you, or this case you've just heard. It was really fun to put that article together because the reality is that we believe play therapy helps, so why not use play therapy to help in yet this other arena of helping ourselves externalize, contain, project, discharge, and manage.

Sori: I will be looking for that article! I remember when I came for my training in family play therapy you showed a video of a family from Monica's doing a puppet interview. You didn't tell us anything at all about them, and then you stopped it and you had us do a drawing. That was so powerful! I will never forget that.

Gil: Wasn't it great! I loved that. And I think more and more it is an attempt to access those reactions that are intuitive if you want to call it that—responses that we all have and sometimes we just ignore them. Or we certainly don't spend as much time with them as we could. They offer a lot in terms of looking at the family or what might be going on, or to clarify the directions that we really want or need to take.

Sori: That's great! I'm glad you're writing about that.

Once again, Gil turns to the topic of the many benefits of play for both children and adult clients, and the value of laughter for promoting attachment. She emphasized the primary goal of family play therapy, which is to enhance family interactions, provide opportunities for people to view one another differently, and offer chances for mutual enjoyment. She then emphasized the benefits of this type of work for the clinician in preventing burnout.

Sori (continued): Any specific benefits that play has for children or adults, and what are the goals of family play therapy?

Gil: I think it's sad to watch how over the years people become more and more distant from opportunities to play. It's disheartening that it occurs with the frequency it does. When you bring families and children together you're giving them a chance to make different kinds of contact with each other. If it's happening spontaneously, then that's great, but in the families that I work with, that isn't what's happening. The opposite is true. There's tension, there's anger, there's secrecy, there's emotional disconnect. Injecting play into the family interaction enhances opportunities for them to connect. Laughing together creates opportunities for attachment. It creates contacts that are really important, it helps people see each other in different lights. If you've got a dad who's got big wizard puppets and is able to use big voices and move the body in certain ways and tell stories that are interesting, that forever changes the kid's perceptions of dad. Because now they've had an opportunity to see something that maybe they haven't seen before. If they can see Dad in a softened way, if they can see Mom in a more nurturing way, if they can do some joint activity that's fun, creative, energetic—that all tends to make the contact grow. I think that's a goal of family play therapy, to enhance interactions between family members, to give them chances to see each other differently and have mutual pleasure. After family play therapy sessions, family members can leave the office together saying, "Wow, we've had a good time together doing that!" They've had an opportunity to put something together that's concrete, where a contribution has been made by each family member so that the individuality is identified and acknowledged, but at the same time there's a collective product. The overall goals of trying to have the family function better together and see each other in a different way have been achieved. And when these sessions work well, everyone has a sense of well-being (the research shows) from playing together. If families can leave feeling a little bit better than they felt before they arrived it might motivate them to try to reproduce that feeling. These are the things that we really need to promote in an effort to have some positive impact, to shine some light into a dark corner.

Sori: I am thinking about all the research about the benefits of humor and the physiological functions and endorphins …

Gil: For me when I have families who are laughing together I think this is great!

Sori: And it's good for you, too!

Gil: Absolutely! And that's a good point to make, because it helps to prevent my own burnout. I remember times being in verbal therapy sessions where I felt like I was sinking deeper and deeper into the chair. In order to combat that in myself, I always wanted to move—to move my body, move my creativity, move something, and I find that with families too. When they are depressed they get more still. So this actually can interject some energy and some difference in their lives and they end up feeling like this session was—at a minimum—an interesting thing to do. At a maximum they may feel that it was enjoyable and they really felt connected for a period of time, and sometimes they spontaneously do more of it. Which is great!

Sori: And it is energizing!

In the following section, Gil discussed how she utilizes play therapy to accomplish specific goals in family therapy, and how she designs play interventions to fit the particular child and family situation. She provided a moving case example to illustrate how her interventions flow from the family and their issues and dynamics.

Sori (continued): Is there a difference in how you use play to engage a child and a family member and in how you would use play to intervene?

Gil: Yes, probably flowing is the best word. I am a family play therapist when they come into the room. I introduce myself that way. Now, that means a couple of things: That I am going to be interested in seeing the child with the family or parts of the family, or at some point the child alone. I talk about the value of play therapy and that it is really useful for everyone, as few or as many family members as may be available. So, those two things are said up front. It's also a huge family play therapy room, so they see the toys right away. So it hasn't been too jarring for people when I do invite them to come in. For the most part I do it with every family that I see at some point or another. Because I've worked a lot in the context of a sex abuse program, I do a beginning stage with the kids alone because I really want them to become comfortable with me. As soon as I have a good feeling of that, I start trying to work with as many family members as possible. We always have family therapy sessions in the middle and end phases of treatment. That's the model that I utilize.

As a play therapist my task is to identify and utilize play therapy techniques to promote specific goals. If you are talking to a psychiatrist you would say, I wonder what medicine I could give them to make them feel better. Or if you are talking to a cognitive behavior person they are going to talk about what might shape this behavior differently. I am constantly thinking about what kind of play I can bring in to help them look at that particular issue. So I design some specific options for people.

Sori: Could you give a couple of examples?

Gil: Well, I was working with a family once, where there was an issue of neglect, and the mother had not provided food for the children. Now it's many years later and they are doing a reunification process, but the kids never quite stopped having that anxiety about the mother, even though we talked a lot with the mom about food that would be in the house. I wanted to address the issue of food and at the same time do something that would be family play therapy. Just as the aquarium project is done to have an individual and then a collective projective experience, I had this family do a fruit salad. Their task was for each to pick a fruit—whatever fruit they wanted, and then to bring it back into the office. Then everyone would help to cut the pieces and shape them the way they wanted. They made the salad, and the last part was to put a salad dressing on it. Interestingly enough, the shopping together, the working with food together, the parent providing the limits around sharp objects, and then the group collectively coming up with what would meet everyone's needs in terms of a dressing was a wonderful cooperative venture in the area of food. That was really something I thought worked out very well for that family and really arose from the issue that was most pressing for them.

Sori: That kind of changed the dynamic of how they talked about food and …

Gil: … experienced it, and worked with it. It really helped a lot, and the anxiety about food seemed to decrease after that. They had real fun.

Sori: Your goals—your interventions and ideas, come from looking at the needs of a family and how you can address those needs in a playful way.

Gil moved on to discuss possible limitations to using family play therapy with some clients, and offered a few case examples to illustrate. She then described some of her favorite family play therapy interventions.

Sori (continued): Any cautions about using play? Are there any times that you think play wouldn't fit or be good for a child or an adult?

Gil: I haven't encountered too many situations like that. I have had two very memorable occasions where the family could not do anything playful together at all. I think that is very diagnostic in and of itself. One was at Monica's where the family could not put a story together with a beginning, middle, and an end. In that family nobody was related to anybody in the family. There were no blood relationships, so there was this long story about them but they really weren't connected. They really didn't function as a whole. In the second family the mother had already made a decision to place her children for adoption but hadn't told them. They could not put a family story or a sandtray or anything together. I've always been struck by that. There are some families who will not respond to play therapy at all. I worked with a mom who refused to participate in a family puppet story. We ended suggesting that maybe she could be part of the audience, and we could listen together to her children. And she was able to do that. But in terms of counterindications, I can't say that I know of any. I would exercise the same caution in verbal therapy that I would in any kind of play therapy. If you begin to see that this is not useful or if it is going to produce a situation that's going to be dangerous or threatening, then you better stop it. I personally haven't had any of those experiences. But I'm always conscious that the environment is safe and the therapy is of use to people.

Sori: So this is where you trust your intuition. I look at how many creative family play interventions you've developed and to me they just seem to make the invisible visible, or what can't be talked about, be able to be talked about. I wonder what are your favorite family play interventions?

Gil: Well, I really do love the play genogram; it is not a static technique. It's something that keeps growing all the time, and I have really enjoyed the process of watching what people do with it. I love the aquarium project. Of all the things that I do, I lean toward it. It's a water metaphor, and there is so much life in metaphors. There's so many projections onto fish—dolphins and sharks. I also like the gardening intervention. Anything that sparks creativity in people is really of interest to me. With the kids I like the environment project because you can learn a lot about kids, and they are learning as well. That was something Barbara Sobol, my art therapy supervisor, developed with her colleague and there is something about that project that is very compelling.

Sori: Those are some of my favorites too.

Gil: And of course, I love the puppet interviews. I think the puppet stories are incredible.

The importance of process and content in family play were explained in the next segment of the interview. Then Gil described her thoughts on processing play activities, and trusting the process and one's own intuitive reactions. She emphasized the need to be more fully present with clients and to respond to their stories, rather than focusing cognitively on what questions to ask when processing play activities.

Sori: Well, that leads into the value of process and content. You talk about how both are important. Could you comment on each and give some examples?

Gil: I think that there's the product, there's the story, there's the art, there's whatever they are doing together and whatever it is that comes out, and that's content and that's metaphor. In addition, the process piece is the observation of how the family works together: the nonverbal communication; the level of tension or spontaneity; the unspoken demands that are being made; differential encouragement of a family member. Sometimes families can create a product that says one thing but utilize a process that says something else. I think they are equally important. It's important to observe both. Otherwise you could say to someone, I'd like for you to go do this, and just call me when you're done. But then you've missed so much in terms of looking at what it is that may be getting in their way of having a successful experience together. People can say things that are devalued by the posture of their body or the tone of their voice. You won't really know that unless you happen to be in that room. I think that's the more complete way of doing an assessment.

Sori: Can you talk about using process in a different way? I think the hardest time trainees have is learning how to process an activity with a family after they've done, say, an aquarium. You can give them a list of questions and ideas and things, but it doesn't flow. How do you help people get that flow?

Gil: Working with students in the training process is very interesting because it takes me back to my own process when I was starting out. What I remember the most was the anxiety that I had. "I'm supposed to do something now, right? I'm supposed to say something now, but what is it? What if it is the wrong thing?" I remember that so clearly. Part of doing the experiential piece is learning to be interested in what you are doing, giving yourself a chance to really understand there is no right or wrong action, it's just whatever reaction *you* are having that is happening for some good reason. You need to trust the process. Probably that's my mantra. I say to students all the time, you have to trust the process. *So what* if they don't say anything? What's the worst thing that can happen? It's the anxiety. I say to them, you need to be present, to stop thinking about what you are going to say and do, and just be present with the person, with the story, with the artwork, with whatever it is, and see if you can just respond yourself to what is going on. Just model interest, introspection, curiosity—model it yourself. The other part of it is you don't have to do anything. Invite *them* to do it. Turn to them and say, "I'm wondering what thoughts, feelings, reactions you are having as you look at this now," or "I'm wondering if there's anything you want to ask each other?" I wish that there was some way that students could relax more and be more present. The moment that you start thinking ahead to what the client is thinking, you aren't there any more. Throughout the process, if you start to be analytical, you aren't there anymore.

And that's the hardest thing to teach. One of the best ways to do that is to have them experience play therapy themselves or with trusted others, and then maybe watch it on video. We spend a lot of time going through tapes and then having students generate 10 or 15 responses to the client. Then we talk about each idea they come up with in terms of its potential.

Sori: Then the collective process of everybody …

Gil: Yes, and working with each other. I do show tapes of myself working, but I hesitate to do too much of that because then their creative thinking tends to be decreased by their interest in copying. There isn't anything unique or unusual about what I do. It's a response I'm having to the family I'm with. They have responses as well. Sometimes if they start "over watching" someone then they want to give the response that they think you would give, and that doesn't work.

Sori: That's a good point! The first live session I ever saw was Carl Whitaker, and I'm thinking about him saying …

Gil: … You don't have to do something! I was also really struck with that videotape where he fell asleep and then he got up and he said, so "I wonder what it is about you that made me fall asleep?" And I thought, wow, that's really interesting that he would do that and he really meant it. He was always in the context of the system. All of the responses that occurred within that context had to do with that and his responses to that.

In this final section, Gil returned to the topic of the benefits of play for therapists, and their ability to play. Then she discussed the important concept of "staying in the metaphor" when doing family play therapy, and offered a case example to illustrate the powerful benefits of nonverbal play therapy with an individual adult. The interview ended with Gil once again emphasizing the importance of "trusting the process."

Sori: I recall Whitaker's comment that if he didn't have an experience in a session or didn't feel more fully alive, then it probably wasn't a good session for the client. I'm wondering if using play does that for you.

Gil: Yes. I mentioned that one of the other motivating reasons for doing play is that I believe it is so good for me as well, and I do think it helps prevent burnout in myself. There's a certain openness that comes with play, a certain availability that you have to people when you are playing with them. When I sit down to play something opens up and I become more energetic, more available, more spunky. And having the client experience that in me sometimes is catchy, and it gives them permission and it gives them freedom.

Obviously you can get into problems there if you have a family that has a lot of depression; you don't want to polarize and end up with them feeling that the happier you are the more depressed they can get. It's not about being happy. It's about being more available, being available in a different way. In many of those sessions where there is playfulness going on and there is an experience of play, you can leave feeling pretty satisfied, like you've done something productive, or had a deeper experience for some reason or another. Now that presumes that I can participate on that level. I think where the problem comes in with some therapists is that playing doesn't feel natural for them. It isn't something that helps them feel more available. For some people, playing is hard work and they feel mechanical.

Sori: Constrained.

Gil: Constrained and false. Do you have to be an artist to do art therapy? I think the answer is no. Do you have to be able to play to do play therapy? Maybe the answer is probably. If you can't really value and appreciate it on that level and allow yourself to experience that, it is going to be a little bit harder to encourage it or allow it in other people.

Sori: You don't think you can teach this to everybody?

Gil: I've had the experience of teaching enough that I do think there is a percentage of people who engage in it very cognitively and yet it doesn't feel natural to them. They will find a way to do it, but they can't reach a deeper level.

Sori: Not spontaneous … more proscribed.

Gil: Yes, more proscribed. So maybe you could teach it, it's just a question of whether they would ever learn it at a level where they would have greater availability to people because they are experiencing it.

Sori: I like that, availability. That really captures what happens. I think of the word "fully alive."

Gil: Yes, fully alive works for me, too.

Sori: I talk all the time to my students about staying in the metaphor ...

Gil: There's a couple of places that are hard for people when they are doing this training, and that's one of them. Staying in the metaphor. They really want to go to the real life thing that is happening that *causes* this metaphor to occur, as opposed to staying *in* it. I have some examples that I give of that. A client [an adult] once said, "Here's how I feel—I'm sinking in quicksand." I stopped at that point and I said I'd like you to come over here. We went over to the play therapy area and recreated the sinking in quicksand. We put the quicksand in Tupperware and I asked him to choose a figure that could represent him. He picked a guy with a briefcase and put it in the quicksand. I said, "There you are sinking in quicksand, and I would like for you to just look." He looked and all of a sudden you could see the wheels spinning. He got a life raft, and a tree, and a helicopter, and a rope. It was pretty interesting to watch because he literally created a rescue. Then he took some water and washed and dried the figure, and put it back. I asked what that was like for him to do and he said, "Suddenly I feel like there are things I have to do." That was his internal process, that was his metaphor, and it was making his metaphor concrete that allowed him to then respond to it differently.

Once he has done that, he now takes his metaphor of sinking in quicksand back into his psyche with the potential for rescue. Anytime he ever thinks about the sinking in quicksand metaphor, he will always recall the rescue as well. Probably that possibility was always available to him, but now he has made it concrete. So there is something about the miniaturizing of problems, there's something about it being something you touch and something you can clean and something that you can work with, that I think allows for that energy to be activated.

It was a great example of how the metaphor works. We never really talked about what he needed to do in his life, what changes he was going to go make, or why he felt like he was sinking in that quicksand, he just went and did it.

Sori: And he didn't need to go to the left brain and talk about it and analyze it

Gil: No, he didn't. That is another example of how I followed his lead. Had he begun to talk about it, I would have followed, but he didn't. I didn't need to know because he had already made the change he needed to make. It's called trusting the process. The trainee would need more explanations and understanding than I do. I trust that whatever it is that needed to happen, happened.

Sori: And you don't have to do research on it, you know it happened.

Gil: Exactly. But it's great to ponder the process that ignites in people who play.

Sori: That's fascinating. Thank you so much for sharing your time and your passion about family play therapy!

SUGGESTED READING

Briere, J., & Gil, E. (1998). Self-mutilation in clinical and general population samples: Incidence, correlates, and functions. *American Journal of Orthopsychiatry, (68)*4, 604–620.

Gil, E. (1981). Protecting the rights of children in institutions. Protecting children through the legal system. *American Bar Association.* (National Legal Resource Center for Child Advocacy and Protection, Ed.).

Gil, E. (1982). Defining institutional abuse. *Child and Youth Services, 4,* 1–2, 7–13. New York: Haworth.

Gil, E. (1984). Foster parents: Set up to fail. *Child abuse and neglect, 8*(1), 121–123.

Gil, E. (1988). *Treatment of adult survivors of childhood abuse.* Rockville, MD: Launch Press.

Gil, E. (1991). *The healing power of play: Therapy with abused children.* New York: Guilford.

Gil, E. (1993). *Foster parenting abused children* (2nd ed.). Chicago: National Committee on Child Abuse Prevention.

Gil, E. (1994). *Play in family therapy.* New York: Guilford.

Gil, E. (1995). *A training curriculum for mandated reporters on the California child abuse reporting law.* California Department of Social Services: Office of Child Abuse Prevention. Sacramento: California Consortium to Prevent Child Abuse.

Gil, E. (1996a). *Systemic treatment of families who abuse.* San Francisco: Jossey-Bass.

Gil, E. (1996b). *Treating abused adolescents.* New York: Guilford.

Gil, E. (2003). Play genograms. In C. F. Sori, L. L. Hecker, & Associates, *The therapist's notebook for children and adolescents: Homework, handouts, and activities for use in psychotherapy* (pp. 49–56). Binghamton, NY: Haworth.

Gil, E. (In press-a). *Moving mountains: Transforming children's trauma using collaborative therapeutic play.* Rockville, MD: Launch Press.

Gil, E. (In press-b). *Sex and the single child: A parent's guide to children's sexual development*. New York: Guilford.

Gil, E., & Baxter, K. (1979). Abuse of children in institutions. *International Journal of Child Abuse and Neglect, 3,* 3–4.

Gil, E., & Bogart, K. (1982). An exploratory study of self-esteem and quality of care of 100 children in foster care. *Children and Youth Services Review, 4*(4), 351–363.

Gil, E., & Bogart, K. (1982). A study of children's perceptions of foster care. *Children Today, 11,* 1.

Gil, E., & Drewes, A. A. (2005). *Cultural issues in play therapy*. New York: Guilford.

Gil, E., & Edwards, D. (1986). *Breaking the cycle*. Santa Monica, CA: Association for Advanced Training.

Gil, E., & Johnson, T. C. (1993). *Sexualized children: Assessment and treatment of sexualized children and children who molest*. Rockville, MD: Launch Press.

Gil, E., & Sobol, B. (2000). Engaging families in therapeutic play. In C. E. Bailey (Ed.) *Children in therapy: Using the family as a resource* (pp. 341–392). New York: Norton.

CHAPTER 5

Filial Therapy

An Interview with Rise VanFleet

CATHERINE FORD SORI, PH.D.

> Many parents come in and are anxious or serious, it is hard to get them to smile; they are worried about their kids. Then they enter this playroom and they see the delight on their children's faces, and it's contagious. We're also teaching parents how to play with their children in specific ways. And as they apply that they start feeling ... joy. That really comes when you're playing and laughing together. Filial helps us to regain sight of one of the greatest ways that there is to bond in our relationships, which is to be able to sit down and laugh together about something.
>
> **—Rise VanFleet, 2005**

Rise VanFleet, Ph.D., is one of the leading proponents of filial therapy, having studied with the founders of this method and the relationship enhancement approach, Bernard and Louise Guerney at Pennsylvania State University. She has authored numerous books, book chapters, journal articles, and training videos on this topic. Dr. VanFleet has trained and supervised thousands of clinicians, and is in demand to present the filial therapy model internationally. She is a past president/board chair of the Association for Play Therapy, and served for many years on the editorial board of the *International Journal of Play Therapy*. Her books have been translated into numerous languages.

* * *

In this interview, Rise VanFleet began by introducing readers to her background and training, and then offered an overview of how the model of filial therapy was developed in the 1960s by Bernard and Louise Guerney. She summarized early and more recent research on filial therapy, which is a psychoeducational, integrative approach that trains parents to conduct nondirective play sessions with their children. VanFleet also addresses the reaction of the field to this model, which empowers parents to be the change-agents for their children.

Sori: Rise, you are so enthusiastic and knowledgeable about the fields of family therapy, play therapy, and especially filial therapy. First will you talk a bit about your background and how you became interested in all those diverse areas?

VanFleet: I started as a biophysics major at the University of Pennsylvania. Eventually, I became aware that it was not a field for me. I also had a work study job in the psychiatric ward of a hospital, part of Penn's Psychiatry Department. There I learned to do some psychological testing under supervision and attended case conferences, so I got interested in the field then. I did really well in psychology and went on for my master's, which is in clinical community psychology. For years I worked in residential programs for children and adults who were seriously and persistently mentally ill, and with developmentally disabled adults. I really enjoyed this, and worked my way up the ranks, and became the director of a four-county residential program in Pennsylvania.

I had always planned to return to school to get my doctorate. How I ended up in play therapy was by an interesting route. I was working part time doing some individual therapy and marital cases, and did not know exactly what to do with them. So I took training with Bernard Guerney at Penn State. I loved the model, which was a psychoeducational model of doing marital therapy. He is known for his relationship enhancement approach, and it really resonated with my beliefs and personality. I decided to study with Bernie, and went into the Human Development and Family Studies Program at Penn State. Bernie suggested I take Louise Guerney's courses on play therapy and filial therapy. After three sessions with a little girl as part of my training I was amazed at how magnificently it worked. Filial therapy has been my first love since that time.

Sori: So you were convinced! Would you give us some background on filial therapy?

VanFleet: Yes. Filial therapy was conceived by Bernard Guerney Jr. back in the late '50s. He and his wife, Louise, were psychologists, and both had been trained in play therapy. They were so impressed with how powerful play therapy was, and I think that they were way ahead of their time in conceptualizing what play could do with families. Bernard had the idea that if it works well with therapists, why would it not work even better if the primary caregivers for these kids, the parents, were involved in the process. The first article that appeared in professional journals about filial therapy was in 1964 in the *Journal of Consulting Psychology.* It was not very well received by the professional community. This idea, which was extremely novel for the time, was sharing what we know about psychology with family members, and using parents as primary change agents for their own children. Objections from the professional community propelled Guerney to start an extensive research program on filial. Some of the early research used videotaped sessions of parents and therapists doing play sessions for raters who were blind as to condition, and low and behold, there were no statistically significant differences.

Sori: Between the parents and the therapists?

VanFleet: Yes, which shows that parents *can* learn this particular set of skills. The word filial comes from the Latin, meaning son or daughter. I have loosely translated it into parent/child play therapy. For a while I used the term filial play therapy. Now it is most widely known by its original name, filial therapy. In essence it is a family therapy intervention. It is theoretically integrative, taking the best of many different theories and blending them together. I think of it as family therapy. We train parents to conduct special nondirective play sessions with their own children. We then supervise parents and help them to become more skillful in conducting these play sessions. We also help parents understand more about their children's play themes, which in essence translates into understanding more about their child's development, what is on their child's mind, and what motivates their child. We supervise the whole process until the parents reach a level of competence and confidence in doing these play sessions. Then they switch over to the home setting where we are not directly supervising them, yet we still monitor what is going on. We still meet with the parent for a period of time to make sure that the transition goes well, and eventually the parent can continue play sessions. At the very end of filial therapy we deliberately help parents generalize what they have learned and apply some of the skills and attitudes they have developed during these play sessions to their day-to-day lives.

Sori: How empowering for parents to be able to learn so much!

VanFleet: That's the real strength of it. I am going to be involved with a big research study in London on using filial therapy with foster families as a kind of continuum of care through residential, foster care treatment, and into adoption, or reunification of biological families. There were a couple of longitudinal studies of filial therapy that looked at the gains that families made after three years and five years, and found that the gains were maintained. Those were done with the original Guerney model, which was a group model. It's a little bit longer than the individual model which I've described in my filial therapy book that was published in 1994, and then in the second edition recently in 2005.

Sori: Will you discuss why you think filial therapy has been somewhat overlooked by many in the field, despite the research findings and the clinical success?

VanFleet: Yes, and let me add one more thought about the research. I think filial therapy research has been very consistent. It doesn't really matter which model people have used. What they have found very consistently is that parents' acceptance and enjoyment of their children has increased, and parents' stress levels have decreased. Parents' basic childrearing skills have increased, and child behavior problems decreased. Those findings have been pretty consistent. Certainly we need more and stronger research with bigger numbers of subjects. But I just wrote a chapter with Scott Ryan and Shelly Smith, published by the American Psychological Association, [for a book] called *Empirically Based Play Interventions for Children.* We did the chapter on filial therapy. It's a nice summary of the research, an empirical history, and some of the more recent studies that have been done.

Here VanFleet returned to the question of why filial therapy has, to some degree, not received wide popularity within the general field of psychotherapy, despite the body of research supporting its clinical effectiveness. She explains that filial therapy is a model that integrates several major psychotherapy theo-

ries, and addresses common objections or lack of understanding that both individual therapists and family therapists sometimes have to this approach.

VanFleet (continued): Back to the question. It has not quite been overlooked, but I have a few theories. When it was first conceived by the Guerneys, it was way ahead of its time. They were pioneers, really, in the field and people just didn't believe that you could use one family member to serve as a therapeutic agent for another family member. So I think that was one reason. Another is that filial therapy is not based on the medical model. It is truly a psychoeducational model. You used the word empowerment earlier. I think that is exactly on target. It is about teaching people how to apply new knowledge and skills so that they can solve a lot of their problems. In parallel process, especially with nondirective or child centered play therapy, we really believe that if we create the right climate of acceptance and safety, kids will solve a lot of their own problems. They move in a direction of health. Filial therapists really believe the same about parents. If we create a climate of safety and acceptance for them, and give them the skills that they may never have had an opportunity to learn, they will use those to move in a very healthy kind of direction, which will lead to more satisfying relationships and lives for them. I have been doing filial therapy since 1980 or 1981, and just see that over and over again. The medical model is an expert model, where people come in with their illnesses and the doctor is going to fix them up, tell them what to do, and so on. In the psychological sense there is still that idea if I go to the expert, the expert is going to tell me what to do, or tell my child what to do differently, and then everything is going to be better for us. I think there are some professionals who really would be reluctant to let go of that expert role, because that's what they are used to and they may not share the belief that parents can do as well as they can, once they are supported in that process.

Another thought that has occurred to me recently is that when you think of this theoretical integration of filial therapy, it draws from psychodynamic theory, from humanistic, cognitive behavioral, from social learning theory, interpersonal theory …

Sori: It seems like it is Rogerian, being client-centered.

VanFleet: Yes, client-centered is probably the one that people think of most prominently because of the humanistic approach used with the child, and in terms of being so accepting of the parents. Also developmental theory and family systems theory, and attachment theory. Filial therapy incorporates a whole range of theories. The Guerneys combined the best aspects of those different theoretical orientations, and they are orientations you would not ordinarily see working together. So I had the idea of late that maybe that theoretical integration has gotten in the way of people embracing it, because I think there is still a tendency to align yourself with one theory or another. As professionals align themselves with different theoretical orientations, it may actually stop them from seeing the huge value of filial, because it has drawn from so many theories.

Sori: I agree. Training programs often focus on one or two models, and people come out and do what they feel comfortable with. To train people to integrate several theories is difficult. Filial has this vast array of theories that all fit together so well. I think the idea of empowering parents and seeing them as experts also fits with postmodernism. There is still that dichotomy between individual and family approaches, so it seems that there are a lot of obstacles to get people to see the broader application of this.

VanFleet: Right. When I do training I get some people who are oriented to doing individual work. It's sometimes hard for them to see how this could possibly work, the intricacies involved in filial therapy, where you are shifting the entire family system. At the same time family therapists sometimes say, "Oh, you don't have the whole family in the room together all the time? That's not family therapy!" I think that's a narrow view of what family therapy is. Everybody in the family may not always be involved in the same room at the same time; there are dyadic play sessions because families are made up of dyadic relationships. Also, having one parent and one child in a play session helps both parents develop all the skills, instead of where one parent is the disciplinarian and the other is the nurturing one. Filial therapy *does* involve all family members in the process.

VanFleet next explained how filial therapy can be useful to reduce polarization between couples who have different views on parenting, to break up parent-child coalitions, and to address sibling rivalry.

Sori: Well, I can see that could really bring together couples that are polarized.

VanFleet: Yes, it often does. My experience is that people have their own parenting style that they have either adopted from the way that they were parented, or perhaps in opposition to the way they were parented, or perhaps whatever seems to work with their personality. As each parent learns how to use empathic listening and imaginary play, limit setting, and all those skills, it really moves them more to the center. They have a more consistent approach with each other, and it embraces the strengths that each person has. So if you have a parent who really is quite good with limit setting, then they might need more help with the nurturing piece, but we really recognize the strengths they have, and this is done in a very positive way. We have parents watch each other as they have these play sessions, and they learn vicariously from each other, from the reinforcement that the therapist gives them. The couple appreciates each other in a way that they have not before. Instead of their focusing on things that are frustrating, both parents begin appreciating each other for the positive things the therapist has recognized. It is a very, very positive type of feedback that parents get from the therapist. It puts the whole marital relationship, as well as their parenting relationship, in a very positive focus, instead of focusing on what they are doing wrong.

Sori: It seems like having both parents play with a child could also be useful for breaking up a coalition that a child may be in with one parent, while being distant from the other. Do you find that happens?

VanFleet: Yes, I think it does. For example, you may have one parent who is very close with the children and may worry that family changes might upset that nice relationship he or she has with the kids. I really help them understand that it doesn't take away from their relationship with their kids to have the other parent in a relationship with the kids too. It draws parents to a place where they can alter aspects of the family and not feel threatened. If you feel like you have a lot of confidence and a great relationship with your children, then it is easier to feel like you can share the kids. You want the best for the kids, and we know that generally speaking, it is best for the kids to have strong relationships with both their parents.

Sori: Absolutely, I can also see that would help with issues of sibling rivalry because you are helping the parents to do this type of play with each of the children so that no child is left out.

VanFleet: Right. Rivalry doesn't always stop, because it's a normal part of development, but filial therapy can reduce it substantially. The parents are embracing each child through this play session format, which is the child's language and way of communicating. Parents are saying, "You are unique and you are wonderful, and I accept you as that unique human being." That acceptance includes some of the cranky feelings they have about their sibling, but it gives them an outlet for their feelings. The opportunity to really be accepted just the way they are goes a long way.

Sori: What a wonderful way to move a child out of the scapegoating role in the family, to be accepted like that!

The many benefits of filial therapy are described in the next segment of the interview, including how it involves all family members, can facilitate acceptance, boundary making, and enhance parent-child attachment.

VanFleet: One of the strengths in filial is that we do involve all the kids in the family. Sometimes you have very large families and it may not be real practical, but as much as possible we have the parents do play sessions with each child, roughly three to twelve, and with older children some type of special times. Parents have that dedicated half-hour a week to spend in a play session or special time with each of the children, where they are deliberately focusing on being really accepting of the child and hearing the child.

Sori: How do children benefit from their parents doing filial therapy with them?

VanFleet: They benefit in a number of different ways. First, just by having someone who can play with you, and allow you to play in the way that you need. And that acceptance is important. But boundaries are important as well. The safety piece comes with the boundaries, and helps kids be responsible for themselves. That undivided attention that kids get from their parents has got to feel very good, especially in this day and age where families are so busy, and sometimes lead very structured or chaotic lives, where families are not always connecting. The real power comes in the attachment, and while filial therapy has not typically been described in terms of attachment language, I think it is creating that secure base, that attunement, all the features of a healthy attachment that we know helps kids by providing a buffer, that safe haven for them when facing stresses in the world. And it does the same for the parents. We are able to create healthier or stronger relationships, which is helping these families reconnect. Then the kids start feeling more of that security that is really essential for good development.

Sori: That's wonderful! I can see this working so well with children in foster care or those from multicrisis families who have been fragmented.

Next, VanFleet is asked to address methods to involve overwhelmed or reluctant parents in the process of training them to be change agents for their children. She emphasized the importance of empathy and acceptance in building parental confidence in this collaborative approach, and discussed how filial therapy is different from parent training models.

Sori (continued): I am wondering how you help a parent who may be overwhelmed with their own environment or their own issues, their living conditions or their socioeconomic situation. How do you help them overcome a reluctance to doing this, to taking the time to learn all these skills and acquire the materials that are necessary to make this kind of investment?

VanFleet: Well, as a filial therapist, you want to be a model of the attitudes and skills that you eventually want them to be able to use with their children. So we spend a lot of time thinking about acceptance and empathy, really trying to see the world through someone else's eyes. And so when we work with a parent who has a tough lot in life, a lot of pressures or difficulties, whether it's financial or emotional, the first and perhaps the most important thing we do is be empathic with them. We really do try to see the world through their eyes. While there might be certain things we don't like about their behavior, there are reasons why they are the way they are. We try to understand their emotions and motivations. In filial therapy we never push people hard in a particular direction; it really needs to be their choice. The difficulty of convincing parents to try filial usually comes at the beginning. And once they get the sense of the empowerment of it, it is no longer difficult. So I just have to get them over the hurdle, and sometimes I try to keep in mind that they have probably tried most, if not all of the resources they have. No matter how they present themselves to us they are still in a vulnerable position. They have tried everything and it hasn't worked, and it is easy for them to feel like a failure. And sometimes our "systems" also reinforce that idea that they are a bad parent. So spending a significant amount of time just hearing them out, listening to them, empathizing with the feelings and difficulties they have usually helps them get a sense that this is a little bit different. I don't start out saying, "Try this, or try that." I first listen. It is really the whole idea of a partnership. Sometime parents are feeling overwhelmed and they will say, "Look, I've tried everything, now you do it. You've got the training and background." My response to that has always been, "Well I do have an expertise in this particular method of working with a family, and this has been used a lot; it's been very effective with families with similar problems to yours. That's my area of expertise, but you have an area of expertise that is totally essential to this process too, and that is you know your family, and you know your kids. You know them better than I will ever know them, and you know how they react under different circumstances. So if we can put together what you know and your expertise with what I know in terms of this particular method, we might make a pretty unbeatable team." And this way really has great possibilities and great hopefulness for making some changes in their lives.

So it's a matter of trying to hear them, trying to help them see that what I am offering through filial therapy does, indeed, address their needs. If they are frustrated and burned out with their kids I am going to be offering them something that will likely reduce the frustration and allow them to get their energy back. I am offering them an alternative. And not only am I offering them an alternative, but I am going to stick by them while they put it into practice.

That's another part of filial that is quite different than parenting skills programs. I say, "In the beginning of filial therapy I just want you to try this half-hour experiment every week, and I am going to be here to help you with it." So we don't ask them to change much in their day-to-day lives unless there is something abusive going on, and we have to intervene in that first. But otherwise we are saying, "You don't have to change a whole lot about your day-to-day lives yet, let's just focus on this a half hour a week. We will see if this will work, and if it works, which I think it will, we'll worry later about spreading it in your daily lives." Sometimes you have to give them a little something to help bring the stress down to a level where they can focus on this, but I think many parents experience that as a relief, that first of all we are recognizing that they know something important. Second, we are not expecting them to change everything. Third, we are going to be there and assist them as they make the changes, and do everything that we can to make sure it fits their family. Those kinds of things help families start to realize that this might be useful for them, and that there might be some hope after all.

Sori: That's an excellent way to present it. It's empowering them and being willing to be a team with them during the process, while recognizing their strengths. I really like that.

VanFleet: And related to that, I always explain to parents that they are the most important people in their children's lives. And I believe that with all my heart. Parents don't always believe it and sometimes they point to their kids' behavior as "proof." The children are not really listening to them and don't seem to respect what the parent is saying. So they say, "See, my kids don't care what I think." I tell them, "The kid's behavior doesn't really show it, but that's not where you look. It's really in their hearts and minds; underneath it all, you are still the most important person in their lives. We just have to help change or strengthen the relationship, or give you some additional tool that will help reduce the behavior that is so frustrating, and help you start enjoying each other more."

Sori: That's wonderful! That changes their whole lives, to go from being angry or frustrated with a child to enjoying them.

The goals of filial therapy are addressed in the next section of the interview, and then VanFleet described the benefits that occur when families laugh and play together.

Sori (continued): Can you discuss the goals for filial therapy?

VanFleet: The primary goal is really to strengthen all of the relationships in the family, to strengthen the family as a whole. We can have goals for the child, which would mean reduction in problematic behavior, more adaptive kinds of behavior, children better able to express their feelings and have their needs be met, a greater sense of security, all those kinds of things. Parents might have specific goals as well, in terms of helping them understand their children better, being more consistent with setting limits, and so forth. I think the real goals have more to do with what makes a strong family.

Sori: It seems like you are building in resiliency.

VanFleet: Today we are so much more aware of what is going on in the world in terms of all the really awful news we get. We live fast-paced lives and lose sight of how important playfulness and humor are. Not only as something that makes life worth living, but also something that helps us cope when times get really intense. That's another thing I've always liked about filial, it lightens families up. Kids will play naturally, and it's their way of making sense of the world. It's a wonderful coping mechanism that we have certainly downplayed in Western culture in lieu of work. Many parents come in and are anxious or serious, it is hard to get them to smile; they are worried about their kids. Then they enter this playroom and they see the delight on their children's faces, and it's contagious. We're also teaching parents how to play with their children in specific ways. And as they apply that they start feeling, I don't know of a better word for it than joy. That really comes when you're playing and laughing together. Filial helps us to regain sight of one of the greatest ways that there is to bond in our relationships, which is to be able to sit down and laugh together about something.

Sori: That reminds me of Whitaker's experiential model of being more fully alive. Plopping kids in front of the TV or video games is not the same as enjoying something together that builds relationships.

VanFleet: Yes, I think that's really true.

Next, VanFleet provided an overview of the filial therapy training model, and then she emphasized the importance of using positive feedback to shape parents' skill development.

Sori: Will you give an overview of filial therapy and the steps that you use in training parents?

VanFleet: Yes. First I talk with parents about what filial is all about. I like for them to have a concrete example of what it looks like, so the first step in the training process is for the parents to watch me while I have a half-hour play session with each of their children. The play sessions are nondirective, or child centered in nature, basically the same methods that I will eventually be teaching the parents. So they get to see what it looks like and how their child responds to it. That's usually one session. Then there is another session where it's a combination of some didactic material, where I explain the four basic skills that they use in the playroom. I cover what those skills are and why we use them and how you actually do them, and then I have the parent practice with me for the latter part of that session. I pretend I'm a child and play, and I have them practice just empathic listening to me as I play. I give them feedback as we go along, so I am stopping periodically and saying, "Yes, that's the idea!" or "That's good, you're able to recognize my feelings." I sometimes use prompting or cueing. I'll say, "Well, look at my facial expression; how do you think I'm feeling?" Or sometimes I use modeling for them, where I'll suggest, "Maybe you can say something like this: 'You are really happy to be decorating that house the way you want it,'" or something like that. So I use a variety of teaching methods. It's very experiential, and we practice just the empathic listening skills that week. The didactic and the practice of the empathic listening are done together. At the end of that practice we have a more dedicated time to talk about what that felt like to the parent. I usually start with the parent's reaction first, and what they felt comfortable with and didn't feel comfortable with. Then I give them some more specific skills feedback, usually just a couple suggestions of what to work on. Overwhelmingly, what we are telling them is what they are doing right. Basically, we use a behavioral shaping method right in the moment, and then feedback at the end, saying, "This was good, you're paying attention, you're not telling me what to do. You're describing what I'm doing. That's all great! The next time I'd like you to concentrate a bit more on identifying feelings." Or something like that.

After that I would do two sessions, which we call mock or pretend play sessions. I have parents practice all four skills. We go in the playroom and I pretend I'm a child again, only this time I not only play by myself when they practice listening skills, but I also involve them in a role play. I pretend to break a limit so they can practice doing limit setting skills. I am playing as a child, but I stop momentarily and tell them that they are on track, with maybe a brief suggestion on how they can make it better. Then we stop the role play and go to the feedback process again. The parents watch each other's practices because they really learn an awful lot from watching each other and hearing each other's feedback.

We do two weeks of those role play sessions, and then they start with their own children. We actually consider the first several play sessions with their children to be practice, too. As the parents get better and better with their skills, the kids learn to trust. "Gee, when we have these play sessions they really listen to me, and they really follow through on what they say!" As the parent skills go up, kids' trust in their parents goes up too, as the parents are able to put it into practice better. We continue giving them feedback on their skills, but once they start with their own kids, we add in discussions about what the play might mean. That's done in a very contextual way, so that is another skill that is learned in vivo. I might say, "In looking at these patterns in your children's play, what are some possible things that might relate to?" We are always looking at the context of the kids' play and family life. What's going on in their lives helps us come up with some tentative hypotheses about what the child might be expressing or working on.

Sori: So you are shaping the parent's behavior by giving them a lot of positive feedback. Again, that has to be empowering for parents who have felt like they were failures or they couldn't manage their children.

VanFleet: Yes. Many parents have grown up hearing about what they've done wrong, not what they do right. It is a unique experience to get feedback on what they're doing well.

VanFleet explained the four specific skills that are targeted in training parents to do filial therapy with their children in the following portion of the interview. These include structuring skills, empathic listening, child-centered imaginary play skills, and limit setting.

Sori: Can you explain more about those four skills that you train parents in?

VanFleet: Yes. The first skill that we teach parents is a structuring skill that involves helping the child understand what is about to happen in the play session. There is a room entry statement that the parents make to the children to let them know that they can do almost anything they want, but if there is anything they may not do, the parent will let them know. We do not give kids a big list of no-no's to start with, because that would put a damper on things; we just set limits as they are needed. So it does not have a controlling, punitive feel at the beginning. Part of the structuring skill is also leaving the playroom. That involves giving kids a 5-minute warning that the play session is about to end, then a 1-minute warning, and then a final statement from the parent to help the child leave the playroom. Transitions can be difficult for kids, so the structuring skill gives the child the general tone of the play session, and the overall boundaries around it.

The empathic listening skill, or reflective listening, is the core of what we are teaching the parents to do. It is trying to see the world through the child's eyes, to enter the child's imaginative world. Parents describe aloud what they see in their own words, showing the child their undivided attention, and stating the feelings being expressed either on the child's face or through the character the child is playing with. The parent does not lead the play in any way; the child chooses what to play with and how to play with it, which is the nondirective flavor of this. Bernie once said that empathy is really an attitude, and I always liked that, the attitude of really trying to see the world through someone else's eyes. We want the parents to do that with the children.

The third skill is a child-centered imaginary play skill where the child invites the parent to play a role of some sort, like "Let's play school," or "Let's play store." We want the parent to get into that role and use faces and voices, and enjoy playing the role. The key is to *play the role the way the child wants them to,* not the way they want to, and their job is not to entertain the child, but to go along with the play and do it the way the child wants them to. We help parents learn to engage in play, which they may not have done since they were children. Some may never have had that opportunity. Recently I've been thinking of the imaginary play skill as another form of empathy or attunement, if you can really understand what your child wants without asking a bunch of questions. You just sense from what they have told you, how they have either dressed you up or what characters they have given you, and you look at the context of their play and then you just join in that play, knowing that the child will correct you if you don't have it right. To me that is another form of empathy. We ask parents to avoid asking questions at that particular time unless they are totally lost about what to do, just to make their best estimate of what their child wants and to try that, and then watch for the child's reaction.

Finally, there is a limit-setting skill that is very clear and gives the child a couple of chances to self-correct. If they don't, then we end the play session. That is a very quick way of reasserting parental authority when needed. It is very rare that kids ever push things that far, and if they ever do, they almost never do it again. It helps the parent to have a strong consequence, but the process first entails just telling the child what the rule is, and then redirecting their play. So, "One of the things you may not do is throw the toys at me, but you may do almost anything else." Then the second phase is a warning phase. Some empathy there is good, too. "I can see you really want to throw that toy at me, but remember I told you that you can't do that. If you try to do that one more time then we will have to leave the playroom for the day. You can do almost anything else." Sort of reset the tone. Then if the child breaks the same limit three times, they are basically giving the parent the message, "I guess I need you to take control of this situation for me," and that's when we would end the play session. When you say you can't splash the water on me but you can do anything else, it becomes the child's responsibility to figure out where they are going to throw the toy or splash the water, or what they are going to do next that is within bounds. Children become more responsible for their own behavior, and the outcomes of their behavior.

Sori: I like that better than giving them suggestions that they have to comply with or not comply with. This way they come up with their own alternative.

VanFleet: It doesn't become more of a power struggle, especially with kids that are more oppositional. Also, the parent isn't saying, "You can't solve this problem. I am going to solve it for you." It gives the child more of a chance to do that.

Sori: It is more empowering to the child that way. I can see this model is about empowerment.

VanFleet: Yes, I think it is.

The more advanced skills that parents need in order to recognize and explore play themes that emerge in filial therapy sessions are addressed in the next part of the interview. VanFleet also illustrated the important role parents play in interpreting the meaning of children's play.

Sori: Will you explain how you help parents become aware of themes in their children's play?

VanFleet: Yes. Usually parents are quite good at recognizing play themes, even though they may not have thought of them that way before. We are looking for patterns in the play, or it might be particularly intense play. Perhaps the parents are reminded of something, like "Oh! He is pretending to have a car accident with a toy car, and we just had an accident with our car!" They might notice some similarities to their daily play.

We also teach parents how to reflect children's intentions in their play. So it's right there in the open, yet it's not reading a whole lot into what the child is doing. The theme discussion is just between the therapist and the parent, and it's geared toward helping the parent have a better understanding of the child's motivation and of their relationship. Initially it is more of a dialogue. I'll just say to the parent, "What did you notice about their play?" or other questions that are a little bit more specific, like, "Did you notice any pattern, or any particular points where your child's play was particularly intense or when he or she was really into it?" Parents usually point out those things, and if they don't, I will. Then we start talking about what this process is about. We look for alternative hypotheses; there is not one right way of looking at it because we really don't know, and we take context heavily into account. Sometimes parents don't recognize things that I see; sometimes they pick up on things that I don't always understand.

One classic example of this was a little 4-year-old boy who was doing filial therapy with his grandmother. His parents were divorced and there was a lot of tension and chaos in his life, but he visited his grandparents regularly. He was really focused on little play eggs that I had in my playroom, and he was playing with a rubber chicken that's hollow inside. He got these eggs and kept saying, "Do these eggs crack? Do these eggs crack?" He started feeding the eggs to the chicken, and they would roll out the other end of the chicken, as if the chicken was laying the egg. Depending on your theoretical orientation, there were a lot of different ways that you might interpret that play. Was it about birth? Nurturance? Limits and boundaries? But this shows the importance of the parent and the context of the situation: When I met with the grandmother afterwards I asked her what she thought of his play. She mentioned the chicken and egg play. She mentioned that when the boy was at her house every other weekend, she did a lot of baking. It was his job to crack the eggs. That opened a whole new way of thinking about that play, which might have been about the child's role in the family. We spent time talking about how important the grandmother's role was, that she was baking with him, that he could feel part of things and had his place where he could belong, especially because there was so much attachment disruption for him. So that's one case where the context made all the difference in how we viewed his play, and what was going on for him.

Sori: That's an excellent example of exploring themes, and the important role parents play.

At this point, the interview shifted to a discussion of moving filial therapy sessions from the office to the home, and the typical number of sessions needed for training. VanFleet also addressed how individual sessions and other theories are often integrated with filial therapy training.

Sori (continued): So how do you know when people are ready to do home sessions? What is the skill level that you need to see before you let parents do home sessions on their own?

VanFleet: Before they go home, I watch parents anywhere from four to six times each. They might be playing with different kids for those sessions. Even if they catch on to the skills very quickly, it's nice to see the play themes emerging. Sometimes that takes a few sessions. Skill wise, before they start doing the play sessions at home, I want them to be very good. The home setting presents new challenges because kids are more likely to test some of the limits. Basically, as long as the parents are consistently using the four skills and are able to recognize feelings, even if sometimes they might miss the intensity a bit, I am inclined to start the home sessions.

Sori: What's the total number of sessions that you would typically have?

VanFleet: Well, based on an hour-long session, I typically do between 15, maybe 17 sessions. If I have a choice in the matter, I probably would do about 20 sessions with each family. I rarely have trouble with both public and private funding sources for 15 or 20 sessions, if I can educate the right people about what we are doing, what the goals are, what the outcomes are, and what the research has been.

Sori: That's wonderful.

VanFleet: Sometime it's longer. For example, Cindy Smscak (LPC, RPT-S) runs the Beech Street Program, a practice I'm affiliated with. We work almost entirely with highly traumatized and attachment-disruptive children there. Some of these kids have extreme behaviors and frightening triggers, and sometimes the parents are exhausted. So we use filial therapy as sort of a center piece. We do other interventions as well, but in those cases where there is so much trauma, we might do filial therapy for longer periods.

Sori: So you might integrate individual or family sessions with filial. What do you do when a parent comes in, and instead of doing the training, wants to complain each week about what the child has done wrong? Do you ever have trouble refocusing them?

VanFleet: I have learned how to refocus people. I think it's a matter of listening initially, then helping the parent understand that we are doing filial therapy to help with those kinds of problems. That's why we are trying to create this relationship that will help them know more and more about what to do with all these different situations. If we really focus on the relationship, a lot of those day-to-day things that are so troublesome are likely to disappear, which is often the case. Often, after just a handful of play sessions, the parents' attitudes toward the kids are a little bit different, and the kid's behavior and attitudes toward the parents is a little bit different, so they get some relief from that.

But certainly there are times when you might do some individual play therapy or other individual therapies, whether it is art, drama, bibliotherapy with children alone, with parents alone, etc. Filial therapy doesn't preclude any of that happening. Filial actually blends nicely if, for example, you want to continue with some marital therapy, especially the relationship enhancement method that is based on the same principles.

The next segment addressed the types of materials parents need to acquire for home filial therapy sessions, and how many of these objects can be purchased inexpensively.

Sori: So you can integrate other therapies with filial. Can you talk about the types of toys that are needed, and why it is important for parents to have a separate set of toys at home? Do you have any suggestions about how parents might accumulate these special toys inexpensively?

VanFleet: Yes. We want the parents to have a variety of toys available. I help the parents develop a play kit of their own that they eventually will use. They need to have a variety of toys that will elicit a lot of different feelings. We give parents a list of some basic toys for the toy kit at the early stages of filial therapy, and ask them to accumulate them. Sometimes they draw from the toys the kids have, but have not been really been playing with. Other times yard sales or dollar stores—there's lots of opportunities to find things inexpensively if you keep your eye out and you know what types of toys you are looking for. Sometimes we put together toy kits that are loaned to families who have few resources. Toy catalog companies that sell party supplies and novelties, like the Oriental Trading Company or Rhode Island Novelties, are good; you can buy inexpensive items by the dozen. Sometimes I will put together just a small starter kit, with a clown nose, a mask, and some very inexpensive puppets. Sometimes people have toy-making sessions for the parents. You can make puppets out of socks, or you can get a basic puppet form from Lakeshore Learning. Some clients who couldn't afford a dollhouse made one out of four shoe boxes. There really are a lot of things you can make for almost nothing. If kids complain about the toys, I suggest that parents reflect, "You are disappointed, and wish you had a better dollhouse." I tell them to keep in mind that they, the parent, are really their child's favorite toy. It's really about the relationship, and while the toys are helpful, it is not essential to have magnificent toys to do filial therapy.

Sori: What are some of the basic categories of toys that parents need to get started?

VanFleet: Some family-related nurturance toys, a set of dishes, and something that holds water. A baby doll and a blanket, and it's nice to have a little family set: a mother, father, brother, sister, and baby. You also want some aggressive toys because we want to help kids learn how to channel their aggression in more appropriate ways. They can't do that unless they are allowed to play aggressively. That's one of the things we really focus on with parents. So some aggressive toys like an inflatable bop bag, or soldiers. The big noodles for swimming pools can be cut down in size to make a fairly safe "sword" for kids to use. We want to communicate to kids that it's OK to express aggression. Then little vehicles like cars, school buses, ambulances, fire trucks, rescue vehicles, and maybe some construction equipment. Also, art materials, some type of modeling substance or clay, markers, paper, crayons. Things where kids can be expressive in those ways, too.

Sori: A lot of those things can also be gotten inexpensively at garage sales.

Here, VanFleet offered a moving case example to illustrate the power filial therapy has to change children's and parents' lives.

Sori: You have covered so much about filial therapy. Is there a particular case that comes to mind that illustrates how effective this approach can be?

VanFleet: Yes. I'll tell you about a little guy. I am going to change some of the details so that he is not identifiable. He was 11 years old, and in a fairly typical situation that you hear about in foster care. His mother had a lot of boyfriends, and some of the boyfriends had physically abused him. When he was about 8 he was placed in foster care. Mom was in and out of his life. She seemed to keep going back to men that were not good for him, and eventually she agreed to terminate her parental rights. He had a lot of anger about that because he felt like she was picking these men over him. He was placed in several different foster homes, and suffered some abuse there also. He was hit by one foster parent, and molested in another placement. He was put up for adoption, and had two adoptions that fell through. In one foster placement he did quite well, but there were some changes in the family and they couldn't have him anymore. He was not given any notice that he was going to move from their home. One day he was just moved.

After that his behavior deteriorated. He was not a bad kid, but there was serious attachment disruption in his life. His acting out was fairly predictable, when there were transitions in his life. He longed to be part of a family. The two adoptions fell through because the families just didn't know how to handle his bad behavior. More rejection for him. Finally he ended up in a foster home, and through that placement he ended up coming to our practice.

We did filial therapy with the foster mom and she did a beautiful job learning to do the play sessions. He went through his same acting-out behaviors, but because they were doing the play sessions it was really minimized. He was able to play some of the aggressive feelings, under which there was tremendous anxiety. Other people were looking at him on the surface and saying, "Oh, he is so aggressive!" But really he was very anxious and just scared about his life and his future, and not being wanted anywhere. So this woman, through the play sessions, was really able to "get it." She was able to tune in to how he was feeling, and he actually opened up more and more with her in his daily life, talking about his feelings. They had this feeling language in common, that had arisen from the play sessions. He became quite stable. He still acted out when things were stressful, but they were able to use the play sessions to help him express more of his feelings. That also led to them doing more playful kinds of things together.

What eventually happened, and I would love to see this implemented more, was the funding source actually agreed to pay for the next adoptive family to do filial therapy with him, as well. So first we informed the adoptive family about what they could expect. We then went through the filial therapy training with the adoptive parents prior to the adoption. As he visited the preadoptive family more, they started doing the filial play sessions with him. That became part of his visits, and he spent longer periods of time with them. When he was placed, he had already had a series of play sessions with them. It made that transition much smoother for him. The attachment that he had formed with the foster mom gave him a template of what healthy relationships are like. Then, instead of ending that relationship abruptly and moving him on to the next placement, which would have triggered all his frightened feelings, we were able to help the adoptive parents also learn to do the play sessions. They actually created a relationship with him through the filial play sessions before he was ever placed with them. It was like he was moving from one healthy attachment to another healthy attachment, instead of having to end one relationship to start the next one. It really made a huge difference in this child's ability to adjust to an adoptive placement. The previous pattern of acting out during transitions was greatly diminished, because the adoptive parents were able to be part of the process. The other nice thing is that it stabilized his foster placement, and it stabilized the adoptive placement, because of the attachment features of filial. And the foster mom did keep in touch with him afterward and, to my knowledge, she still does keep in touch.

Sori: So that third adoption was then successful. That is such a success story and a wonderful example of how this model can change the course of a child's life.

VanFleet: Yes, and that's the model I am hoping that we will do in the London project, where they are setting up a whole new system that would incorporate filial sessions with other therapies that may be needed. But filial therapy would be a common thread throughout the process. This is the way people create relationships, have fun together and learn about their new families.

Sori: So you will be training foster parents and then adoptive parents, or reunifying families in London. That is exciting.

The next part of the interview addressed the international interest in filial therapy, as well as values and special cultural issues.

Sori (continued): Do you want to say something about the global interest in filial?

VanFleet: Yes, there has been tremendous interest, and I get e-mails from people all over the world. I have been spending quite a bit of time over the last four years in the UK. I am going to Korea in the fall, and have been invited to go to Turkey. People have come here to train with me from India, Israel, Bahrain, Saudi Arabia, Korea, Japan, South Africa, and other countries. There is this interest all over.

The relevance of filial to transcultural work is great. I think it is because, first of all, play is universal. Kids throughout the world play if given the opportunity, and they play within their own cultural context. They also play within their own family culture. I think of cultural differences not just in the broad category, but in more subtle ways as well. Every family has its own culture. So there is great diversity even within cultural groups, and within families. But the play is within that context. The difficulty that we sometimes have is that we all have our own cultural biases, our own worldview, and our own way of seeing and interpreting things that happen. Our biases are there, but when the parents are present they can correct us, the same way that grandmother knew about the little guy and his chicken and his egg-cracking business, which was sort of a family cultural practice. And she educated me about that. If I am working with someone who is culturally different from me, the parents are partners in the process. We start with their interpretation and say, "What do you think this means?" and sometimes they hit on things that I never would, because they know what it means in the context of their family.

I think most values are shared by people throughout the world, in terms of wanting to have a strong family. Now how they define a strong family, or how they might define family roles might be very different. But, nevertheless, they value family. That is part of our human condition, that we are social and family beings. So the values of filial therapy really fit well across cultures because it is such a respectful and empowering approach. There is this dialogue that takes place where we invite families to educate us, when what we are suggesting does not fit. It is collaborative, and the collaborativeness of it really allows for the biases that stand between us and the people we work with to be dealt with in a very open, relationship-based way.

My own feeling about multicultural sensitivity is that the training that we get is very valuable and alerts us to areas where we have differences and need to be more sensitive, looking at our own cultural identity and how that plays into the mixture with the clients we work with. But at the same time, filial therapy has triggered my thinking in this way: It's about the relationship. We can create a relationship that is open and honest, where we really are empathic with the clients we are working with, and they are free to say, "No, where we come from we do it a different way." Then we can have a dialogue about that, and ultimately understand that it is their choice how they are going to do something. The flexibility of filial therapy is great when working with different cultures. The *Parent's Handbook of Filial Therapy* [VanFleet, 2000] is being translated into Arabic, Chinese, Korean, Spanish, and Romanian. So there is this worldwide interest, because filial can be adapted across cultures. For example, one woman told me that with some of the families that she works with, while the father has a relationship with the children, the childrearing is left primarily to the mother. Her use of filial therapy has to be with the mother because of the cultural and religious practices in her culture, but her "take" on it was quite unique, in that filial therapy not only strengthens the relationship between that mother and child, but it also allows the mother to perform her role in the family more effectively. This would then have implications for the relationship with her husband. He might really appreciate that she is making the effort to learn and to try something new with her children.

Sori: That is a fascinating discussion about all the cultural implications and ramifications of filial therapy.

In this final segment of the interview, VanFleet described how filial therapy seems to have come into its time in the 21st century.

VanFleet: There is this worldwide interest. It is almost like the time really has come. The world of mental health has changed, and family therapy has moved around to a more prominent place. This method is still unique, even among a lot of family therapists, in that we are using that parent as the primary change agent for their own child. And I still hear reluctance in the voices of professionals, to really trust that this is OK. But less and less reluctance all the time. So as word spreads, I think it is entering a new phase.

Sori: That is very exciting. If people are interested in learning more about filial therapy they could see some of the material you have written or contact you at your Web site?

VanFleet: Yes they certainly could.

Sori: This was excellent. We have covered quite a bit of ground, Rise, and I want to thank you for sharing so enthusiastically!

SUGGESTED READING

Guerney, L. (1997). Filial therapy. In K. O'Connor & L. M. Braverman (Eds.), *Play therapy theory and practice: A comparative presentation* (pp. 131–159). New York: John Wiley & Sons.

VanFleet, R. (1992). Using filial therapy to strengthen families with chronically ill children. In L. VandeCreek, S. Knapp, & T. L. Jackson (Eds.), *Innovations in clinical practice: A source book, Vol. 11* (pp. 87–97). Sarasota, FL: Professional Resource Press.

VanFleet, R. (1993). Strengthening families with storytelling. In L. VandeCreek, S. Knapp, & T. L. Jackson (Eds.), *Innovations in clinical practice: A source book, Vol. 12* (pp. 147–154). Sarasota, FL: Professional Resource Press.

VanFleet, R. (1994). Filial therapy for adoptive children and parents. In K. O'Connor & C. Schaefer (Eds.), *Handbook of play therapy, Vol. II* (pp. 371–385). New York: Wiley & Sons.

VanFleet, R. (1997). Play and perfectionism: Putting fun back into families. In H. G. Kaduson, D. Cangelosi, & C. Schaefer (Eds.), *The playing cure* (pp. 61–82). New York: Jason Aronson.

VanFleet, R. (1998). A parent's guide to filial therapy. In L. VandeCreek, S. Knapp, & T. Jackson (Eds.), *Innovations in clinical practice: A source book, Vol. 16* (pp. 457–463). Sarasota, FL: Professional Resource Press.

VanFleet, R. (2000). *A parent's handbook of filial play therapy*. Boiling Springs, PA: Play Therapy Press. (Translations into Spanish, Korean, Chinese, Romanian, and Arabic currently underway.)

VanFleet, R. (2000). Short-term play therapy for families with chronic illness. In H. Kaduson & C. Schaefer (Eds.), *Short-term play therapy interventions with children* (pp. 175–193). New York: Guilford.

VanFleet, R. (2000). Understanding and overcoming parent resistance to play therapy. *International Journal of Play Therapy, 9*(1), 35–46.

VanFleet, R. (2001). Disaster dinosaurs. In H. G. Kaduson & C. E. Schaefer (Eds.), *101 more favorite play therapy techniques* (pp. 328–330). New York: Jason Aronson.

VanFleet, R. (2001). Dynamic dinosaurs. In H. G. Kaduson & C. E. Schaefer (Eds.), *101 more favorite play therapy techniques* (pp. 357–361). New York: Jason Aronson.

VanFleet, R. (2001). Make me laugh. In H. G. Kaduson & C. E. Schaefer (Eds.), *101 more favorite play therapy techniques* (pp. 203–206). New York: Jason Aronson.

VanFleet, R. (2001). The gallery of goofy art. In H. G. Kaduson & C. E. Schaefer (Eds.), *101 more favorite play therapy techniques* (pp. 372–374). New York: Jason Aronson.

VanFleet, R. (2003). Filial therapy with adolescent parents. In R. VanFleet & L. Guerney (Eds.), *Casebook of filial therapy* (pp. 163–170). Boiling Springs, PA: Play Therapy Press.

VanFleet, R. (2003). Filial therapy with adoptive children and parents. In R. VanFleet & L. Guerney (Eds.), *Casebook of filial therapy* (pp. 259–278). Boiling Springs, PA: Play Therapy Press. (Adapted and reprinted from VanFleet, 1994.)

VanFleet, R. (2003). Short-term filial therapy for families with chronic illness. In R. VanFleet & L. Guerney (Eds.), *Casebook of filial therapy* (pp. 65–84). Boiling Springs, PA: Play Therapy Press. (Adapted and reprinted from VanFleet, 2000.)

VanFleet, R. (2003). Strengthening parent-child attachment with play: Filial play therapy. In C. F. Sori, L. L. Hecker, & Associates. *The therapist's notebook for children and adolescents: Homework, handouts, and activities for use in psychotherapy* (pp. 57–63). Binghamton, NY: Haworth.

VanFleet, R. (2005). ***Filial therapy: Strengthening parent-child relationships through play,*** 2nd ed. Sarasota, FL: Professional Resource Press. (Japanese translation, 2004, by Masashi Kushizaki for Tuttle-Mori Agency, Inc., Tokyo.) (Original work published 1994.)

VanFleet, R., & Guerney, L. (Eds.). (2003). ***Casebook of filial therapy***. Boiling Springs, PA: Play Therapy Press.

VanFleet, R., & Kaduson, H. (In press). ***Play therapy for traumatic events***. Boiling Springs, PA: Play Therapy Press.

VanFleet, R., Lilly, J. P., & Kaduson, H. (1999). Play therapy for children exposed to violence: Individual, family, and community interventions. ***International Journal of Play Therapy,*** *8*(1), 27–42.

VanFleet, R., Ryan, S. D., & Smith, S. (2005). Filial therapy: A critical review. In L. Reddy, T. Files-Hall, & C. E. Schaefer (Eds.), ***Empirically-based play interventions for children*** (pp. 241–264). Washington, DC: American Psychological Association.

VanFleet, R., & Sniscak, C. C. (2003). Filial therapy for children exposed to traumatic events. In R. VanFleet & L. Guerney (Eds.), ***Casebook of filial therapy*** (pp. 113–137). Boiling Springs, PA: Play Therapy Press.

VanFleet, R., & Sniscak, C. C. (2003). Filial therapy for attachment-disrupted and disordered children. In R. VanFleet & L. Guerney (Eds.), ***Casebook of filial therapy*** (pp. 279–308). Boiling Springs, PA: Play Therapy Press.

CHAPTER 6

A Playful Postmodern Approach to Counseling Children and Families

An Interview with Lee Shilts

CATHERINE FORD SORI, PH.D.

> You know, when working with children you have to be playful, so I said to her to note my carpet in my office. I said, "Do you know what this carpet is made out of?" She said, "No, I don't." I said, "It is made out of monster ashes. Because once we get the monster down to a certain size we can stamp it right into the ground, grind it in, and then it is gone."
>
> **—Lee Shilts, 2005**

Dr. Lee Shilts is a prominent family therapist in the area of solution focus therapy, where he has worked closely with Insoo Kim Berg and the late Steve de Shazer, who were the founders and leading experts in this therapeutic modality. In addition to being a professor in the Family Therapy Program at

Nova Southeastern University in Fort Lauderdale, Florida, Shilts is currently involved in a solution-focused brief therapy training project with Insoo Kim Berg that includes trainers across North America.

Lee Shilts began his extensive professional career as a counselor in special education programs that were both school and residential based. He has worked in programs in the areas of early childhood, learning disabilities, the emotionally disturbed, educable mentally retarded, trainable mentally retarded, multiple handicapped, and with school-aged mothers.

Since receiving his Ph.D. in marriage and family therapy from Virginia Tech, Dr. Shilts has taught since 1990, is licensed in the state of Florida, and has been an AAMFT-approved supervisor for many years. His special teaching interests include the areas of clinical practice, especially solution-focused therapy, teaching and supervision in systemic therapies, the application of solution-focused therapy in nontraditional settings, Ericksonian hypnotherapy, writing therapeutic letters, and the importance of language systems. Dr. Shilts is widely published, especially in the areas of the applications of solution-focused therapy and aspects of supervision.

* * *

To begin this interview, Dr. Shilts first explained several areas that delineate modern and postmodern theoretical approaches.

Sori: Lee, I know you work predominately from a solution-focused perspective, and that you incorporate narrative techniques in your approach. Before you discuss how you integrate the two theories, I would like to explore how you became interested in doing postmodern, brief therapy, especially in working with children.

Shilts: OK. Why don't I start out by talking a little bit about the theory behind how I work, how I go about delineating, and how I look at the work theoretically and how that relates to therapy. Then, I thought that I would talk about how this has influenced my work over the years.

Sori: That sounds excellent.

Shilts: What I do with my work is to look at nine different areas that I think are highly influential in any type of therapy that goes on. Then, I try to delineate between these nine areas from a modernistic versus a post modernistic approach. Let me relate this to how this would work, say working in the field of addictions.

The first area has to do with how we view symptoms. From a modernistic approach, for someone who had an addiction we would see that as an individual pathology, and there would be an internal focus. It would be physiological and we would have the DSM nomenclature to go along with that. From a postmodernistic view, when we view symptoms we would look at that as a communication about a relationship. It is a positive statement. A symptom is looked at as something ready for growth. It is a form of self-correction, and that would be the whole Batesonian idea on hitting bottom, say with alcoholism. So, that is the first area that I look at.

The second one is in the area of pathology, which is closely related. Again, if we were looking at an addictive personality from a modernistic approach, that would be an individual biology-based approach to pathology. We would say that this is probably hereditary and we have twin studies that show that alcoholism is biological, sometimes hereditarily influenced. This would be something internal within the individual. Now, if we looked at this idea of pathology from a postmodern perspective we would probably say that these are ordinary problems that are being mishandled, that the individual is not ready to change directions, and that the problem is seen through the language. It is contextual and socially constructive, so a major shift there.

In the third area, I look at the whole concept of resistance. From a modernistic approach to the addictive person you would say that resistance is extremely present. There is excessive denial going on and they will resist any attempts to stop doing drugs. From a postmodern perspective, we would look at this whole thing of resistance as a type of cooperation. It is one of several responses that the client can make to suggestions and is a product of the client-therapist relationship. So resistance is just looked at as another form of cooperation. It is another shift.

Sori: Yes, that is a very different way of viewing resistance.

Shilts: Number four is the area of change. We have to look at how change influences our work in therapy. If one was to view it through a modernistic lens, again we would say that change comes from within. One is powerless over anything they have to do, and they need to surrender and then change will occur. From a postmodern perspective, we have a much more optimistic look at change, in that the family or the individual will restructure themselves given time, kind of that whole second order idea of change. Change is meaningful through the language you use in therapy. So again, it is very much the language base from the postmodern ideas.

Number five is goals. This is a real distinction here. The modernistic approach would say that you have to have clearly defined goals because goals are universal and they are necessary to assess progress and define success. From a postmodern perspective, I like to use the idea that de Shazer wrote about regarding goals. He said that interventions only need to fit so that a solution evolves. Do something different. Again, a whole different perspective there.

Sori: Kind of a twist on that idea of doing something different from the MRI [Mental Research Institute]?

Shilts: Exactly. Number six in delineating theoretically between modernistic and postmodernistic is the idea of diagnosis. If we were to approach an addictive person from a modernistic perspective, we again would use the DSM. It would be very much physiological symptoms and universal kinds of diagnoses. From a postmodern perspective there would be no diagnosis, only descriptions of what is going on as presented by the client and family. We would only diagnose in terms of how the family would explain that to us. That is our only diagnosis.

Sori: So that is much less pathologizing.

Shilts: Oh, tremendously. Yes, a tremendous shift. The seventh area is in the area of interventions and how we intervene in therapy. From a modernistic perspective, working with addictions again, you would see advice giving, prescriptions, the 12-step approach, focus groups, AA, NA, and things of that nature. The type of interventions that I would see myself, working with addictions, would be White's idea of externalization, attending to the language, exceptions, and coauthoring the story. So, again, very heavily language-based.

Eighth is the role of the therapist, and again a big distinction there. The role of the therapist from the modernistic approach would be hierarchical. The therapist is the expert and he or she stands at a position to direct the clients in their work. From the postmodern perspective the role of the therapist would be collaborative. The therapist and clients bring different resources to the relationship. There would be a "not-knowing" kind of position, a less directive stance.

Sori: So do you see this as a more respectful approach to working with clients?

Shilts: Absolutely. As I go on it will become very clear that when you take this not knowing position and you are less directive, it is not only less authoritarian, but it frees you up as a therapist to do a lot of different things because you are relying on your client to set the pace.

The final area, and then I want to go on and talk about how this has influenced my work, is how we would view a family, as defined from modernistic versus postmodernistic approach. We would see from the modernistic side that an unhealthy family would be rigid, maladaptive, pathological, have generational problems, bad genes, hereditary dispositions, and this is how we would define an addictive family. From a postmodern perspective we would see the family as flexible enough to change their rules, and easily structured to adapt to changing life circumstances. Again, it is this idea that families come to us with all the necessary ingredients or resources to change.

So I like to look at it this way, Kate: From a modernistic approach you are very static, reified and objective. From a postmodern perspective it is continually flowing, changing, and you take a subjective position. Once I started applying the postmodern approach my work became my inspiration, and how I view families, and work with families, children, and anyone.

Next, Shilts described his early work as a school psychologist, what sparked his interest in solution-focused therapy, and how he began using it when counseling children in a school setting.

Sori: Can you talk a little bit more about that, about how it became your inspiration?

Shilts: Sure, I think that would tell you how I was influenced. I started out originally as a school psychologist many years ago, about 25 years ago. I did not realize it, but at that point I was very modernistic in my work. I assessed children. We had to label them because that was the law, and that was the only way we could help children get certain services. There was constant diagnosing. Because of the diagnosis the child became this entity that we looked at, learning disabled, emotionally disturbed, and what have you. There was very little flexibility. I really did not spend a lot of time in the early part of my career counseling kids. I just tested them, gave them a label, wrote up a prescription, and thought I had done a marvelous job.

Sori: So the person was the problem?

Shilts: Yes, certainly in the person there was a genetic, environmental, or what have you predisposition, and this is the way this child was. It was very limiting. Then an epiphany occurred in the early 1980s and I started consulting with Insoo Kim Berg and

Steve de Shazer. I started learning their ideas about therapy and the solution-focused approach.

Sori: How did that epiphany occur?

Shilts: The first time I saw Insoo work she was working with a person who was supposedly clinically depressed. I will never forget this. The first question Insoo asked the woman was, "Can you tell me a time when you are not depressed?" My jaw dropped because I thought that was the queerest question anybody could ask. I thought that the client would say, "You are not listening to me. I am clinically depressed." Yet, the client went on to talk about a time when she was not depressed. I could not believe that it would really work.

So I started doing that with kids in the schools I was working in. I started just toying around and experimenting with it. I was amazed how kids could tell me times when they did well in school, times when they did like school, and times when they liked their teacher, etc. When Johnny was referred for testing because he was having behavioral problems, I started talking to Johnny about times when the problem was not there. I started talking to teachers about that, and the referrals started to go down. The problem was that my boss at that time, now when I reflect back it made sense, was saying, "You are the school psychologist and you are supposed to be *testing* kids, not *talking* to kids." That is when I had to make a career decision, and I decided to go back and pursue my doctorate degree in family therapy. I continued my relationship with Insoo and Steve over the years and began exploring this whole idea of more of a postmodern lens when working with all clients, but I found it increasingly interesting with students. This led to my work in the schools today with Insoo on the WOWW project.

In this segment of the interview, Shilts described the WOWW program that he and Insoo Kim Berg developed, which has been implemented successfully in many schools and is currently under empirical investigation.

Sori: Can you talk a little bit about that?

Shilts: Sure. I am married to a teacher for 25 years. The last few years Insoo comes down here doing trainings and she stays with us. One day my wife said, "Insoo, I would like you to see one of my kids. He is never in his chair." I remember Insoo was in the kitchen cleaning vegetables, and she said, "I would be more than interested, but I am going to want to know what is going on when he is *in* his chair." My wife's jaw dropped. She said she had never thought of it that way.

Sori: Sounds like that was a big shift for her. A paradigm shift?

Shilts: Yes. So from that we met with this boy. He did wonderful when we were in the classroom, and we wrote him a letter at the end of the day explaining how well he did. From that we became inspired to look at working with kids within the school's classroom, instead of removing them. I have always been a big proponent of not taking kids out of the classroom; they don't want to leave the classroom. It stigmatizes them and singles them out.

Sori: It takes them out of their context.

Shilts: And it takes them out of the context where the situation is occurring with the key players, other students, teachers, etc. We started putting counselors in the classroom. At the school where I am at, the Nova Southeastern University, we have master's programs, so we had interns and had the luxury of a lot of people who would work on the project. We call them coaches, and they go into the classroom. The first test that they do is to just sit in the classroom and write down their observations on things they see going well in the classroom.

Sori: That is very different from what normally occurs during a classroom observation. Usually it is marking down bad behaviors.

Shilts: Right, exactly, and trying to get a behavioral baseline on why Johnny is a problem. We go in and we get, if you want to use that term, a baseline of what *is* working. At the end of the class the coach reports this to the students. For example, "I saw Johnny share his pencil with Mary" or "I noticed when someone knocked at the door one of you kids got up and answered it and helped out the teacher." Or, "I noticed that everybody was raising their hand today" or "I noticed that Billy smiled when I came in." Anything that is positive.

Sori: So it is not just about the targeted child? That is terrific.

Shilts: It is about the classroom. Kate, we prefer not to say, "Here is Johnny. Here is the problem, work with him." We will try to come in and work with the whole classroom. We are more interested in what you are doing right in the classroom.

Sori: That is so much more systemic than removing the child, targeting him, and seeing him as the problem.

Shilts: From there, once we developed kind of what I like to call from Erickson, a "yes set," the class develops the goals they want to work on. This is pretty easy because most classes have goals. We stress with the teachers that the goals need to be collaborative and that the children should have some input. Usually the students and teachers can agree on things that could be good goals. Once the goals have been established, then we as coaches continue to go in. We continue to look at what is working, but we also look at the goals, and at the end of our session we have the teacher put up on the wall what we call the classroom success scale. Each day the class rates themselves, on a scale of 1 to 10, how they think they did that particular day, with a comment. Now we have that data ongoing, even when we are not there, but we try to get in there once a week. From that the class collaboratively, with the teachers, decides how they are doing. And it is very focused on what is working. Hence the WOWW, which stands for "Working On What Works." This is our third year at the particular school that we work at and we hope this year to start collecting some evidence-based data to see if, in fact, what we are doing is having a positive influence in the classroom. We are getting a lot of teacher feedback saying that it is working for them.

Sori: Well, that is tremendous.

Shilts: We are pretty optimistic. Insoo and I wrote one manual which is out, and we just finished the coach's manual. Last year we were up to 30 teachers. It has just taken off. This year a lot of our teachers say, "I don't need the coach anymore. I know exactly what I need to do."

Sori: So they have gotten it and internalized it. That is incredible.

Shilts: So, it is working.

Sori: It is so exciting because next to the family the school is the most important environment that the children are in. Too often family therapists neglect working with the schools to help the children adapt and do better in school.

Shilts: Not only that, but I have long thought that we take these kids and we work with them as counselors and we never involve the teachers. What I am finding out from the WOWW project is that the teachers want to be involved. There is a need for the teachers to feel they are competent in dealing with these things and it makes them better teachers. They feel better. One teacher who has been working with WOWW said that she did not go home with a headache anymore.

Sori: So WOWW stands for "Working On What Works!" That is clever.

Shilts: I always noticed that whenever Insoo is working, she always says, "Wow!" My students have picked that up over the years so I thought about how I could acknowledge that "wow" thing. It was just one of those things found its way out of my head.

The focus of the interview shifted next to Shilts describing the major interventions he utilizes in his competency-based, postmodern approach to working with children: Externalization from narrative therapy, and scaling questions from a solution-focused perspective. He then provided a case example to illustrate his playful method of integrating these two models.

Sori: That is excellent. From there would you talk about some of the major interventions in solution-focused and narrative approaches, and how you integrate them and adapt them for use with children?

Shilts: Well, I use mainly the two models together when working with children at an age or mental ability where they are not able to abstract well. I use two specific interventions from both models, White's externalization along with de Shazer and everyone else's scaling question. The kids that I use this with are not able to abstract, so we do what is called a visual scaling [see Shilts & Duncan, 2003].

Sori: So a visual scale works with children who cannot think abstractly. What sorts of problems do the children you work with experience?

Shilts: I have used visual scaling over the years with a wide variety of cases involving kids who are referred for specific things; fear, fear of school, phobias, and temper tantrums. I recently worked with a young girl who was not able to sleep in her own bedroom. She ended up in the parent's bedroom every night. She had a real fear of the dark, which is the way she and her mother explained it to me. I worked with the girl and her mother. She, I will call her Megan, was probably about 8, and I started out by getting a description as to what the concerns were with the family. Using White's idea of externalization, we came up with the idea of the fear monster.

Sori: The fear monster!

Shilts: Yes. My first session I took quite a bit of time finding out about this monster, exploring his habits, how he pushed her around, and times when the monster appeared to be at his very worst. This was my idea of getting an accurate description of the problem as viewed by Megan and Mom. So, bringing in the visual scaling, I asked Megan to stand up on a chair in my office, reach up as high as she could, and show how big the monster is when at its very worst, pushing her around and influencing her. Finally it pushes her into Mom and Dad's bedroom. I asked, "Is this the way it is when the monster is this big?" They both nodded. Mom was beginning to understand where we were going, so she was very cooperative and was part of the dialogue. Next, I introduced the idea of how would we go about shrinking the monster. I went down about five inches on my office wall from where it was at the worst, and put a mark on the wall. I asked Megan and Mom what would be going on if the monster was this size, five inches shorter.

Sori: So you were very concrete.

Shilts: It has to be very concrete because this is the only way that children at that age, from a developmental standpoint, can understand this. What I have found when I have asked this question is that they start telling me all kinds of things that would be different. In this particular situation, Megan started talking about how she would probably be sleeping one night in her own room, not spending as much time in her parents' room, and all kinds of things that would be back to a more normal situation. We started talking about the possibility that she would be sleeping on her own, in her own room. So, that is how the first session ended. The task was to measure the size of the fear monster each day, based on how Megan did at night with the dark and her sleeping arrangements. We then set up a second session. In the second session I asked the size of the fear monster and how they recorded it on a daily basis. Megan reported that the monster had shrunk in height on three different nights during that past week.

Sori: Was she actually standing on a chair at home and doing the same thing?

Shilts: Well, you know clients are so resourceful and so clever; they went to a local store and bought a chart where you can actually measure a kid's growth. They put it on the refrigerator.

Sori: How clever! Again, very visual and concrete.

Shilts: They were very clever, and they came in with this thing and had it all measured out. I again complimented them and said, "Wow, I never would have thought of doing it that way." It was so convenient and kept a very nice record.

Sori: There's the "Wow!" And I like how you give them credit for being so creative.

Shilts: So she talked about how she actually spent a couple of nights in her own bed, and her mother echoed the same results. We saw that as tremendous progress. Then we talked about what would be going on if the monster was this size, and I went even lower. Now Megan was like a snowball going down a mountain, really picking up a lot of energy with this. She said that if we got it to this point, she would be doing everything they wanted her to be doing more and more consistently. You know, when working with children you have to be playful, so I said to her to note my carpet in my office. I said, "Do you know what this carpet is made out of?" She said, "No, I don't." I said, "It is made out of monster ashes. Because once we get the monster down to a certain size we can stamp it right into the ground, grind it in, and then it is gone."

Sori: I love that! How very playful.

Shilts: I make them go through stamping their feet on the ground; it is kind of a ritual thing. I say you will know when you are ready to stamp it out completely. The third session she came in and it was a marvelous end to the story. She was ready to stamp it out. They reported two weeks of her sleeping in her own room. So, we stamped it out and at the end I said, "You know these monsters can be tricky and other monsters or other things can come back, but now you know what you need to do, you and Mom. In the future, if this fear monster or any other thing comes back, you measure it at its worst, and then you start shrinking it and stamping it out." Again, what is that saying? Not just giving them fish but learning how to catch the fish kind of thing.

Sori: You had a monster-stomping party!

Shilts: Right, and on follow-up she continued to do very well. I like to ask the clients at the end, what made the most sense for you in our work. The mother said, "You know I think she enjoyed the monster stuff, but I think that you gave my daughter a sense that she was capable of overcoming this, plus you never from the get-go made her feel like she was a failure."

Sori: That is so empowering, looking at strengths and competencies.

Shilts: Yes, competency. Right from the get-go I think it is really important that we see them as very competent individuals who will get to a better place. By doing that our work is easier and then all these ideas from these models make so much sense. Certainly, if we see our clients as competent and resourceful, then why would we not expect them to get to a better place?

Sori: Right, and you help them be able to literally visualize what that is going to look like.

Shilts: Right, exactly.

Sori: That is wonderful. Was she able to articulate exactly what she did to reduce his size?

Shilts: Basically, we established it in very concrete terms. She said that the monster would start shrinking in size when she would be able to stay in her own bed, to work through that on her own. Of course, mother was trying a nightlight and things like that. She would know that things were getting better because rather than getting out of bed she would talk to herself. She could call Mom in and say, "What do you think here, Mom?" The whole idea was that, "I will stay within my room and work this through." She was not able to articulate this and I do not go fishing for this, but what happened is that once she was able to see that she could do it, it was like a snowball effect again. It started taking on its own energy and became fun for her. The whole idea of being fearful went away and was replaced by the feeling that, "Hey, I overcame this!"

Sori: It changed her whole view of herself. That is a wonderful example.

Shilts: It was a wonderful case.

Next, Shilts explained how he uses the Miracle Question with families in a way that allows all family members, even teens, to participate. He also addressed common problems that clinicians often experience in using the miracle question with clients.

Sori: You have written a lot about the miracle question, how you simplify it and break it down, and help clients address parts of the miracle question to bring about and maintain change. Do you use the miracle question with children and if so, do you adapt it for kids?

Shilts: I don't really adapt it for kids, but I will give you a good example of how I simplify it in working with a family. Often, when you work with parents and an adolescent, their miracles are very different. People often ask what to do with that, and it is really confusing. So what I do is I ask the miracle question to the whole family. First of all, I start out getting a description of what brings them there. I think that is essential. I pretty much expect that, of course, 15-year-old Tom is going to have a whole different idea of what the miracle would look like than Mom and Dad. You might as well just accept it; that is going to be the rule. I tell my students, the day that all family members agree on the same miracle, document that because it would be a first. Then what I do is I write down everything that they say. I say, "Who wants to start? OK we will start with you, Mom. So this miracle occurs, how would you know it?" And she gives me her information. Then I ask who wants to go next, and the family decides. You get all these different versions of the miracle. I tell them that this is a huge miracle, and it is probably too much to expect right off the bat. We need to simplify it and make it a little more doable. I say, "Each of you pick one piece that, when you see it happening this week, would be a sure sign to you, and possibly to the other family members, that things are beginning to get better." They each have their own piece of the miracle and that is fine, and we work that way. So, it is kind of an interactive thing. Everybody is invested in getting to a better place.

What happened to me in the past and where, I think, people get bogged down and perhaps even burned out, is that therapists usually take one of two directions. When you have a family referred to you who is having some behavioral problems with an adolescent, you either have to join with the parent to try to coerce this kid to change, which is usually a dead end.

Sori: Yes, and then you lose the child.

Shilts: Sure, you lose the child. Or, you can become an advocate for the child, and the parents do not show up anymore with the kid. What I have learned is that if I am going to get anywhere, everyone has to feel invested in the miracle or have a goal that makes sense. When it works, what you find is that the family is able to make the necessary adjustments; they are able to loosen up a little and make a bit of a shift to accommodate the others. Perhaps a miracle would be that Tom is going to school, and that is his parents' miracle. But why is he going to school? Because the parents are not nagging him all the time. We continue to massage and work that and see where it goes. Once they start feeling success, the system changes and things start heading to a better place. That is an example of how I would use the miracle question working with a family.

Sori: Some counselors have a difficult time initially with the miracle question because people will say things like, "Well, I will win the lottery." Or a child will say, "My miracle would be that my mommy is not dead anymore," or "My parents are not divorced anymore." How would you encourage people to work with clients who come up with responses like that?

Shilts: Yes, that is tough. I would say that one key word is patience. You have to be patient with your clients. If you are really sincere and patient, they will calibrate to a miracle that is more realistic. I will try to impose some humor in it. I tell my clients right off of the bat, if their miracle is the lotto and they win it, they have to split it 50/50 with their therapist.

Sori: That is great!

Shilts: That kind of gets them to refocus. Here is a funny story. I asked this young guy who was having dating problems about the miracle. I said, "So you wake up tomorrow morning and come down from bed and the miracle has occurred. How would you know it?" He said someone like Jessica Simpson would be in his kitchen making breakfast for him. He went into a whole thing. Then he stopped, waited, and said, "You really want me to answer it realistically, don't you?" He then brought it down. So, patience is one thing. Obviously, when people first hear it maybe they throw something out, but I think if you are just patient and work with them they will do it.

Your other question, which I think is really good, "My mother would be alive." That one really threw me a couple of years ago, and I consulted with Insoo. I will give you the case example. I was working with a woman who was depressed. I had very little history on her depression. I did not really care about a history because that is the way I prefer to work. She came to me and I asked her the miracle question and she said, "My two sons who I lost in the Vietnam War would be alive." Well that threw me for a loop. I wanted to just say, "Time out and I will get back to you." I forget now how I ended the session. I think probably by just allowing her to emote and vent that experience of losing two sons. I consulted Insoo and she said next time to ask her how the boys would know that the miracle in Mom has occurred.

So, I asked her and do you know what she said? I got chills running up my spine when she looked at me and said, "The boys would say to me—'Mom it is OK. Get out of bed and start living your life again.'" From that things just changed in our relationship, and slowly but surely, she started figuring out what a miracle would be with her sons involved in it.

Sori: That is brilliant. It is like she invoked those sons!

Shilts: Yes. Those are some ideas that people might want to try. Again, the key word is patience.

The therapeutic use of humor, playfulness, and metaphors are discussed in the next part of the interview. Shilts also commented on the importance of safety when counseling children.

Sori: Right! That is a very good approach to it. You have mentioned humor, and play, and playfulness. Will you talk more about that? Do you ever use any toys or props with children?

Shilts: I am not a big one on props or toys. I mean if kids bring things I will certainly try to evoke that into my therapy. But, when I work with kids I try to use as much humor as I can with any client of any age. Obviously you do not want to use humor when it has to do with death and dying, but I have gotten the lotto thing a lot. They laugh and we laugh and it is kind of like, now let's get real here.

Again, if we are talking specifically with children, I feel humor, playfulness, is a beautiful way to develop fit and join with clients. If you don't do that, all of these interventions and things we talk about will not go anywhere. So humor, metaphors, analogies, and things like that are a wonderful way to develop fit with children. Because think about it, it is a very unnatural environment to bring a child into therapy. I mean, I have yet to have a kid call me and refer themselves for therapy. So one of the things I do with kids is I try to be very observant, and watch what they wear or bring to the therapy session. With boys, for example, I look at the baseball hat they are wearing, or the shirts. With girls, their clothing and what kinds of earrings, or things like that. From that you can start developing a conversation that really helps you to get to know those kids. Invoking a little humor makes it more playful, and kids like that. So I will have a child come in and, because I am in Florida, they will have a Dolphins shirt on. Because I am originally from Wisconsin, I say, "Oh the Dolphins, they are terrible!" Just kind of playing with them and teasing them a little bit. From simple little playful and humorous things like that, then when I start to ask them "What brought you here?" or "How come you are here?" I am amazed over the years how kids will start talking. I really believe it is simply because now they feel comfortable and they are confident. They have a better connection with you because they have seen that playful side of you.

Sori: I think that it also creates safety. Don't you think it is essential that kids feel safe and that the therapist is a safe person?

Shilts: Certainly. I think that it is somewhat analogous to a kid going to the doctor or dentist. First and foremost is, "Am I going to be OK here? Is this a safe environment?" This is reflected in the parents, too. You start being playful and humorous with your kids and notice how parents react to that. It is a very good barometer, how comfortable the parents feel their children are with you, and it makes the parents comfortable. A lot of residual things that come out of that.

Sori: And is it also vice versa? When kids see that the parents are comfortable with someone, they get more relaxed. That makes sense because too often kids feel going to a counselor or therapist is like going to the principal's office. I think those are great ideas!

Shilts: Yes, they see it more as a punishment or something that is going to be painful. When you can impress upon them that this is a safe place, and can actually be a fun place to learn more about yourself, kids will respond much, much differently.

Cultural considerations when counseling children and families are addressed next, and Shilts provided an example of how to work with families whose cultural beliefs may be at odds with the laws and the dominant cultural norms in the United States.

Sori: Excellent. I am curious if you see any problems when you work across cultures. I know that in Florida you have a lot of cultural diversity. Do you have to do any adapting of this method? Do you find that some cultures do not take as readily to this postmodernism approach?

Shilts: You know I am a big proponent that people are people. I try not to get too reified into certain cultures and how they respond. However, I will have to say that living in South Florida now for the past almost 20 years, there are certain cultures that you have to be aware of. Certain rules and structures in their culture do not really fit into the therapeutic world as we know it. I will give you a good example. When you are working down here and a family from the Caribbean area, Jamaica or the Bahamas, is referred to you, our laws and rules on parental abuse and punishment are very different from their culture. Their culture says that when you spank a child and it leaves a mark, that is actually being a good parent. In our society, if their child goes to school and there is a mark they can be referred to the Department of Children and Families, or what have you. I have learned a lot about cultures and certainly how they discipline their children and how they view discipline. However, if they are referred to me and they have unfortunately gotten involved in the system, I have to be aware of their beliefs. But again, my basis is still, "How do we need to get to a better place? What do we need to do to get past this?" The miracle question: "How will you know?" I still look at the family, no matter what their cultural background, as capable of change and moving on to a better place in their lives. Again, there are certain rules or structures that different cultures have. But to answer the other part of your question, I find it really kind of self-defeating as a therapist to ever position myself that just because this family is from this culture, I cannot work with them. I feel that everybody has the resources to get to a better place and it does not matter what their culture or background is.

Next, Shilts was asked to address the question of whether a solution-focused approach might not fit for some clients who may want to talk more about problems than solutions.

Sori: Do you find that there are some people who just do not take to focusing more on solutions than on problems? They just want to continue, week after week, talking about how awful their child or their partner is?

Shilts: You know, that is an excellent question. I have tossed this around in my head and have suggested it to students as possible dissertation projects, to see if we could come up with any kind of data. I have often wondered why some clients never stay in therapy long. Basically, I think there are a couple of reasons. Maybe because of the way we work, looking at what is working, they may say, "Oh hey! I got this figured out." Other people might not come back because they say, "No, that is not going to work for us. The guy is just looking at how we are going to do better, and is not talking about the problem."

Sori: Or he is not seeing it from my point of view?

Shilts: I have never really had a client say that, "Hey, I don't like your approach. I have to find somebody else." I think they just politely make that decision, but they never give us that feedback or data. People pretty much realize that this is the way I view the world, and this is how I work. I am pretty up front about that in the referral process, so they have a pretty good understanding. My underlying feeling is that most people want to get to a better place and they want to feel better, so why would they not be open to this kind of an approach? To be honest with you, I have never had anyone say, "You are too solution-focused and I don't get it."

Sori: Do you ever find that parents just continue to berate their children and give you the laundry list of all their bad behavior?

Shilts: No. When parents come to you they really see that their children need to get to a better place. So I work from the understanding that there is no such thing as a bad parent. Parents can become bad, but I do not think that people go into this thing called parenting and say, "I am going to be a bad parent." I think circumstances along the way may make them a bad parent, but I like to work from the idea that when parents come, they are invested in anything that will help their children feel better about themselves or about the situation. I really think parents are in it for the best for their children. I think it is just inherent in us as parents.

In the final segment of the interview, Shilts elaborated on the use of metaphors in therapy, and offerd a creative metaphor to use with parents who are launching children.

Sori: One thing I am really interested in is the difference between play and playfulness and play therapy. You have talked about playfulness and metaphor, and I am wondering if you could give us maybe a couple more concrete examples of how you use metaphors.

Shilts: OK, I have a wonderful metaphor that I would like to share with you. Many times I will have parents come in presenting the concern that their adolescent children are disobedient and break the rules. They are never where they are supposed to be. They are always defying the parents, etc. From the child's perspective, they need more freedom. "I am 18 years old now and they need to trust that I know what I am doing, and just because I am going out with that person it does not necessarily mean that I am going to get in trouble." This causes a tremendous amount of stress in the parent-adolescent relationship. I have used the metaphor of ship building with that. This may sound like I am erring on the side of the child, but in many of these cases the adolescent is right. The only way they are going to grow up is if the parent will let them try this stuff.

I use the metaphor that as parents, we are all ship builders and our children are the ships. We spend a lifetime building this ship, making a safe and sturdy ship, teaching it and putting all this effort into it so that it is solid and well structured. We have it tied to the dock. We lavish it and continue to make it look better. If it needs a new paint job we will run out and get that for it, etc., etc. We have the ship to a point where it is beautiful. Somewhere along the line, we have to cut the rope to see if it floats.

Sori: To see if it is seaworthy.

Shilts: I like that! I have had parents get teary-eyed with that story of building the ship. Somewhere we have to cut the rope and see if it floats, see if it is seaworthy—I am going to use that! I say, "You know, if it is built well and we have done the job right, it will float and it will find its way back to the dock. You will always have that ship."

Sori: It will find its way back to the safe harbor.

Shilts: Yes, the safe harbor. I sometimes talk that way to families. I guess that I am giving them another story.

Sori: I love that because we even use the word "launching" in terms of letting our children go! So it fits with the ship metaphor perfectly.

Shilts: Right. So that is one of the metaphors or analogies that I use. I think that it just loosens up everybody and gives them a different way of looking at it. I have had people come back the next session and had the young "ship" report, "They let me try to sail this week and it was kind of neat!" It is a reality, and I try to tell the parents, "Hey, look I agree with you that keeping them tied to that safe harbor sure makes a whole lot of sense. Why not? It is a tough sea out there." But I say that we have built the ship and it is kind of ludicrous that we do not see if it is seaworthy. It gives them a whole different perspective on the situation.

Sori: That is a beautiful metaphor! Well, you have covered a lot, and I appreciate the depth of your answers.

Shilts: OK. I have really enjoyed this.

Sori: Lee, this was tremendous and I can't thank you enough for sharing so many of your thoughts!

SUGGESTED READING

Berg, I. K., & Shilts, L. (2004). *Classroom solutions: WOWW approach*. Milwaukee, WI: BFTC Press.

Berg, I. K, & Shilts, L. (2005). Keeping the solutions inside the classroom: WOWW approach. *School Counselor, July/August*, 30–35.

Berg, I. K., & Shilts, L. (2005). *Classroom solutions: WOWW coaching*. Milwaukee, WI: BFTC Press.

de Shazer, S. (1988). *Clues: Investigating solutions in brief therapy*. New York: W. W. Norton & Co.

Green, S., Shilts, L., & Bacigalupe, G. (2001). When approved is not enough: Development of a supervision consultation model. *Journal of Marital and Family Therapy, 27*(4), 515–525.

Nau, D. S., & Shilts, L. (2000). When to use the miracle question: Clues from a qualitative study of four SFBT practitioners. *Journal of Systemic Therapies, 19*(1), 129–135.

Protinsky, H., & Shilts, L. (1990). Adolescent substance use and family cohesion. *Family Therapy, 17*(2), 173–175.

Reiter, M. D., & Shilts, L. (1998). Using circular scaling questions to deconstruct depression: A case study. *Crisis Intervention and Time-Limited Treatment, 4*(2–3), 227–237.

Rudes, J., Shilts, L., & Berg, I. K. (1997). Focused supervision seen through a recursive frame analysis. *Journal of Marital and Family Therapy, 23*(2), 203–215.

Shilts, L. (1991). The relationship of early adolescent substance use to extracurricular activities, peer influence, and personal attitudes. *Adolescent, 26*(103), 613–617.

Shilts, L., & Aronson, J. (1993). Circular hearing: Working through the muddles of supervision. *Journal of Family Psychotherapy, 4*(1), 57–67.

Shilts, L., & Duncan, B. L. (2003). Integrating externalization and scaling questions: Using visual scaling to amplify children's voices. In C. F. Sori, L. L. Hecker, & Associates, *The therapist's notebook for children and adolescents: Homework, handouts, and activities for use in psychotherapy* (pp. 230–236). Binghamton, NY: Haworth.

Shilts, L., Filippino, C., & Nau, D. S. (1994). Client-informed therapy. *Journal of Systemic Therapies, 13*(4), 39–52.

Shilts, L., & Gordon, A. B. (1996). What to do after the miracle occurs. *Journal of Family Psychotherapy, 7*(1), 15–22.

Shilts, L., & Knapik-Esposito, M. (1993). Playback of the therapeutic process: He said, she said, they said. *Journal of Systemic Therapies, 12*(2), 41–54.

Shilts, L., Rambo, A., & Hernandez, L. (1997). Clients helping therapists find solutions to their therapy. *Contemporary Family Therapy: An International Journal, 19*(1), 117–132.

Shilts, L., Rambo, A., & Huntley, E. (2003). The collaborative miracle: When to slow down the pace of brief therapy. *Journal of Systemic Therapies, 22*(2), 65–73.

Shilts, L., & Ray, W. (1991). Therapeutic letters: Pacing with the system. *Journal of Strategic & Systemic Therapies, 19*(3–4), 92–99.

Shilts, L., & Reiter, M. D. (2000). Integrating externalization and scaling questions: Using "visual" scaling to amplify children's voices. *Journal of Systemic Therapies, 19*(1), 82–89.

Shilts, L., Rudes, J., & Madigan, S. (1993). The use of a solution-focused interview with a reflecting team format: Evolving thoughts from clinical practice. *Journal of Systemic Therapies, 12*(1), 1–10.

White, M., & Epston, D. (1990). *Narrative means to therapeutic ends*. New York: W. W. Norton & Co.

PART III

Conceptual, Practical, and Ethical Issues in Counseling Children and Families

CHAPTER 7

Involving Children in Family Counseling and Involving Parents in Children's Counseling

Theoretical and Practical Guidelines

CATHERINE FORD SORI, PH.D., SHANNON DERMER, PH.D., AND GENE WESOLOWSKI, A.M.

Many counselors who wish to work with both children and their families are faced with two major obstacles: Knowing when and how to involve children in family sessions, as well as how to actively engage parents who want the counselor to work individually to "fix" their child. Some of the questions that counselors grapple with include, "How do I persuade parents to participate in therapy without blaming them? Should I just see the child for a couple of sessions and then focus treatment on the parents? If I focus treatment on the parents, do I stop treating the child? If I involved both parents and children in sessions, *how* would I do it?" (Bailey & Sori, 2000, p. 475).

The goal of counseling should be, whenever possible, to help parents to help their children, with a focus on strengthening the parent-child relationship. When parents are excluded from counseling, the child remains the "problem," and often the only relationship that is strengthened is between the child and the counselor. If we ignore contextual factors, such as the child's relationships within the family, at school, with peers, and in other settings, we run the risk of providing only symptom relief and not long-term systemic treatment goals (Bailey & Sori, 2000). It is especially vital to involve parents when working with children who have multiple risk factors (e.g., marital discord, parental psychopathology, social-cognitive deficits, socioeconomic disadvantage). Estrada and Pinsof (1995) report that children from these families show fewer gains in therapy and are less likely to maintain those gains over time. In addition, children may be the ticket to working with adults to address some of these issues.

This chapter addresses the decision-making process of who to see, and emphasizes a multimodal approach based on the fluctuating needs of family members. Practical suggestions for engaging both children and parents are also discussed.

DECISION MAKING: WHO TO SEE?

When working with children and families, one of the first decisions a counselor has to make is who should be asked to attend counseling. Deciding whom to invite to session is based on one's theoretical perspective, the presenting concern, developmental needs, relationship issues, and the emotional availability of those involved. Counselors need to take all of these factors into account when making a decision about whom to see in counseling.

Individual Perspective

The individual perspective has its historical roots firmly planted in the psychoanalytic tradition of seeing problems as a result of dysfunctional regulation of internal processes. These deficiencies were seen as individual and as separate from social influences (Gil & Kaplan, 1994). The assumption is that the key to individual problems and solutions lies within the individual with the presenting concern. The individual has either behavioral deficits, skewed thinking, is developmentally "stuck," or unable to reconcile internal struggles. From this perspective, individual counseling makes sense (Griffin, 1993). Such a focus on the intrapersonal dimensions of a client meant that at best families were not needed in treatment, and at worst including them could be harmful to the progress of individual clients.

In the psychoanalytic approach, the therapist uses play to gain access to the child's inner life. Thus, the main focus of therapy is on the child's intrapsychic process and exploring the unconscious. A thorough assessment of the child's development is made to determine if the child has not successfully progressed through the stages of development and is stuck at a point that inhibits the child from progressing to an age-appropriate level. If so, the child would engage in a psychologically significant relationship with the counselor, through the use of techniques including free play. The goal is for the child to move forward at an age-appropriate pace through the developmental stages.

Play therapists may engage a child in play to help him/her express and resolve a traumatic experience. Meeting with the child alone is seen as the best way from this perspective to directly diminish child distress and suffering. The counselor endeavors to create a safe environment where the child can explore and express feelings either symbolically through self-directed play, or directly through conversation with the counselor. The role of parents is to provide crucial information about the child's development and their relationship with the child during the assessment process. Parents often meet regularly with the counselor in a supportive role and to ensure that they can permit the psychological growth of the child. However, parents are usually not informed about the content of what goes on in the child's therapy (Landreth, 1991), as this is kept confidential.

Family Systems Perspective

Those steeped in a family systems perspective assert that the best way to deal with individuals is in the context of families. Griffin (1993) goes so far as to assert that besides problems related to genetic or organic origins, all child and adolescent problems should be treated as family problems. Interpersonal relationships are seen as the key to understanding someone's context and are the crux of intervention. Involving all children, not just children identified with a problem, is important because everyone is affected by and may affect what is perceived to be an individual issue.

From a family systems perspective, when a child is the identified client, including family is especially important. "The family is a child's primary resource system. Children are born into, grow up within, and learn a fundamental world view within their families ..." (Combrinck-Graham, 1989, p. ix). Including everyone in the family in counseling has the benefit of providing the counselor with a more accurate view of family life, family rules, and family reactions to individual members. Integrating children into family sessions makes them available for direct intervention, and making sure to include all family members lets them be known from direct contact, rather than from third-party descriptions. In addition, children add a unique point of view, and tend to be spontaneous and candid (Chasin & White, 1989). Children are quite creative and can offer a unique perspective on problems and solutions.

Despite the fact that many systems-oriented clinicians hold to the theoretical belief that children *should* be included in sessions, research has shown that they are often excluded (Johnson & Thomas, 1999; Korner & Brown, 1990). This holds true even when the presenting problem is child related. Too often children are delegated to the waiting room or parents are asked to leave them at home because clinicians lack the skills and comfort to work with children individually or in a family setting (Johnson & Thomas, 1999; Sori, 2006d; Sori & Sprenkle, 2004).

Parents Only

In Parent Management Training, the caretakers of a child are seen as the point of intervention. Parents create the structure and environment in which children live; they are the most powerful force in children's lives. Consequently, in this approach, parents become the center of intervention and children are not included in sessions. Utilizing ideas from behaviorism and social learning theory, parents are taught skills that will decrease their child's problem behavior, increase desired behavior, and help alter parent/child interactions. Although the purpose of intervention with the parents is to change child behavior, children are not present in the session. Parent management training is supported by empirical data and has gained acceptance as an effective approach for contending with a wide range of childhood problems (see Estrada & Pinsof, 1995).

Multimodal Perspective

The authors believe that it is important to assess and treat both individual as well as relationship issues. We advocate for using a multimodal approach, which is supported in the research (Sori, 2006c; Sori & Sprenkle, 2004). According to Bailey and Sori (2000), counselors need to be able to assess the functioning of and treat six different areas: (a) the individual child who is the identified patient; (b) the functioning of each individual parent and each sibling; (c) the relationship between each child and each parent; (d) the couple's relationship; (e) relationships among siblings; and (f) the overall functioning of the family and their relationships, including multigenerational relationships. To this list we add (g) the role of the child in the couple's and family relationships.

In general, we advocate for some individual session time with all children (Wachtel, 1991), especially when the child is the focus of counseling. It is important to see the child alone at some point to help get to know the child "apart from the problem" (Freeman, Epston, & Lobovits, 1997, p. 35), as well as to assess the impact of parents' problems on the child (Sori, 2006c; Sori & Sprenkle, 2004). Individual sessions may also be needed to help children heal from trauma, address internalized conflicts, gain a sense of mastery over their environment (Bailey & Sori, 2000), or to process their grief in a supportive environment. Individual sessions may also be useful to help children develop skills such as impulse control, or to tolerate frustration (Wachtel, 1991). Children can be coached, and skills can be role-played and then shared with the family. Information gleaned in individual sessions should be used to develop interventions that include the parents and other siblings.

Wachtel (1991) cautions that individual sessions with children should always be part of the larger context of working with the whole family.

When working with multiple subsystems of the family, the issue of confidentiality may come up when family members are seen individually. This issue is addressed at length in the ethics chapter in this volume (see chapter 8). Caution must be taken not to compromise the work with the whole family while honoring each individual's boundaries.

Wachtel (1991) contends that there are two good reasons to hold individual sessions with children. The first is that it is simply harder to get to know children than adults. Individual sessions allow us to get to know children better and to learn things about them, such as their coping style, degree of emotional openness, or social skills. The second reason is that even when family issues are resolved, children may have individual issues that have not been addressed. Individual sessions offer the child direct help in handling problems, such as how to deal with peers, cope with losses, abuse, poverty, illnesses or disabilities, or to coach a child in changing his or her part in problematic interactions (Combrinck-Graham, 1989; Wachtel, 1991). This information can be useful in planning family interventions that also target children's individual issues (Wachtel, 1991). However, time spent alone with a child or teen should be structured and goal oriented, and kids should understand that material may be brought back to the family, if deemed relevant by the counselor (Taffel, 1991). When the child is uncomfortable with the parent's response, e.g., the parent lectures the child, when parents are not differentiated enough to accept the child's issues as separate from their own, or if complete confidentiality has been promised, then caution must be used when bringing the material back to the family (see Sori & Hecker, 2006).

Clinicians also may want to hold individual sessions with parents for various reasons. For example, unresolved issues from the past tend to surface and get played out in parent-child conflicts. Often family-of-origin issues may need to be addressed in order to help parents make effective changes in their interactions with their children or spouse (Bailey & Sori, 2000).

In addition to working on individual issues, it is necessary to examine dyadic relationships in families. This includes the child's relationship to each parent. If there are problems (such as disengagement, enmeshment, neglect, or abuse) the child will likely continue to manifest problems even after "successful" individual treatment (Bailey & Sori, 2000). Sibling relationships are important to assess (see Sori, 2006d), as this is where children first learn the rules of socializing, negotiating, and conflict resolution.

Counselors also must determine how the child is impacted by the couple's relationship. Research demonstrates the negative impact of marital discord on children's adjustment (Gottman, 1999), and often marital conflict is detoured through a child (Minuchin, 1974). Finally, it is important to observe how the child functions as part of the family's overall interactions.

GUIDELINES FOR DECISION MAKING

As stated earlier, decisions about whom to include must be well thought-out. They should be based on what is best for a particular child and family with their specific presenting problem. Decisions should not be based solely on therapist preference or comfort level (Sori, 2006d; Sori & Sprenkle, 2004). Given that, how does one make informed decisions about involving children in family sessions, and involving parents in children's counseling?

The one study that examined the issue of children's inclusion in family therapy sessions found that experts in the field agreed that children should generally be included in family sessions, and should only be excluded for a few specific reasons (Sori, 2006d; Sori & Sprenkle, 2004). These included when parents are talking explicitly about sex, or when they are discussing how to share sensitive information with a child, such as the impending death of a parent, or that one partner is homosexual. Children generally know what is going on, so it is best to include them. Even when they are excluded, these panelists suggest that they be included at some point in order to assess the impact of parental or family problems on them. In addition, Minuchin observes that dynamics between a couple change when young children are present (Sori, 2006e).

Parents Not Emotionally Available

One time that it is especially advisable to hold individual sessions with a child is when there is no parent or caretaker who is emotionally available to help them during a difficult time. For example, when a child experiences the death of a parent or sibling, the parent(s) often are so steeped in their own grief that they are just not able to offer the comfort and support the child needs. Too often these children are left to try to make sense of the loss and to grieve on their own. A child may try to comfort or take care of a bereft parent, which can result in role reversal, or may begin acting out to distract a grieving parent (Biank & Sori, 2006). The same may occur when parents divorce, or when a parent is addicted or has a mental illness, such as depression or bipolar disorder. Younger children are egocentric and often blame themselves for such situations, and if these magical thoughts are not addressed they can lead to serious psychopathology as the child develops (Fogarty, 2000). The counseling relationship can offer children a safe place to explore these difficult emotions, which eventually may be addressed in family sessions, once a parent becomes more emotionally available.

Adolescents' Need for Autonomy

For many adolescents, achieving autonomy is a gradual process that begins during the preteen years and ends in young adulthood. This can be a very important issue to consider when developing a plan for counseling the adolescent and the family. Is the teen psychologically connected to his or her parents and siblings in a way that suits everyone being seen together as a family? Or is the teen attempting to make decisions on his or her own and be more independent of the family? Can the family support this attempt at individuation? Is the teen only interested in being with peers, or can he or she relate to a helpful adult? These factors regarding the adolescent's striving for autonomy need to be considered when planning how the adolescent and the family will be seen in counseling.

In discussing teens, Berg and Steiner (2003), coming from a solution-focused perspective, suggest:

> When parents are so frustrated with their teenager that no matter what the topic of conversation is, the parent repeatedly returns to the child's problems or appears to be preoccupied with the child's problems for various reasons, it is time to see them separately. Likewise when several attempts to change the topic to what the child has done well or to some positive changes the child made since the appointment was set are unsuccessful, then it is best to see them separately. There are times when the child is irritated and it seems impossible to create an atmosphere of cooperation and respect for each other or with you. (p. 51)

In these situations, it may be best to divide a session between the child and parents, coaching each on how to change their part in the interactions, and encouraging all parties to notice small gains. Berg and Steiner (2003) suggest bringing parents and children together when "there are noticeable changes toward the positive directions, both at home and at school" (p. 53). When this occurs counselors can punctuate success in the family, what parents as well as children are doing well and how they might continue to improve, while giving credit to everyone for the positive changes.

OVERCOMING OBSTACLES TO INVOLVING PARENTS

There is strong evidence that child problems may be influenced by many factors (Bailey & Sori, 2000). There has been a long-held notion in the field of family therapy that child problems are an expression of marital issues (Cummings & Davies, 1994; Fincham, 1998) or some type of family dysfunction (Montalvo & Haley, 1973; Olson, 1970). However, research indicates that many other issues contribute to child problems, including genetics (Plomin & Rutter, 1998), temperamental factors (Sanson & Rothbart, 1995), physical illness or a disability (Rolland, 1994), parental psychopathology (Field, 1995), difficulties with sibling relationships (Brody & Stonemen, 1996), economic and social factors (Hoff-Ginsberg & Tardif, 1995), and problems with peer relationships (Ladd & Le Sieur, 1995). Parents need to be involved to assess and treat children grappling with any of these issues.

Parents can provide important information about a child's developmental history, family genogram, educational history, and medical history, as well as the history of the problem and how they have tried to resolve it (Bailey & Sori, 2000). One practical suggestion to engage parents is to let them know that they are the experts on their children and that they are a vital resource for their child. Counselors can stress that the child needs their support to make and maintain any changes. In this way parents are invited to play a positive role in helping their child reach therapeutic goals (Bailey & Sori, 2000).

It is vital for the counselor to see how parents interact with their children, how they function in the parental role, and to assess the emotional climate in the family. Parents are often overwhelmed and frustrated with their child, and they need support, encouragement, and hope. Some may blame themselves (or their spouse) and feel inadequate and confused about how to help their child. Counselors can offer a supportive environment to help parents begin to get a larger picture of the problem and to see solutions they have not previously considered. They can be helped to see their own role in maintaining the problems, as well as to become aware of strengths and resources that have not been previously utilized. Counselors should highlight parental strengths, such as their love, concern, and determination to help their child. We believe it is vital to shift parental focus from deficits to individual and family strengths and examples of resiliencies (Bailey & Sori, 2000; Walsh, 1998). Bailey and Sori (2000) state, "Unless a therapist disarms the parents' fear and defensiveness by establishing a relationship of safety and trust, parents will remain resistant to change and want the therapy to stay focused on their child" (p. 479).

The family may present with child problems, but often children's problems really *do* reflect parental or family problems, such as marital discord, lack of structure, parental depression, or substance abuse. If parents are not included it is difficult to discern if the couple's relationship, family problems, or a parent's individual issues are impeding a child's progress in counseling (Bailey & Sori, 2000). By including parents these problems may be able to be addressed at some point in family therapy.

Often parents will need to be educated about a systems approach to counseling. One of our favorite analogies is that of a mobile: When one part is moved all the other parts are set in motion. The same thing happens in families: When one person has a problem it impacts other family members, so everyone needs to be involved in order to accurately determine how each person is affected by the problem (Bailey & Sori, 2000; Carr, 1994).

Narrative therapists Freeman, Epston, and Lobovits (1997) suggest numerous roles that parents may play. These include brainstorming ideas and solutions with the child, working together to oppose the problem, and witnessing and celebrating children's behavior changes. These authors also explain how playfulness can help parents to "bypass" guilt and the problem, while encouraging creative new solutions.

Case example of involving parents. One of our interns was referred a family for counseling, and she asked that the whole family come for the first session. The mother, 13-year-old son, and 11-year-old daughter arrived for the session. They said that the father is an alcoholic and refused to come in. The family then spent most of the session talking about how the father's alcoholism affects them. The counselor assessed that the mother was avoiding dealing with marital problems, and that the children were brought into the marital conflict when they would rather be doing child things. The counselor asked them each to "do something different" with Dad. They weren't to tell anybody else what they did, and this would then be discussed in the following session. Everyone was surprised when the father came for the next session. He decided to come after noticing changes in his family. The homework was processed, the father was integrated into the therapy, and he continued to participate in the sessions. The counselor turned the negative complaints into a positive action and the result was a systemic change that benefited the whole family.

OVERCOMING OBSTACLES TO INVOLVING CHILDREN

Counselors need to become comfortable and knowledgeable about how to work with children in order to avoid making decisions based on personal preference. Therapists may be put off by children because they often are either withdrawn and silent, or disruptive and out of control (Carr, 1994). Therapist attributes and skills that were found to be important in engaging and working with children include genuinely liking, respecting, and appreciating children and their ways of being. Clinicians also need to be comfortable with very little children—who are excluded most often. Comfort comes with good supervision as well as experience in seeing many different types of families with children from all stages of development. Counselors also must be able to use their own creative selves in the process of therapy (Sori, 2006d; Sori & Sprenkle, 2004). This means being brave enough to trust one's own instincts (Rober, 1998) and to risk looking silly or "unprofessional" to parents. Using humor and being playful are excellent ways to connect with children.

Taffel (1991) believes that children often make great cotherapists because they know so well what they need from their parents. Once children are engaged they are often more motivated as clients than their parents. Berg and Steiner (2003) state, "When you have fun with children, they will learn that they are fun to be around, which will contribute to their sense of well-being as unique individuals" (pp. 13–14).

How to Talk to Children

Young children think very concretely, so counselors must be careful to speak clearly and simply, but not to talk down to children. Language should be accessible to all participants (Chasin & White, 1989). However, too many counselors use only verbal methods to communicate instead of experiential playful ways to talk with children (Rober, 1998). Playful metaphors are excellent ways to intervene, pointing out problems in the hierarchy or role reversals (see Sori, 2006e). For example, in a family that enjoys football, the counselor might ask, "So in your family, who calls the plays? The head coach or the quarterback? Who protects the quarterback?"

Taffel (1991) suggests that a counselor's approach to children should reflect the child's developmental stage, and he offers ideas to guide counselors on how to approach children of different ages. Children ages 5 to 8 are egocentric and use magical thinking, so they may blame themselves for family problems, such as marital conflict. Short sentences are recommended for these concrete thinkers. Children this age need safety, order, and to be soothed by their parents. Tools, such as feeling charts, can be used to teach children simple feeling words. Children can be asked to draw what happened, or to use dolls or puppets to enact a sequence of events (see also Bailey & Sori, 2000; Carr, 1994). Taffel emphasizes the importance of avoiding *why* questions; and instead to use who, what, when, where, and how questions for younger children. When seeing children alone the counselor may ask what their biggest worry is, and what they wish they could change about their family, school, or friendships. While some counselors promise children complete confidentiality during individual sessions (see Sori & Hecker, 2006), Taffel contends that children, especially younger ones, actually *want* the counselor to tell their parents what they have shared. He encourages counselors to give parents some feedback from individual time spent with the child.

Keith and Whitaker (1981) encourage therapists to talk in a silly manner that is pseudo-serious. They believe that telling childlike jokes engages children and it is "a way of enjoying our own stupidity so that our interventions do not appear to emanate from us as paragons of mental health" (p. 250).

Children ages 8 to 12 need a different approach. Taffel (1991) sees these children as often moody, who need counselors (as well as parents) to be "chums" who can reassure them that they are perfectly normal. At the same time children in this age group also need parents to be "cops" who can set firm limits with them. According to Taffel, the fastest way to alienate children this age is to ask them how they feel about something. He suggests avoiding direct eye contact, which they find uncomfortable, and engaging them in side-by-side activities, such as board games. Whereas you should ask younger children about their biggest worries, preteens should be asked about their "gripes" (Taffel, 1991, p. 44), which can evoke powerful responses. These children can be allowed to talk about others (which they love to do) and even to impersonate family members, which are excellent ways to really understand the world of both their family and their peers. According to Taffel, preteens suffer from "age envy" (1991, p. 44), and this can be used to flatter them that they seem older, or to challenge them in this regard.

In discussing teens, Taffel (1991) contends that their key issues are freedom and independence. It is important to remember that while teens may want to rebel, they do not really want to be totally separated from their families. Many counselors dread trying to counsel silent, sullen adolescents, who can be the most difficult to engage. Taffel suggests letting teens know up front that they are not expected to contribute anything, but that it is the parents who need help in dealing with the situation. This can be quite disarming for resistant teens. Taffel captured the mood when he wrote, "Most adolescents, who shuffle in like captured guerrillas condemned to the firing squad, respond with a look of surprised hope—maybe they've been granted amnesty!" (1991, p. 45). But he cautions counselors to beware of teens who share too much too soon, since they may regret this and not return. Although preteens want to be like everyone else, Taffel believes when seeing teens alone it is important to emphasize their uniqueness, and to recognize all the drama in their lives. He suggests asking them to enact their struggle for freedom, and to help them learn how to negotiate with their parents. These kids live in two worlds—the world of the family and the peer group—and counselors need to be skilled in weaving quickly between issues related to the family, then the peer group, and then back to the family once again (Taffel, 1991). This seems to be an excellent suggestion for an additional reason—the short attention span of teens who are conditioned to quick-action video games and MTV!

When seeing families with children it is important to discover the children's concerns, according to Berg and Steiner (2003). They suggest that counselors avoid the temptation to teach, lecture, or give advice, but instead focus on children's thoughts, ideas, and beliefs. Saying, "You must have a good reason for ..." (Berg & Steiner, p. 204) can open the door to discover explanations for an inappropriate behavior that will begin to make sense, or that can be used to begin to articulate goals.

How to Listen to Children

Because children are limited by their language skills they may not be able to express their worries or concerns. Many have written about using puppets or dolls, stories, or drawings to engage children and help them share their stories and their views of what is happening in their world (i.e., Berg & Steiner, 2003; Carr, 1994; Freeman, Epston, & Lobovits, 1997; Gil, 1994; Oaklander, 1988; Sori & Hecker, 2003).

Wachtel (1991) believes that children are more open and self-revealing in the context of a game, and suggests board games that are designed to help children express feelings (e.g., "The Talking, Feeling, and Doing Game"; "The

Ungame"). Making up squiggle stories (Gil, 1994; Wachtel, 1991) can help children express what they are struggling with in a safe way that the counselor is able to hear.

Carefully observing nonverbal cues of children and families at play is another way to listen—to the facial expressions, tones of voice, energy level, amount of enjoyment, degree of engagement, and the emotional process as family members interact with one another and with the play materials. In addition, the product or content of their play is often a metaphor for what is happening in real life (see Gil, 1994; Sori, 2006b). For example, a puppet story about an animal that is lost and can't find his way home may be the child's way of expressing loss and confusion following a divorce.

Involuntary Clients

Most children and adolescents do not initiate counseling on their own, but are referred or forced to attend counseling by an adult. We should not expect them to be happy about it, as it often implies that there is something wrong with them, or they are "abnormal" (Berg & Steiner, 2003). Children often have no idea about what counseling is about, or about the role of a counselor. They may see it as punishment, much like being sent to the principal's office, and may anticipate being embarrassed or shamed. Berg and Steiner suggest that counselors explain to children what will happen from the onset and throughout the treatment process.

Use of Play

From a developmental perspective it is crucial to understand the role of play in children's lives. Play is their language, and through playing they explore and make sense of their world. Landreth (1991) states:

> Children are able to use toys to say what they cannot say, do things they would feel uncomfortable doing, and express feelings they might be reprimanded for verbalizing. Play is the child's symbolic language of self-expression and can reveal (1) what the child has experienced; (2) reactions to what was experienced; (3) feelings about what was experienced; (4) what the child wishes, wants, or needs; and (5) the child's perception of self (p. 15).

Because young children often cannot express this verbally, parents are often unaware of what their child is feeling or experiencing. Involving parents—either by being playful, or incorporating family play therapy (see Sori, 2006b) or filial play therapy (see Sori, 2006c) in treatment is critical to helping children in the most optimal way, within the context of the family.

Family Play

Eliana Gil (1994) is responsible for uniting the diverse fields of family therapy and play therapy (see Sori, 2006b), to develop an approach that engages both parents and children in conjoint play activities. During family play sessions the clinician has an opportunity to observe the family interactions and dynamics. Family play therapy moves treatment from the intellectual, cerebral, abstract world familiar to adults, to the world of imagination, spontaneity, metaphor, and creativity that is familiar to children (Bailey & Sori, 2000). Both children and parents will express feelings and experiences through play that they otherwise may not feel comfortable or have the capacity to do verbally. Parents gain insight into their child's world, and clinicians recognize how the play tells the family's story in metaphor. Family play can infuse energy into sessions, can help families to reconnect and communicate on a deeper, more meaningful level. Play breaks down defenses and offers families (and counselors!) a positive, enjoyable experience that can breathe new life and hope into distressed families (see Gil, 1994, 2003; Gil & Sobol, 2000; Sori, 2006b). When a family has a playful interaction around a problem, they can no longer experience that problem in the same manner, because the context of the problem has been changed to a positive one (Ariel, Carel, & Tyano, 1985; Sori, 1998).

Family play also allows the therapist to enter the family's metaphor to explore, question, challenge, and encourage new interactions or ways of approaching a problem. Families are encouraged to discuss their experiences following play sessions, and to explore any parallels between their play and their real life situation (Gil, 1994). Family play allows clinicians to both observe and intervene in vivo, and it is a very effective approach to use as part of an overall treatment plan that may include individual sessions with a parent, individual play sessions, marital therapy, and traditional family talk therapy (Bailey & Sori, 2000).

Gil & Sobol (2000) discuss many creative playful techniques that facilitate the metaphoric expression of children's and family's experiences, such as sandtray, family aquarium, family genogram, and the family puppet interview. After observing how the family interacts and the content of the play, the therapist can begin to understand what is bothering the child, and can design family or individual interventions to address these metaphorically expressed concerns. By engaging parents in playful interventions, such as games or storytelling that are targeted to address the child's concerns, positive changes in family interactions often occur (Wachtel, 1991). See Wark (2003) for suggestions on how to introduce the concept of using play in family counseling.

Counseling Room and Materials

Numerous experts have written about how to design a counseling room that is child-friendly, and have offered suggestions for toys and play materials (e.g., Chasin & White, 1989; Gil, 1991; VanFleet, 1994; Zilbach, 1986). A large room with a one-way mirror that allows for observations by the clinician or parents is optimal. The room should be divided between a play area, with carpet and play materials readily available, and a family area for conventional talk therapy. Because many children seen in counseling have poor impulse control or are inattentive, it is best if toys are kept in cabinets, closets, or storage boxes so as not to be too distracting. A bulletin board to display children's artwork is useful. Other suggested materials include a sandtray and miniatures, construction and drawing paper, art supplies, clay, a baby doll and bottle, blocks, toy telephones, a doctor's kit, a doll or stuffed animal family, puppets, toy dart games, play guns and knives, handcuffs, games such as checkers, chess, Uno, as well as therapeutic games for the whole family. A dollhouse is also essential to allow children to depict domestic scenes, and a second dollhouse enables children of divorce to play out what happens at each house (see Hecker & Sori, 2006). There are numerous therapeutic books on topics such as divorce, ADD, death, or abuse that can be used to engage children, educate parents, and strengthen the parent-child bond when read by parents. (See Wark, Johnson, and Abrahamson [2003] for a detailed list of books by topic.)

The First Session

One of the first decisions that must be made is who should attend the first session. Some see the parents alone first, in order to hear their concerns, empathize, and gather a history of the problem and the child's developmental history (VanFleet, 1994). If parents seem extremely angry with a child over the phone this might be a good approach in order to allow them to vent their frustrations and to feel heard before bringing in the child. Others believe that the whole family should be present at the first interview. Keith and Whitaker (1981) strongly favored having children present at all interviews, and had toys available to engage them. Berg and Steiner (2003) invite "whoever will be most helpful in finding the right solution for the child" (p. 48).

However, studies show that whoever attends the initial session has implications for who will be involved in future counseling sessions (Brock & Barnard, 1999). Those who are there initially are more likely to be committed over time than those who have to be lured in. Clinicians should initiate the "battle for structure" (Napier & Whitaker, 1978) at the telephone intake.

Berg and Steiner (2003) propose acknowledging that the child probably would have preferred to stay home and watch TV or hang out with friends, and to normalize that feeling. This can then lead into an explanation of what will happen in the session. For example, a clinician might explain that first she would like to talk with everyone together and find out what they like to do and what they are good at (Berg & Steiner, 2003). Then explain that you will explore what everyone would like to have different in the family. You might invite children to draw a picture of their family doing something, or show young children where some quiet toys are that they can play with while everyone talks for a few minutes. Explain that sometimes you might meet alone for a while with just the parents or just the child, and then have everyone come back together again at the end of the session. While parents may request that the child be seen alone first, Berg and Steiner (2003) caution that it is important not to have the parents leave the room until the child seems calm and comfortable with the counselor.

Zilbach (1986) emphasizes the importance of learning exactly what children have been told about coming to counseling. Sometimes children are cajoled, promised treats, or even lied to about where they are going. This can be especially problematic with reluctant teens. According to Zilbach (1986) and Rober (1998), it is important to listen to what children have been told without contradicting parents, and then explain counseling in a way that is reassuring and creates a safe therapeutic environment. Children might be told that counseling is where everyone can share their likes and their dislikes, what's going well, and what they wish were different in their family. In addition, children need to be assured that they will not be berated or punished for what they say or do in a counseling session (Rober, 1998).

Goals

Selekman (1997) points out that in family therapy the parents' goals often take precedence over the wishes of the children. He invites children to share their goals, which often include goals for parents, such as yelling less. Chasin and White (1989) emphasize that it is important in the first session to have each person state a goal, or some way for the family to be better. They suggest emphasizing "finding ways to make things better for everyone in the family" (p. 14). Goals need to be concrete enough so they can be visualized, and they need to be meaningful. Complaints or blaming statements should be turned into goals. For example, if a mother wants her children to stop fighting, ask what she'd like them to do instead. Solution focus therapists often use the miracle question to elicit goals from children and adults, perhaps with the aid of a "magic wand" (Berg & Steiner, 2003). Shilts (in Sori, 2006a) also utilizes the narrative approach of externalization, followed by scaling questions to both set goals and measure children's progress. Some families may do a family drawing of their goal, and Chasin and White (1989) suggest families enact how the family might look when the goals are met. When families are unable to set goals, Chasin and White suggest exploring the problem further before asking what they want to be different that would make things better.

Berg and Steiner (2003) point out that often parents believe all will be well if only their child would change, while children, especially teens, simply want their parents to change. It is not unusual for parents and children (especially teens) to have conflicting goals. When this occurs, Berg and Steiner propose that clinicians listen to both sides of the problem while staying neutral, asking questions to determine how things might be different if each person made even some very small changes that the other wants. While this takes much patience on the part of the counselor, often a path can be forged toward a common goal, such as more peace in the home or everyone getting along better.

Beyond the First Session

In using a multimodal approach, the counselor will be making decisions about when to see people individually, in dyads, or as a family unit throughout the course of treatment, irrespective of the theoretical approach(es) being used. Joining is an ongoing process (Minuchin, 1974) with adults and children, so we encourage counselors to continue to utilize the above suggestions on how to talk to, listen to, and actively engage both children and parents. In addition, playfulness and family play techniques can be integrated into any theoretical approach (see Dermer, Olund, & Sori, 2006).

CONCLUSION

The decision of whom to see in a session should never be taken lightly. Family sessions with children can be emotionally loaded, chaotic, and draining. There is a danger, especially for individually trained clinicians, to quickly become overwhelmed and to take the easiest course, and meet only with individuals or couples. When this occurs, the therapist has lost the ability to think objectively and systemically, thereby missing the opportunity to change the family system to support the child's needs. Good supervision is helpful in making decisions that are best for the child and family, not simply what is easiest or most comfortable for the clinician.

There is an art to conducting family sessions with children that calls for right-brained creativity and playfulness on the part of the counselor. Letting go of the need to know what to do and following one's instincts are vital therapist attributes. We were all once children, and if we've forgotten how to be playful, we can allow our child clients to show us. This will help not only our clients, but us as professionals, to be more fully engaged and alive.

REFERENCES

Ariel, S., Carel, C., & Tyano, S. (1985). Uses of children's make-believe play in family therapy: Theory and clinical examples. *Journal of Marital and Family Therapy, 11*(1), 47–60.

Bailey, C. E., & Sori, C. E. F. (2000). Involving parents in children's therapy. In C. E. Bailey (Ed.), *Children in therapy: Using the family as a resource* (pp. 475–502). New York: W. W. Norton & Company.

Berg, I. K., & Steiner, T. (2003). *Children's solution work.* New York: W. W. Norton & Company.

Biank, N. M., & Sori, C. F. (2006). Helping children cope with the death of a family member, chap. 12 in this volume.

Brock, G. W., & Barnard, C. P. (1999). *Procedures in marriage and family therapy* (3rd ed.). Boston: Allyn and Bacon.

Brody, G. H., & Stoneman, Z. (1996). A risk-amelioration model of sibling relationships: Conceptual underpinnings and preliminary findings. In G. H. Brody (Ed.), *Sibling relationships: Their causes and consequences* (pp. 231–247). Norwood, NJ: Ablex Publishing Corporation.

Carr, A. (1994). Involving children in family therapy and systemic consultation. *Journal of Family Psychotherapy, 5*(1), 41–59.

Chasin, R., & White, T. B. (1989). The child in family therapy: Guidelines for active engagement across the age span. In L. Combrinck-Graham (Ed.), *Children in family contexts: Perspectives on treatment* (pp. 5–25). New York: Guilford.

Combrinck-Graham, L. (1989). *Children in family contexts: Perspectives on treatment.* New York: Guilford.

Cummings, E. M., & Davies, P. (1994). *Children and marital conflict: The impact of family dispute and resolution.* New York: Guilford.

Dermer, S., Olund, S., & Sori, C. F. (2006). Integrating play in family therapy theories, chap. 3 in this volume.

Estrada, A. U., & Pinsof, W. M. (1995). The effectiveness of family therapies for selected behavioral disorders of childhood. *Journal of Marital and Family Therapy, 21*(4), 403–440.

Field, T. (1995). Psychologically depressed parents. In M. H. Bornstein (Ed.), *Handbook of parenting: Vol. 4. Applied and practical parenting* (pp. 85–99). Mahwah, NJ: Lawrence Erlbaum Associates.

Fincham, F. D. (1998). Child development and marital relations. *Child Development, 69,* 543–574.

Fogarty, J. A. (2000). *The magical thoughts of grieving children: Treating children with complicated mourning and advice for parents.* Amityville, NY: Baywood Publishing Co.

Freeman, J., Epston, D., & Lobovits, D. (1997). *Playful approaches to serious problems: Narrative therapy with children and their families.* New York: W. W. Norton & Company.

Gil, E. (1991). *The healing power of play: Working with abused children.* New York: Guilford.

Gil, E. (1994). *Play in family therapy.* New York: Guilford.

Gil, E. (2003). Play genograms. In C. F. Sori, L. L. Hecker, & Associates, *The therapist's notebook for children and adolescents: Homework, handouts, and activities for use in psychotherapy* (pp. 49–56). Binghamton, NY: Haworth.

Gil, E., & Kaplan, K. (1994). A history of family therapy and its use of play. In E. Gil, *Play in family therapy* (pp. 15–32). New York: Guilford.

Gil, E. & Sobol, B. (2000). Engaging families in therapeutic play. In C. E. Bailey (Ed.) *Children in therapy: Using the family as a resource* (pp. 341–482). New York: W. W. Norton & Company.

Gottman, J. M. (1999). *The marriage clinic: A scientifically based marital therapy.* New York: Norton.

Griffin, W. A. (1993). *Family therapy: Fundamentals of theory and practice.* Bristol, PA: Brunner/Mazel.

Hecker, L. L., & Sori, C. F. (2006). Divorce and stepfamily issues, chap. 9 in this volume.

Hoff-Ginsberg, E., & Tardif, T. (1995). Socioeconomic status and parenting. In M. H. Bornstein (Ed.), *Handbook of parenting: Vol. 2. Biology and ecology of parenting* (pp. 161–188). Mahwah, NJ: Lawrence Erlbaum Associates.

Johnson, L., & Thomas, V. (1999). Influences on the inclusion of children in family therapy. *Journal of Marital and Family Therapy, 25*(1), 117–123.

Keith, D. V., & Whitaker, C. A. (1981). Play therapy: A paradigm for work with families. *Journal of Marital and Family Therapy, 7,* 243–254.

Korner, S., & Brown, G. (1990). Exclusion of children from family psychotherapy: Family therapists' beliefs and practices. *Journal of Family Psychology, 3*(4), 420–430.

Ladd, G. W., & Le Sieur, K. D. (1995). Parents and children's peer relationships. In M. H. Bornstein (Ed.), *Handbook of parenting: Vol. 4. Applied and practical parenting* (pp. 377–436). Mahwah, NJ: Lawrence Erlbaum.

Landreth, G. L. (1991). *Play therapy: The art of the relationship.* Bristol, PA: Accelerated Development.

Minuchin, S. (1974). *Families and family therapy.* Cambridge, MA: Harvard University Press.

Montalvo, B., & Haley, J. (1973). In defense of child therapy. *Family Process, 12,* 227–244.

Napier, A., & Whitaker, C. A. (1978). *The family crucible.* New York: Harper & Row.

Oaklander, V. (1988). *Windows to our children.* Highland, NY: Gestalt Journal Press.

Olson, D. H. (1970). Marital and family therapy: Integrative review and critique. *Journal of Marriage and the Family, 32,* 501–538.

Plomin, R., & Rutter, M. (1998). Child development, molecular genetics, and what to do with genes once they are found. *Child Development, 69,* 1223–1242.

Rober, P. (1998). Reflections on ways to create a safe therapeutic culture for children in family therapy. *Family Process, 37*(2), 201–213.

Rolland, J. (1994). *Families, illness, & disability: An integrative treatment model.* New York: Basic Books.

Sanson, A., & Rothbart, M. K. (1995). Child temperament and parenting. In M. H. Bornstein, (Ed.), *Handbook of parenting: Vol. 4. Applied and practical parenting* (pp. 299–321). Mahwah, NJ: Lawrence Erlbaum Associates.

Selekman, M. D. (1997). *Solution-focused therapy with children: Harnessing family strengths for systemic change.* New York: Guilford.
Sori, C. E. F. (1998). Involving children in family therapy: Making family movies. In L. Hecker and S. Deacon (Eds.), *The therapist's notebook: Homework, handouts, and activities for use in psychotherapy.* Binghamton, NY: Haworth.
Sori, C. F. (2006a). A playful postmodern approach to counseling children and families: An interview with Lee Shilts, chap. 6 in this volume.
Sori, C. F. (2006b). Family play therapy: An interview with Eliana Gil, chap. 4 in this volume.
Sori, C. F. (2006c). Filial therapy: An interview with Rise VanFleet, chap. 5 in this volume.
Sori, C. F. (2006d). On counseling children and families: Recommendations from the experts, chap. 1 in this volume.
Sori, C. F. (2006e). Reflections on children in family therapy: An interview with Salvador Minuchin, chap. 2 in this volume.
Sori, C. F., & Hecker, L. L. (2006). Ethical and legal considerations when counseling children and families, chap. 8 in this volume.
Sori, C. F., Hecker, L. L., & Associates (2003). *The therapist's notebook for children and adolescents: Homework, handouts, and activities for use in psychotherapy.* Binghamton, NY: Haworth.
Sori, C. F., & Sprenkle, D. H. (2004). Training family therapists to work with children and families: A modified Delphi study. *Journal of Marital and Family Therapy (30)*4, 479–495.
Taffel, R. (1991). How to talk with kids. *Networker, 15*(4), 39–45; 68–70.
VanFleet, R. (1994). *Filial therapy: Strengthening parent-child relationships through play.* Sarasota, FL: Professional Resource Press.
Wachtel, E. F. (1991). How to listen to kids. *Networker, 15*(4), 46–47.
Walsh, F. (1998). *Strengthening family resilience.* New York: Guilford.
Wark, L. (2003). Explaining to parents the use of play in family therapy. In C. F. Sori & L. L. Hecker & Associates, *The therapist's notebook for children and adolescents: Homework, handouts, and activities for use in psychotherapy* (pp. 71–78). Binghamton, NY: Haworth.
Wark, L., Johnson, J., & Abrahamson, L. (2003). Using children's books in family therapy. In C. F. Sori & L. L. Hecker & Associates, *The therapist's notebook for children and adolescents: Homework, handouts, and activities for use in psychotherapy* (pp. 302–322). Binghamton, NY: Haworth.
Zilbach, J. J. (1986). *Young children in family therapy.* Northvale, NJ: Jason Aronson Inc.

CHAPTER 8

Ethical and Legal Considerations When Counseling Children and Families

CATHERINE FORD SORI, PH.D., AND LORNA L. HECKER, PH.D.

THE INTERTWINING OF ETHICAL AND LEGAL ISSUES WITH CHILD COUNSELING

There has been little guidance in mental health literature about ethical issues that may arise in counseling minors outside of a school setting. Even popular ethics textbooks mention issues related to treating minors only briefly, with the exception of breaking confidentiality to report child abuse (Lawrence & Kurpius, 2000). Yet the potential legal and ethical issues when treating children in families are numerous. Common concerns relating to child treatment include the child's right to confidentiality, informed consent, children and divorce, the use of touch, counselor competency, and multicultural issues.

Privacy, Confidentiality, and Privileged Communication

Privacy. Privacy refers to clients' right to choose who has access to information about them (Thompson & Rudolph, 1996). Legally, parents of minors typically make all privacy-related decisions for them. This includes signing consent, releases of information, and access to medical and psychotherapy records. Decisions about protecting children's privacy and confidentiality in counseling must be examined from both legal and ethical lenses.

Confidentiality. The foundation on which counseling is built lies in the ethical obligation to keep information learned in counseling private from others. All codes of ethics in the mental health professions address confidentiality. Clinicians should not share any information with others without authorization in the form of a written release signed by the client(s). What to include in releases is typically dictated by state mental health statutes. In addition, there are limitations to confidentiality dictated by state law, professional ethical codes, common law, and case law (Bartlett, 1996). However, laws are open to interpretation, so one must use careful judgment in making ethical decisions, especially about breaching confidentiality (Thompson & Rudolph, 1996). Access to an attorney familiar with mental health law is a wise investment.

Privilege. Privilege is the legal right protecting the client from having their private therapy information divulged in judicial proceedings. Privilege is established by state statutes. Not all clients hold privilege; it depends upon the type of mental health discipline that is covered in state law. Some states allow privilege to adolescents at the age of 16 for specific issues (Reid, 1999). The legal right to privileged communication can only be waived by the client, although in the process of legal discovery (e.g., in child custody cases), attorneys often subpoena therapists or their records. Unless the client (or potentially the client's parent or legal guardian) has waived privilege, the counselor is obligated to appeal to the court to uphold state statute and keep the counseling information confidential.

There are legally prescribed conditions for which the counselor is not subject to prosecution for withholding information needed by the court in litigation (Bartlett, 1996). Depending upon state law, exceptions to privilege may include client consent; treatment emergencies; duty to warn; duty to protect (see next section); clinical consultations; if the therapist is sued for malpractice; mandatory report statutes (child abuse, elder abuse, disabled adult abuse); if a therapist seeks a restraining order against a former client; or when a client's mental health status is in the legal forum (e.g., child custody cases, civil commitment hearings, competency to stand trial, or civil cases in which the plaintiff claims injury).

CONFIDENTIALITY WHEN WORKING WITH MINOR CHILDREN

One of the most confounding ethical issues that counselors face when seeing children is what and how much information to share with parents (Lawrence & Kurpius, 2000; McCurdy & Murray, 2003; Thompson & Rudolph, 2000). For most counseling issues, parents have the legal right to know what occurs during their child's counseling (Corey, Corey, & Callanan, 2002; Lawrence & Kurpius). Ethically, however, many believe minors should be guaranteed the same confidentiality as is promised to adults (Hendrix, 1991). The setting in which counseling occurs may also influence issues of confidentiality (Taylor & Adelman, 1989). For example, school counselors may not have to disclose the content of individual sessions with minor children to parents, according to the Federal Education Rights and Privacy Act of 1994 (FERPA) (Corey et al., 2002). In states that allow mature minors to access treatment, psychotherapists still have an obligation to notify parents or guardians when it is in the best interests of the minor (Roberts & Dyer, 2004). In some situations, even though minors are legally able to access therapy for mental health treatment, they may not possess the right to authorize the release of information to third parties. While parents also have access to case records, in many situations providers can limit what is divulged to the parent if the information would be harmful to the child if disclosed (Roberts & Dyer, 2004).

Breaching Confidentiality: Duty to Protect, Reporting Issues of Abuse and Neglect

Counselors often must breach confidentiality when mandated by law to act as an agent of social control. Confidentiality must be broken when there are threats of harm to oneself, threats of harm to another, or when it is learned (or in some states merely suspected) that a child or elder is a victim of abuse or neglect.

Harm to self. Any child or adolescent who may be at risk for depression should be interviewed to ascertain if they have any suicidal thoughts, have a plan to harm themselves, and have the means to carry out such a plan. The therapist has a duty to inform parents of the child's suicidal thoughts or intent, and to work with them to take appropriate action. This may include having the child assessed at a hospital, having family members maintain a 24-hour suicide watch to ensure the safety of the child, or a referral to a psychiatrist for an evaluation for the possible use of medication. Care should be taken to document steps taken to protect the child, and clinicians are advised to consult with other professionals to be sure appropriate treatment is undertaken.

Harm to another. The landmark case of *Tarasoff v. Regents of University of California* forever changed the landscape of counseling confidentiality. In 1968, the therapist in this case notified the campus police at University of California that his client, Prosenjit Poddar, had threatened to kill another student, Tatiana Tarasoff. Although she was not named, she was "readily identifiable." The police warned Poddar to stay away from Tarasoff, and proceedings to have Poddar evaluated by a psychiatrist were initiated. Meanwhile, Tarasoff was given no warning regarding the danger to her life. Subsequently, Poddar stabbed and killed Tarasoff, and her parents filed suit against the university for not confining Poddar and for not warning Tarasoff of the threat against her life.

This case gave rise to what is commonly known today as a counselor's *duty to warn* (sometimes also known as *duty to protect*). Duty to warn occurs when the following three conditions are met (*Tarasoff* v. *Regents of University of California,* 1974, p. 346): (1) *Likelihood of harm*. The counselor has established that there is likelihood that the client will cause physical harm, and believes the client is a threat. Some states have statutes requiring that a threat actually be communicated; most do not. (2) *A "special" relationship exists*. Generally a person does not have a duty to control the conduct of another, but counselors have a special obligation due to the nature of their profession. (3) *There is a foreseeable victim*. (Some states have broadened this condition to include unknown victims.)

Counselors must take reasonable steps to satisfy the duty to warn, which always includes warning the intended victim. Counselors may also notify local law enforcement agencies, contact relatives or friends who can apprise the potential victim of danger at hand, or initiate voluntary or involuntary commitment. The failure to warn an individual of a potential threat against his or her life may result in an ethical violation (Thompson & Rudolph, 1996) and is legally actionable.

A more unique aspect of duty to warn arises with issues related to human immunodeficiency virus (HIV) (McCarthy & Sorenson, 1993). While the ethical codes of mental health professionals deal with duty to warn, HIV leads to a gray area in breaching confidentiality. Only the ethics code of the American Counseling Association (1995) directly addresses breaching confidentiality in regard to communicable, contagious, and fatal diseases. Even so, with the advanced pharmacology available today, one could argue HIV is no longer a fatal disease. Counselors must analyze the ethical and legal aspects of duty to warn when seeing a seropositive client. While some believe that an HIV positive client who is having sex or IV drug use with an unsuspecting other meets the criteria for duty to warn, this is a complex issue, both legally and ethically. Schlossberger and Hecker (1996) argue that therapists do not have the same fiduciary duties as physicians, therefore reporting mandates for physicians are not applicable to counselors. Some states, however, do have laws regarding HIV transmission as a crime. So unless a state has a specific law mandating reporting of HIV, *or* if there is a state law making HIV transmission a crime, the counselor is left to decide whether or not to breach confidentiality solely on ethical grounds.

Abuse. All states now have laws that require professionals to report any suspected child abuse or neglect, and in most states failure to do so will result in criminal penalties (Kalichman, 1993; Lawrence & Kurpius, 2000; Thompson & Rudolph, 1996). Clinicians are mandated by law to immediately report child abuse or neglect; some state laws even require reporting of "suspected" abuse or neglect. While there has been a significant increase in the number of cases of suspected child sexual or physical abuse, Kalichman (1993) reports that there are also a substantial number of professionals who fail to report. This contributes to child maltreatment being underestimated, according to Alvarez, Kenny, Donahue, and Carpin (2004).

Many clinicians may hesitate to report abuse because it can permanently damage the therapeutic alliance, both between counselor and child, as well as between counselor and parents. The family may be damaged, and the child may even be removed from the home (Lawrence & Kurpius, 2000). However, failing to report when a child is neglected or abused denies the child the right to be protected and to receive intervention services that may be crucially needed (Alvarez, Kenny, Donohue, & Carpin, 2004). These ethical decisions often place the counselor in the difficult position of choosing to obey the letter of the law against the potential additional harm that may befall a child who may or may not have been abused.

Another problematic issue for counselors is the emotional abuse of a child. Although this type of abuse can severely damage a child, there are few legal resources to address it. While it can be reported, overwhelmed child protective agencies are unlikely to act on the report; some will even refuse to take such a report.

Subpoenas as a Threat to Confidentiality

When a counselor receives a subpoena, *no* confidential information should be released to an attorney just for the asking. Here are a series of steps in responding to a subpoena: First, read the subpoena thoroughly. Is the attorney asking for specific information, for a case file, for testimony via court, or a deposition? Second, talk with the client (or the client's attorney with a written release) with regards to how he or she wants you to handle the subpoena. If the client is amenable to the information being made privy to the attorney, the counselor may release the information *with written consent of the client*(s). If the client does not want the information revealed, let the attorney know that the information is confidential (and/or privileged), and that a signed court order is needed to reveal the information. Third, talk to both parents and the child regarding the dispensation of the information. If confidentiality has been promised to the child and he or she does not want to have this promise violated, the clinician has an ethical obligation to the child to ask the judge to protect the counseling information. If the child consents, the legal parent or guardian must sign the consent to release information. If any others were involved in counseling, do not release any information about them without their written consent. Fourth, a judge may order information to be revealed, in spite of the clinician's stated rationale for why the information should be kept private. Some courts may allow counselors to share privileged information with the judge privately in chambers to determine if the information is necessary to the proceeding, or if public disclosure would be too hurtful to those involved, such as children (Bartlett, 1996). Finally, do not take case records to court unless they are specifically requested in the subpoena. Even if a subpoena asking that records be released is from a judge, it is wise to consult an attorney, especially if clients refuse to sign a release form. Counselors should inform clients why it is necessary to break confidentiality, explain what will be revealed, and invite them to participate in this process (Mappes, Robb, & Engels, 1985).

While most states have laws regarding privilege, Thompson and Rudolph (1996) caution that in states where psychotherapists are not protected by law for privileged communication, "they have no recourse except to reveal the information if subpoenaed" (p. 511). Finally, Bartlett (1996) states, "Failure to observe confidentiality measures may result in a professional liability lawsuit. The therapist must become aware of the myriad of threats to client confidentiality and implement appropriate safeguards" (p. 290). Counselors can avoid misunderstandings if care is taken in the initial session to explain the process (Thompson & Rudolph, 1996).

HIPAA Laws and Minors

The Health Insurance Portability and Accountability Act that many counselors must abide by, depending on the nature of their practice, may affect minors. According to HIPAA regulations, parents have access to children's health information. Mental health treatment would be included in this provision. Adolescents are treated the same as young children (Roberts & Dyer, 2004). However, if state law is more rigorous than HIPAA regulation and allows discretion to disclose or deny access to parents of minor's mental health information, state statute should be followed instead of HIPAA (Chaikind et al., 2003).

Sharing Information with Parents

There is dissent among counseling professionals related to sharing information with parents of children who are seen in individual counseling, or seen individually within the context of family counseling. Because these positions may be a variation from a professional's code of ethics, it is wise to get these permissions in the informed consent or in a special client-therapist contract. Generally, information is shared with parents when it is in the *best interests of the child* (Roberts & Dyer, 2004). However, determining the best interests of the child is left up to the discretion of the therapist in consultation with the parents and child.

There are various options for managing confidentiality with minors. Hendrix (1991) describes four possible positions counselors can take regarding this issue of sharing information with parents; we have added two additional positions to Hendrix's conceptualization of confidentiality options.

The first confidentiality alternative is to promise minors *complete confidentiality* (with the exception of what a professional is mandated by law to report, such as abuse, suicidality, or homicidality). The second is *limited confidentiality* which, according to Lawrence and Kurpius (2000), "requires the minor to waive, in advance, the right to know what will be revealed to the parent or guardian" (p. 134). *Informed forced consent* is the third approach, which occurs when a child has no voice in what is disclosed, but is informed before the disclosure is made. This is a more moderate stance where counselors inform children, teens, and parents up front that they will bring pertinent information back to parents.

The fourth is when *no guarantee of confidentiality* is made to a child. Secrets that are held by a therapist can impede individual and family work. In using this approach it is vital that children and parents be told this at the onset of therapy, both verbally and in writing. This increases parents' trust that the counselor respects their rights to know important facts about their child, while also educating them that the child does need privacy in order to talk about whatever concerns he or she has. The child can be assured that not everything talked about will be shared, and that if something does come up that the counselor decides the parents should know, the counselor will work with the child on how to share the information and to minimize any negative consequences that may result (Taylor & Adelman, 1989).

If this occurs, the counselor could spend time discussing the child's fears in sharing the information, brainstorming and role playing ways for the child to tell the parents, and discussing how to handle fallout after the disclosure. Lawrence and Kurpius (2000) recommend counselors can motivate reluctant children to share information with parents that is deemed to be potentially helpful by explaining the probable benefits and the importance of disclosing. The success of these efforts often depends on the degree of trust and the quality of the professional relationship between counselor and child.

In addition to these, a fifth position is that the counselor may work with the parents and child to come to a *mutual agreement regarding confidentiality* as to what will be disclosed to parents and what will not. For example, some parents will want to know about an adolescent's sexual activity, others will not. Use of alcohol may not need to be disclosed, but what if the counselor learns that the adolescent client is drinking and driving? If the parents and adolescents cannot agree, the parental rights typically prevail.

Finally, some counselors will set up a "*best interests" agreement* with the child and parents. The limits to confidentiality in this agreement are set up by the counselor him or herself, and the children and parents leave the decision to share information solely with her. It is agreed that confidentiality will be maintained unless the counselor believes that the child's best interests are not being served in relation to his or her health, welfare, or significant relationships. If any of these areas are seriously impaired the therapist uses his/her judgment to decide if confidentiality should be breached.

There are advantages and disadvantages to each type of agreement. The more broad the disclosure policy is with regard to what the therapist shares with others, the less likely the child or adolescent will reveal important information in therapy. The narrower the disclosure policy, the more the therapist risks becoming therapeutically immobile if there is important information that parents should know. If a child or adolescent has been promised complete confidentiality, the therapist may be unsure of the ethics of proceeding in therapy with information that may upset parents if they learned of it. Examples may include pregnancy, sexual activity, risky sexual activity or other risky behaviors, especially if the minor client insists that the therapist not tell her parents.

Isaacs and Stone (1999, 2001) suggest that there are two factors that counselors should consider in deciding whether to breach confidentiality: the age of the child and how serious the behavior is in which the minor child is engaging. Less serious behaviors might include smoking or breaking curfew. According to Roberts and Dyer (2004, p. 124), potential high-risk behaviors might include substance abuse, sexual activity, truancy, gang involvement, irresponsible driving behavior, extreme religious practices, unorthodox dieting procedures, fascination with guns or other weapons, or illegal behavior. Roberts and Dyer advocate for a clear description by the therapist as to what constitutes dangerous behavior. Agreements reached should be clearly detailed to avoid undermining trust in the therapeutic relationship between the counselor, parents, and child.

When the therapist has to force disclosure, children can be allowed to decide if they want to tell their parents, if they want the counselor to tell in their presence, or if they want to wait in the hallway while parents are told. Children can also be reassured that the counselor will be available to help the child and parents work through the problem. It is important to prepare parents, reminding them that no one should be punished for anything said in counseling, and to point out that in telling them the child shows courage and trust in the parents.

Group Confidentiality

Although confidentiality is vital in establishing trust among participants in group counseling, there are inherent problems, especially in children's groups

(Thompson & Rudolph, 1996). Complete confidentiality in group counseling is harder to attain (McCarthy & Sorenson, 1993). Time and care must be taken to explain the concept of confidentiality, and to be certain that each child understands the concept, as well as to explore how children might be harmed if participants discuss what is talked about outside of the group. Children should be encouraged to consider the potential limits of confidentiality before disclosing very personal information during group counseling. Salo and Shumate (1993) also advise counselors to explain to group members that privileged communication may not apply to discussions that take place in a group format. Cant (2002) notes confidentiality limitations need to be clarified when working with children in a residential setting, where many staff have access to children's records.

INFORMED CONSENT TO TREAT MINORS

Informed consent "is the formal permission given by a client that signals the beginning of the legal, contractual agreement that allows treatment to be initiated" (Lawrence & Kurpius, 2000, p. 133). Clients need to give informed consent freely, after being appraised of the credentials of the counselor, as well as the consequences and implications of entering into treatment. (See Jensen, McNamara, and Gustafson, 1991, for the results of a study on what to include when discussing informed consent with parents.) Minors may contract for professional counseling either by having parental consent, involuntarily (at the insistence of a parent), or involuntarily through a court order. Without having signed informed consent from parents, guardians, or a court order, the counselor is at risk of being sued. Even in the case of court-ordered treatment, it is advisable to inform parents of treatment as soon as possible (Lawrence & Kurpius, 2000).

Twenty states allow mature minors (see later) to provide consent to access mental health treatment (Roberts & Dyer, 2004). In addition, in some jurisdictions, minors are allowed to consent to treatment without parental knowledge, often when they are facing situations for which they would not access treatment if parental consent was required. Some states may not require parental consent to treat minors for issues such as drug abuse, pregnancy or birth control counseling, sexually transmitted diseases, or following a sexual assault on a minor 12 or older (Lawrence & Kurpius, 2000).

Exceptions to parental consent typically include the mature minor exception, emancipated minors (see below), and for emergency treatment. Court-ordered treatment also is an exception (Plotkin, 1981; Gustafson & McNamara, 1999).

Emancipated minors typically have the rights and obligations granted to adults. Emancipation may occur in several ways, depending upon state law. Typical emancipating actions include: by parental permission, by court order, when the minor marries, has a child, is able to support oneself and live independently, or enlists in the armed forces (Dickson, 1998). Emancipated minors are over the age of 14 or 15 (but under 18). Differences exist by state statute. Emancipated minors are treated as adults with regard to confidentiality and typically privilege, as well. They do not need parental consent for treatment (Bartlett, 1996; Lawrence & Kurpius, 2000).

One important criterion to consider regarding the need for parental consent is the age of the minor child. Bartlett (1996) describes a *mature minor* as one who is thought to be capable of making informed decisions as well as adults. Mature minors may give informed consent for treatment, and may authorize the release of confidential information (see Morrissey, Hofman, & Thrope, 1986). Mature minors are generally children over the age of 16 (Lawrence & Kurpius, 2000), but the age may vary as this status is defined by state statute.

Young minors are usually those under 14 years old, and for these children "the parent or guardian is the legal decision-maker and can legally obtain information about the diagnosis, prognosis, therapy, and so on" (Bartlett, 1996, p. 280). Although some states allow young minors to grant their own informed consent in the case of an emergency when their health or life appears to be endangered, parental consent should still be procured as quickly as possible (Lawrence & Kurpius, 2000).

While there is no general rule that explicitly requires counselors to obtain written permission from parents for children to receive counseling, "obtaining parental consent is good practice for counselors unless potential danger to the minor exists. … The law generally supports parents who forbid counseling of their minor children unless there are extenuating circumstances" (Thompson & Rudolph, 1996, p. 509). It is wise to prevent problems by communicating early with parents, and parents should be made aware their child has sought counseling and be asked to provide informed consent at the onset of treatment. An exception to this may be schools that have policies that allow a child to see a school counselor for a few sessions before parents are informed and asked to give consent.

Obtaining consent to treat a minor. Counselors should ask parents to sign an informed consent form giving their permission to treat the minor children at the first session where children are seen. At this time, release forms allowing communication with other professionals involved in the treatment of the child (e.g., physicians, school counselors) also may be obtained. Counselors always must obtain signed permission from the parent who has legal (not physical) custody of the children, and should insist on being given written proof as to who retains legal custody of the children (Thompson & Rudolph, 1996). It is wise to know state law regarding the rights of noncustodial parents. According to Bartlett (1996), "Only a custodial parent can authorize treatment or release of confidential information" (p. 280). Divorced parents can be polarized on the issue of counseling, with one parent advocating for individual or family counseling, and the other demanding the right to be informed and/or give consent.

Obtaining informed consent can become a contentious issue if the parents are recently separated and custody of the children has not yet been decided (Bartlett, 1996). There is typically a provisional order outlining temporary custody. Clinicians should ask for a copy of this provisional order, as well as a copy of the final divorce decree to understand the custody situation. If there is joint legal custody and one parent is against treatment, this parent would be hard pressed to explain their rationale to the judge to have a court order barring treatment. While this might take care of the legal issue involved in this dilemma, the clinical issues abound. Involvement of the noncustodial parent, as well as loyalty issues for the child about treatment will be difficult.

SPECIAL ETHICAL ISSUES WHEN WORKING WITH CHILDREN

Psychotherapy with children raises numerous ethical issues that are specific to working with this population. The remainder of this chapter discusses several of these issues that warrant special consideration.

Role of the Psychotherapist in Working with Children of Divorce

One area in which counselors are most vulnerable to charges of ethical misconduct is when working with children and families of divorce. Often parents are locked in ongoing bitter legal battles over child custody, visitation, support payments, and a myriad of other postdecree issues. Divorce and postdivorce situations are often emotionally charged, and pull children into destructive loyalty conflicts. In addition, lawyers work within an adversarial system, and therapists work in a collaborative system. These differing systems can lead to misunderstandings and frustrations for both professions.

Counselors can play many potential roles in custody cases. Due to the potential litigation that surrounds custody evaluations, it is wise for counselors to clearly define their roles when working with the child and his or her family. These roles as outlined by Woody (2000, p. 74) include: (a) the *treating therapist* for the child, parents or family (this could occur before, during, or after the divorce); (b) the *evaluator* in the custody dispute, evaluating the psychological characteristics of the relevant adults; (c) the *guardian ad litem* for the child or children; (d) the *mediator* to resolve the disputes between the parents; or (e) the *expert critic*, who evaluates the validity of the testimony given by other mental health professionals.

Bartlett (1996) has several suggestions for counselors working with children of divorce. First, it is vital to clarify your role with the child and the parents. Identify who the real client is, and specify if your role is to provide individual or family treatment, to do a custody evaluation, be a guardian ad litem, or perform mediation with the parents. For example, *if your role is to do family counseling you should not offer an opinion in court regarding the custody of the children.* Make this clear to the family or you risk family members "positioning" to look good, rather than focusing on keeping the children's interests primary to therapy. Second, emphasize to parents the importance of focusing on the child's welfare, and clarify who you will communicate with and how. Explain that you will not take sides, and that harm is done when a child is caught in the middle of parental conflict (also see Hecker & Sori, 2003). Third, establish ground rules and, if doing an evaluation, discuss to whom it will be sent. If permitted in your state, Bartlett (1996) suggests asking parents to sign a waiver of the right to subpoena your records. We suggest doing this whenever families with children are seen, as any couple could decide to divorce at some future date and attempt to subpoena records of past counseling. Such a waiver discourages parents from attempting to negate a child's confidentiality in the throes of a legal battle.

Competencies

All mental health professional codes of ethics prohibit professionals from practicing outside their area of competence (Thompson & Rudolph, 1996). Counselors need to be well trained and follow what is legally referred to as an *appropriate standard of care* (Hecker, 2003), in which a counselor acts in ways that most counselors would treat a case under similar circumstances. Practicing outside one's area of competence is one of the most common types of malpractice claims (Stromberg & Dellinger, 1993).

Special skills and techniques are necessary to work with children individually or in a family setting (Sori, 2006; Sori & Sprenkle, 2004). Lawrence and Kurpius (2000) point out that a counselor who is skilled and effective in working with adults may not have the same level of effectiveness when treating children or adolescents, which requires "areas of knowledge and skills that are unique to working with children" (p. 132). Certain disorders, such as separation anxiety disorder, reactive detachment disorder, oppositional defiant disorder, enuresis, encopresis, ADHD, and trichotillomania, for which parents often seek professional help, mostly affect children. As Lawrence and Kurpius point out, one cannot apply an understanding of adult issues to children's problems. "Because minors are a special, diverse client population, ethical practice mandates distinct education, training, and supervised practice before commencing independent practice that includes minors" (Lawrence & Kurpius, 2000, p. 133). (See Sori [2006] for an in-depth discussion of the training necessary to prepare counselors to work with children and families.) Therefore, counselors who have not had adequate training to treat children are not meeting an appropriate standard of care.

Use of Touch

There is little in the literature regarding ethical considerations about the occurrence of nonerotic touch in therapy. McNeil-Haber (2004) contends that it is difficult to counsel young children without some form of touch. Touch is natural and developmentally appropriate for young children, and is a major component in children's play. When touch is initiated by a child in counseling, it presents an opportunity to discuss personal boundaries and differences in how people feel about being touched. However, care must be taken when discussing child-initiated touch that children don't feel shamed or rejected when the counselor is setting appropriate boundaries.

McNeil-Haber (2004) offers the following guidelines in making case-by-case ethical decisions (p. 128):

- What are the possible benefits of touch? Touch can be reinforcing and calming.
- How might this child perceive the touch? It could enhance self-esteem or make the child feel powerless to comment on it.
- What considerations are related to the counselor? Whose needs are being met? Is touch genuine?
- What safety issues are related to the child? Is it harmful to the child? Does this child have a history of abuse? If so, touch could be alarming. (Abused children have trouble separating fact from fantasy.)
- What in this child's family background might be an issue?
- What are some practical considerations? Culture should be considered, as people from different cultural backgrounds have different attitudes toward using touch as a means of emotional expression, or in socializing children.

At the onset of therapy, counselors should discuss touch with children, inform parents about the use of touch, and ask permission to use touch when appropriate. Parents should be informed as to how touch might be used (e.g., a hug at the end of a session, to prevent a child from harm, or for encouragement). In addition, because a child may act out during session to the degree that the counselor needs to intervene to prevent harm from the child, self, or property, parents should be consulted before individual treatment to explore their wishes with regard to in-session discipline.

Multicultural Considerations When Seeing Children in Families

When seeing children and their families, the context of culture should be assessed before making therapeutic judgments and interventions. Cheung and Hong (2004) note several value differences that may occur when seeing families from other cultures. First, most family therapy models emphasize individualistic orientation, helping members to achieve independence, individuation, identity, and self-esteem. Other non-European-American cultures are collectivistic and "value mutuality and collective welfare, the closeness between parent and children, dependence of children on their parents, and a firm family hierarchy" (Cheung and Hong, p. 14). In addition, dissimilar cultures may embrace different familial values, norms and roles, calling for understanding counselors who have a willingness to examine the constructs of our established theories (Cheung & Hong, p. 15) and to be sensitive to the values of each culture.

CONCLUSION

There is much to consider in avoiding the numerous potential pitfalls that could inadvertently result in legal and ethical problems. Of note is the difference between parental and children's rights in treatment. Children have few rights, and counselors must work to protect the sanctity of the counseling relationship. Therapists should remain cognizant of the vulnerability of children and adolescents, have a broad repertoire of developmental and topical information regarding children, work with the larger systems within which children are embedded (e.g., families, agencies, and schools) and seek education, consultation, and advice (Roberts & Dyer, 2004).

It is important for counselors to review their professional code of ethics regularly, and to refresh their ethical skills and knowledge by gaining continuing education in ethics and legal issues. This training can keep clinicians abreast of new federal laws, state statutes, and case laws. Many professional organizations offer such training at conferences or via home study, and some liability insurance companies provide reduced rates to those who take advantage of additional ethics training. Although client welfare and risk management must be carefully balanced when counseling children, numerous benefits to working with this population can be seen in the child, his family, and, ultimately, the future of our society.

REFERENCES

Alvarez, K. M., Kenny, M. C., Donohue, B., & Carpin, K. M. (2004). Why are professionals failing to initiate mandated reports of child maltreatment, and are there any empirically based training programs to assist professionals in reporting process? *Aggression and Violent Behavior, 9,* 563–578.

American Counseling Association (1995). American Counseling Association, Code of Ethics and Standards of Practice. Alexandria, VA: Author.

Bartlett, E. E. (1996). Protecting the confidentiality of children and adolescents. In J. Lonsdale, S. Powell, & L. Soloman (Eds.), *The Hatherleigh guide to child and adolescent therapy* (pp. 275–290). New York: Hatherleigh Press.

Cant, D. (2002). Joined-up psychotherapy: The place of individual psychotherapy in residential therapeutic provision for children. *Journal of Child Psychotherapy, 28*(3), 267–281.

Chaikind, H. R., Hearne, J., Lyke, B., Redhead, S., Stone, J., Franco, C., et al. (2003). *Health insurance portability and accountability act (HIPAA): Overview and analysis*. Hauppauge, NY: Novinka Books.

Cheung, S., & Hong, G. K. (2004). Family therapy with children: Sociocultural considerations. *The Family Psychologist, 20*(3), 14–16.

Corey, G., Corey, M., & Callanan, P. (2002). *Issues and ethics in the helping professions* (6th ed.). Belmont, CA: Wadsworth-Brooks/Cole.

Dickson, D. T. (1998). *Confidentiality and privacy in social work*. New York: The Free Press.

Gustafson, K. E., & McNamara, J. R. (1999). Confidentiality with minor clients: Issues and guidelines for therapists. In D. N. Bersoff (Ed.), *Ethical conflicts in psychology* (2nd ed.) (pp. 200–204). Washington, DC: American Psychological Association.

Hecker, L.L. (2003). Ethical, legal, and professional issues in marriage and family therapy. In L. L. Hecker & J. L. Wetchler (Eds.), *An introduction to marriage and family therapy* (pp. 493–537). Binghamton, NY: Haworth.

Hecker, L. L., & Sori, C. F. (2003). The parent's guide to good divorce behavior. In C. F. Sori, L. L. Hecker, & Associates, *The therapist's notebook for children and adolescents: Homework, handouts, and activities for use in psychotherapy* (pp. 323–329). Binghamton, NY: Haworth.

Hendrix, D. H. (1991). Ethics and intrafamily confidentiality in counseling with children. *Journal of Mental Health Counseling, 13*(3), 323–333.

Isaacs, M. L., & Stone, C. (1999). School counselors and confidentiality: Factors affecting professional choices. *Professional School Counseling, 2*, 258–266.

Isaacs, M. L., & Stone, C. (2001). Confidentiality with minors: Mental health counselors' attitudes toward breaching or preserving confidentiality. *Journal of Mental Health Counseling, 23*, 342–356.

Jensen, J. A., McNamara, R. J., & Gustafson, K. E. (1991). Parents' and clinicians' attitudes toward the risks and benefits of child psychotherapy: A study of informed-consent content. *Professional Psychology: Research and Practice, 22*(2), 151–170.

Kalichman, S. C. (1993). *Mandated reporting of suspected child abuse: Ethics, law, and policy*. Washington, DC: American Psychological Association.

Lawrence, G., & Kurpius, S. E. R. (2000). Legal and ethical issues involved when counseling minors in nonschool settings. *Journal of Counseling & Development, 78*, 130–136.

Mappes, D., Robb, G., & Engels, D. (1985). Conflicts between ethics and law in counseling and psychotherapy. *Journal of Counseling and Development, 64*, 246–252.

McCarthy, M. M., & Sorenson, G. P. (1993). School counselors and consultants: Legal duties and liabilities. *Journal of Counseling and Development, 72*, 159–167.

McCurdy, K. G., & Murray, K. C. (2003). Confidentiality issues when minor children disclose family secrets in family counseling. *The Family Journal: Counseling and Therapy for Couples and Families*, 22(4), 393–398.

McNeil-Haber, F. M. (2004). Ethical considerations in the use of nonerotic touch in psychotherapy with children. *Ethics & Behavior, 14*(2), 123–140.

Morrissey, J. M., Hofman, A. D., & Thrope, J. C. (1986). Consent and confidentiality in the health care of children and adolescents. New York: The Free Press.

Plotkin, R. (1981). When rights collide: Parents, children and consent to treatment. *Journal of Pediatric Psychology, 6*, 121–130.

Reid, W. H. (1999). *A clinician's guide to legal issues in psychotherapy: Or proceed with caution*. Phoenix, AZ: Zeig, Tucker & Co.

Roberts, L. W., & Dyer, A. R. (2004). *Ethics in mental health care*. Washington, DC: American Psychiatric Publishing, Inc.

Salo, M., & Shumate, S. (1993). Counseling minor clients. In T. Remley Jr. (Ed.), *The ACA Legal Series, Vol. 4*. Alexandria, VA: American Counseling Association.

Schlossberger, E., & Hecker, L. (1996). HIV and duty to warn: A legal and ethical analysis. *Journal of Marital and Family Therapy, 22*(1), 27–40.

Sori, C. F. (2006). On counseling children and families: Recommendations from the experts, chap. 1 in this volume.

Sori, C. F., & Sprenkle, D. H. (2004). Training family therapists to work with children and families: A modified Delphi study. *Journal of Marital and Family Therapy, 30*(4), 479–495.

Stromberg, C., & Dellinger, A. (1993). A legal update on malpractice and other professional liability. *The Psychologist's Legal Update, 3*, 3–15.

Tarasoff v. Regents of University of California. (1974). 13c. D177; 529 p. 2D553; 118 *California Reporter*, 129.

Taylor, L., & Adelman, H. S. (1989). Reframing the confidentiality dilemma to work in children's best interests. *Professional Psychology: Research and Practice, 29*(2), 79–83.

Thompson, C. L., & Rudolph, L. B. (1996). *Counseling children* (4th ed.). Belmont, CA: Wadsworth-Brooks/Cole.

Thompson, C. L., & Rudolph, L. B. (2000). *Counseling children* (5th ed.). Belmont, CA: Wadsworth-Brooks/Cole.

Woody, R. H. (2000). *Child custody: Practice standards, ethical issues, and legal safeguards for mental health professionals*. Sarasota, FL: Professional Resource Press.

PART IV

Children and Family Therapy with Specific Child Issues

CHAPTER 9

Divorce and Stepfamily Issues

LORNA L. HECKER, PH.D., AND CATHERINE FORD SORI, PH.D.

Much research has been done on the effects of divorce on children, as well as how children fare who live in stepfamilies. However, few psychotherapists receive specific training on how to treat children living in nonnuclear family configurations. This chapter provides a summary of important research findings, and offers suggestions to guide counselors to work with these children and their families.

EFFECTS OF DIVORCE ON CHILDREN

It has been well established that children can suffer a variety of problems emanating from divorce. In comparison to intact families, children who undergo the divorce of their parents are more likely to suffer from conduct problems, psychological maladjustment, behavioral problems, problems with both parents, social difficulties, and a decrease in self-concept (Amato & Keith, 1991). However, Amato (1994) notes that these differences need to be understood in context and in comparison to other child problems. The differences are actually small differences, rather than large differences, and the effects of the divorce are relatively weak.

Many of the problems that children of divorce suffer precede the divorce (Kelly, 1993). That is, what we commonly see as "adjustment problems" post-divorce, actually occur before the divorce. These symptoms include conduct disorders, antisocial behaviors, difficulty with peers and authority, depression, and academic and achievement problems (Kelly, 2000, p. 964). As more sophisticated methodology has developed over the years, the results of studies on children of divorce becomes clearer: *Each child is affected differently by divorce.* As we will see later, children are affected by parental conflict as much or more than divorce.

What Helps Children Adjust to Divorce?

Custodial parents also can help children adjust to divorce by *being in good mental health* and by *having good parenting skills.* Poorly adjusted parents put children at much higher risk (Kelly, 2000). Custodial parental strengths and behaviors that help children of divorce include: (a) being accepting (Wolchik et al., 2002) and being affectionate to their child (Amato, 1994); (b) being able to provide adequate supervision (Amato, 1994); (c) exercising a moderate degree of control (Amato, 1994); (d) providing explanations for family rules (Amato, 1994); (e) avoiding harsh discipline (Kelly, 2000); and (f) being consistent with punishment (Amato, 1994).

Yet in the midst of separation and divorce, parenting skills are likely to suffer. Parental anxiety and depression are common immediately following separation. It can be difficult for a custodial parent to regain equilibrium and function in a way that focuses on the child's needs. Impaired parenting is usually temporary, but parents are often underfunctioning at a time when the child is suffering acute stress (Amato, 1994; Wallerstein & Kelly, 1980). There are many factors that may contribute to this decrease in functioning, notwithstanding emotions regarding the marital breakup. Economic hardships increase, task and role overload occurs, and social isolation can increase (e.g., some married friends disappear, or the single parent must move due to economic changes). The distress of court proceedings can be overwhelming, and for some, debilitating. Weary single parents have a harder time doling out discipline, affection, and support.

Other factors that affect children's adjustment include their economic well-being, the number of transitions, and communication by parents about the divorce. Each is discussed here.

Economic hardship increases the risk of psychological and behavioral problems (Amato, 1994), and can precipitate a cascade into other situations that may negatively affect a child: lowered economic opportunities may mean poorer schools, problem-laced neighborhoods, fewer services, and fewer academic resources. McClanahan (1999) notes that economic hardships account for up to half of adjustment problems that are commonly seen in children of divorce.

Transitions to new schools, new neighborhoods, moving, and potentially a new stepparent can decrease children's adjustment to divorce (Amato, 1994). The lowered success rates of remarriage also may mean another divorce and additional adjustments. Generally, the fewer changes for children to navigate, the better they will do.

Children need information about the divorce. Mayes, Gillies, Wilson, and McDonald (2000) found that most parents gave children few details about the divorce and the changes it brings. They found that only about one-third of parents in their research had discussed their child's feelings. Confusion about what divorce means is common. Blame, loss, and fears of separation and abandonment are frequent problems (Pruett & Pruett, 1999). Even young adults complain about the lack of information they receive during the divorce (Lyon, Surrey, & Timms, 1998).

The Role of Interparental Conflict on Child Adjustment

In both intact and divorced families, the largest factor on child well-being is conflict. Children who live in high-conflict intact families are no better off than children of divorced parents. In some situations they may even fare worse (Amato, 1994).

It is not simply conflict that predicts problems for children, but factors within the familial conflict that predict child maladjustment. According to Kelly (2000, p. 964), these factors include: (a) *the severity or intensity of conflict,* which has the largest impact; (b) *the frequency of the conflict*—high frequency conflict has more negative effects on children than low to moderate frequency conflict; (c) *the style of the conflict*—overtly hostile physical and verbal conflict, such as slapping, screaming, contempt, and ridicule/scorn were more strongly linked with both externalizing and internalizing behaviors than were covert styles of conflict (e.g., passive aggressiveness, triangulation, resentment), or the frequency of conflict; however, covert styles were more often linked with depression, anxiety, and withdrawal; (d) *the manner of resolution of the conflict*—chronic unresolved conflict makes children insecure, and they exhibit behaviors such as fear and distress, and children benefit when parents compromise and negotiate, rather than warring verbally; and (e) *the presence of buffers,* which protect children, include having a good relationship with at least one parent (or caregiver), parental warmth, support of siblings, and good self-esteem and peer support for adolescents.

Not surprisingly, children exposed to repeated and severe conflict have difficulties regulating emotional responses, resulting in anger and physical aggression when the child becomes emotionally aroused (Kelly, 2000). In addition to not having proper role models to resolve conflict, it appears that for these children the physiological stress habituates them into a continued state of negative emotional reactivity.

Developmental Tasks of Children Adjusting to a Divorce

Judith Wallerstein (1983) identified six tasks of adjustment for a child undergoing parental divorce.

Acknowledge the reality of the separation. Some children are not surprised when a divorce is announced, especially when there has been fighting between parents. Others are shocked and react accordingly. They also may refuse to acknowledge the reality of the separation and impending divorce and have "rescue" fantasies, such as father coming home to save the day, or mother changing her mind, as if it was all a mistake. Although reconciliation fantasies are normal coping mechanisms and should not necessarily be discouraged, a child also needs to be encouraged to participate in the change, perhaps by helping to choose items for a new bedroom, or finding a transitional object to take between homes.

Disengage from parental conflict and distress, and resume customary pursuits. Children who are not able to do this often feel caught in the middle, suffering from minor inconveniences such as passing notes for parents, to major problems, such as being pawns in parental conflict and legal battles. Children should be allowed to resume their daily life of play, school, and friends without being encumbered by adult stressors.

Resolve loss from the divorce and subsequent changes. Hodges writes: "Mourning is significantly more difficult when the absent parent is either partially absent or completely absent, but alive" (1986, p. 305). This is an ambiguous loss, which is difficult to resolve (Boss, 1999).

Resolve anger and self-blame. Anger is a common theme of children of divorce. Children need help to come to terms with anger, and the underlying feelings. Children often act out their anger; the counselor's task is to begin to link the anger to the underlying feelings. Hodges (1986) recommends linking the anger to feelings of abandonment, unfairness, being attacked, of deprivation, and not feeling loved.

Accept the permanence of the divorce and separation. Reconciliation fantasies are a normal part of divorce for children. While they may help ease a child's pain at the onset of the divorce, eventually children need to navigate the loss so that their development is not delayed.

Achieve realistic hope regarding relationships. Children of divorce can garner the belief that they, too, will fall victim to divorce. Children need to know that healthy relationships will be available to them, and believe that their parents will reach a workable coparenting relationship.

The Role of the Counselor in Custody-Related Issues

Although many counselors find the issue of child custody decisions distasteful, the counselor may be in a position to offer valuable services to the family at the time of transition, as well as to the court in making the difficult decision of child custody. Given what is known about the negative effects of conflict on children, the counselor's main contribution can simply be to help families navigate the tasks of divorce and find ways to decrease parental conflict and increase coparenting efforts. The counselor has expertise in child development that other professionals involved in the divorce litigation may not have, and can help the family by educating others about the situational and developmental needs of the child.

Custody Configurations

Custody arrangements are, thankfully, beginning to be called "parenting arrangements" or "parenting agreements." *Physical custody* refers to the residence and daily care of the child. *Legal custody* refers to who makes decisions for the child in areas such as education, health care, and religious training. "Custodial parent" typically refers to the parent with physical (i.e., residential) custody. (Note: It is imperative for counselors to get signed consent from the parent who has *legal* [not just physical] custody of children in divorce and stepfamily situations [see Sori & Hecker, 2006]). A noncustodial parent would receive what has been referred to historically as "visitation," although many states are moving to the preferable term "coparenting time." Within these two custody delineations, several possible types of custody may occur.

1. Sole legal custody with one parent; sole physical custody with the same parent.
2. Joint legal custody with both parents; sole physical custody with one parent.
3. Joint legal and joint physical custody.
4. Sole legal custody with one parent and joint physical custody with both parents.
5. Sole legal custody with one parent and sole physical custody with the other parent.

Joint legal and sole physical custody is the most common arrangement. An unconventional arrangement is "split custody," whereby one parent has one or more of the children, and the other parent takes the other child(ren), thereby splitting up siblings to the two different homes. Around 5% of parents adopt this arrangement (Hodges, 1991). The attachment and the development needs of the child must be considered when custody arrangements are considered. Child and family counselors need to advocate for their small clients by educating adults as to the needs of the child.

Custody Evaluations and Decisions

Custody evaluations, typically conducted by psychologists or other mental health professionals, aid judges in deciding which parent should gain custody. Guidelines for custody evaluations are provided by the American Psychological Association (1994), and include a focus on parenting capacity, the psychological and developmental needs of the child, and the resulting fit between the parent and child. Specialized training is needed to conduct child custody evaluations. Judges typically use these as part of the information to determine custody; others rely almost primarily on the evaluator's results to determine custody.

Judges attempt to make custody decisions with regard to the "best interests" of the child, though "best interests" from the legal perspective may vary widely from a counseling perspective. Therapists may be consulted by the custody evaluator, and may be subpoenaed or asked to testify by a parent in a custody hearing as a fact witness. This changes the nature of the original therapeutic relationship, when parents attempt to sway the therapist's testimony. It behooves therapists to have a knowledgeable attorney available to consult in these situations, which can become highly litigious for all professionals involved. There are numerous ethical and legal issues that can arise when working with families of divorce or stepfamilies. Readers are referred to Sori and Hecker (2006) for an in-depth discussion of these issues.

Child-Parent Alignments and Coalitions during Divorce

When there is anxiety in a system, alignments and coalitions will form. In many families, there is little that is more stressful than a custody battle. Counselors often see alignments and coalitions that are quite complex. It is important that the counselor understand the impact of anxiety as the family enters into unknown emotional territory, many new transitions in daily life, and for some, their first foray into the adversarial legal system. Some parents may even see custody decisions as life-threatening issues for their children. The power children have in divorce is miniscule, making an alignment with a parent a natural way for a child to gain some mastery and control over a situation that feels out of their control. In highly emotional situations, the assessment, diagnosis, and treatment of children can be particularly convoluted.

Domestic Violence and Custody Disputes

Domestic violence changes the nature of child custody disputes. When the trust for safety between parents has been violated, it is difficult to tell the victimized parent to focus solely on the needs of the child with regard to custody. Even with emotional abuse, some victims will "give in" to the other parent's demands, simply (and often unsuccessfully) to get the abuse to stop.

Mediation

When conflict is high between divorcing partners, the court may order mediation to establish a working parent relationship and to teach strategies to keep the child(ren) out of the conflict. This helps couples develop a workable parenting plan and typically can keep the couple from the stress of a court fight. Mediators may be therapists or attorneys. Some states certify mediators. Interestingly, researchers performing an evaluation project for Strategic Partners (1999), as reported in McIntosh (2000), found that only 4% of mediators had ever directly consulted or met with school-aged children during the course of mediation. Typically, the child's agenda has not been considered when developing parenting plans for divorcing partners.

EMERGENT ISSUES FOR CHILDREN OF DIVORCE

Most family therapists are trained to work with two-parent families and typically have little training that directly relates to alternate family forms. Nuclear families are no longer the "norm," nor do they even represent the majority of family structures in the United States. Family structures now may consist of binuclear families, single-parent families, blended families or remarried families, widowed families, biracial families, and families of affiliation (as opposed to procreation). Therapists (in line with the rest of society) are often biased and see alternate family forms as deficient (Visher & Visher, 1995), and tend to ascribe child problems to the family form itself. Even the language of therapists can be biased as they talk about a "real father" or "real mother" when they are referring to a biological parent who may or may not be involved with children. The terms "stepparent" or "stepchild" also have negative connotations. The phrase "broken home" also lingers. Therapist bias is important to examine when working with divorcing, single parent, or stepfamilies.

The Counselor's Role with Divorce Transitions

Counselors must not become polarized by aligning with one parent over the other. Ehrlich (2001) discusses the danger in working with divorcing parents, especially those in the midst of a high-conflict divorce. Aligning with the distorted view of a client may serve the function of decreasing the counselor's anxiety about confronting the rigid views of the client. It is better for therapists to manage their anxiety about conflict with the client, and help the family find alternatives to aggressive litigation and a hostile relationship with the ex-partner. Ultimately, this will be of much help to the child of the divorcing parents (Ehrlich, 2001).

Decreasing Parental Conflict

Because parental conflict is so central to children's adjustment to divorce (Kelly, 2000), the counselor can best help a child by working with parents to decrease their conflictual behaviors, especially those witnessed by children. There are practical methods to decrease the opportunity for conflict that can be encouraged by the counselor:

- *Encourage alternate forms of communication in place of direct communication* through the use of e-mail, faxes, or letters (*not* to be sent through the children).
- *Suggest neutral drop-off points.* Fast food restaurants are a good neutral place to make exchanges. Most people are less likely to be conflictual in public places.
- *Reframe the coparenting relationship as a "business" relationship.* Parents may have a hard time conceptualizing that they can ever move their relationship from an intimate one to a coparenting one. Reframing the new coparenting relationship as a "business relationship" focused on raising the children can aid a client in reconceptualizing how they view and respond to the coparent.
- *Explore the underlying emotions behind defensive or offensive behaviors of the parent.* Divorce is fraught with emotion, and emotions can be detoured (see Minuchin, 1974) through the children rather than dealt with directly. For example, a lonely parent may turn to a child for emotional support, to fill the role of the missing spouse. Helping parents grapple with their difficult emotions can decrease the need to transfer their angst onto their child.
- *Encourage both parents to work for the best interests of the children.* Helping parents keep the children's needs in mind can ease conflict. At times even placing the child or children's picture in the therapy room may be a physical reminder for them to be constructive with their ex-spouse.
- *Ensure that the parents are not engaging in triangling behaviors with the children.* Sending messages through children, refusing to talk to the ex-spouse, or degrading the parent in front of the child should all be prohibited, with the explanation that these behaviors hurt children. Children's identity is derived in part from both parents; thus their self-esteem will be negatively affected when the ex-spouse is denigrated.
- *Suggest a guardian ad litem when children need additional protection.* If parents are not willing to cooperate in maintaining the best interests of their child, and physical or emotional harm is befalling a child, suggest that a guardian ad litem or like-professional be engaged to represent the child's interests. Although counselors may not be able to have

legal "teeth" in their work with divorcing parents, guardian ad litems do have considerable input into the legal process (Kelly, 2000).

Parental Communication with Children Regarding the Divorce

Parents are often reticent to candidly discuss the divorce with their children. Counselors can help parents constructively tell the child about the divorce, including the when, how, and why in developmentally appropriate ways. Parents should also explain the immediate effects the divorce will have on the child (e.g., moving, a parent moving out, change in school). Be sure parents tell the children *repeatedly* that even though parents are divorcing, parents don't stop loving their children. In addition, parents need to tell their children (throughout different developmental stages) that the divorce is not their fault. See Hecker and Sori (2003) for guidelines and a handout to use with divorced parents or those who are divorcing.

STEPFAMILIES

Most people who divorce remarry fairly quickly, often within two years (Glick & Lin, 1986). Glick (1989) suggests that about 60% of second marriages will eventually end in divorce, and second marriages that do end are not as long lasting as first marriages (Glick, 1984). The implication is that adults (and consequently their children) may experience a number of marital transitions over the course of a few years (Pasley, Dollahite, & Ihinger-Tallman, 1993).

The notion that stepfamilies are usually more dysfunctional than first-married families has not been supported in the literature. Stepfamilies have been found to have lower levels of cohesion and to be more flexible, but the findings were not clinically significant (Pasley, Dollahite, & Ihinger-Tallman, 1993). Visher and Visher (1995) note that less cohesion and greater adaptability are actually functional for stepfamilies, and can indicate health for this family form. Characteristics of well-functioning families, both for step and first-married families, include a strong marital adjustment, strong bonds between biological parents and children, the tendency not to exclude family members, and collaborative decision making. In contrast, both first-married and remarried dysfunctional families were characterized by "strong parent-child coalitions and a lack of mutual decision-making processes" (Pasley, Dollahite, & Ihinger-Tallman, 1993, p. 316) that failed to meet the needs of all family members.

Zill and Schoenborn (1990) report that children from both divorced families and stepfamilies are at greater risk for developing psychological problems and needing mental health services than are children from first marriages. While children in stepfamilies are more apt to experience problems with adjustment, the "average differences are small and individual differences are great" (Dunn, 2002, p. 154). Bray (1995) notes that many of the problems found with children in stepfamilies are not related to the family form per se, but instead reflect problems related to the transitions required in stepfamilies. It is the interactional process of the stepfamily around these transitions that can positively or negatively affect a child.

Stepfamilies in Counseling

Many counselors hear the refrain from stepparents: "If it weren't for the children, our relationship would be perfect." Yet, Martin and Bumpass (1989) found no support that the presence of children in stepfamilies increases the likelihood of divorce. The dynamics of marital interaction around child-related issues does "offer a key for understanding marital outcome and the nature of the spousal relationship" (Pasley, Dollahite, & Ihinger-Tallman, 1993, p. 316). While counselors may want to focus solely on the marital subsystem, it is important to note that the quality of the stepparent-stepchild relationship strongly influences marital satisfaction. That is, in stepfamilies, if a parent sees the stepparent developing a strong bond with his or her child, marital satisfaction increases.

According to Visher and Visher (1995), stepfamilies can be difficult to work with because there is often an emotionally charged atmosphere in the therapy room. Intense feelings that may be expressed include anger, pain from feeling rejected and isolated, depression and sadness over the losses incurred, loyalty conflicts, and anxiety over the fear of further losses. Understanding these feelings and empathizing with the emotional intensity experienced by family members is an excellent way to join family members (Visher & Visher, 1995). It is often useful to look beneath the behavior of an angry stepparent or an acting-out child to understand the fear, anxieties, or attempts to feel in control that may underlie the behavior.

GUIDELINES FOR WORKING WITH STEPFAMILIES

Due to the inherent structural changes stepfamily formation brings, as well as the need for new relationships to develop between parents and children, structural family therapy (Minuchin, 1974) and family play therapy (Gil, 1994; Gil & Sobol, 2000) are helpful modalities when working with stepfamilies. While integrating the available research on stepfamilies with these theories, the following provides guidelines for systematically working with stepfamilies.

First Guideline: Initial Focus on Marital Dyad

Several authors suggest focusing early sessions on the marital dyad, which is important in order to foster more cohesion and to help develop a parental coalition (see Pasley, Dollahite, & Ihinger-Tallman, 1993; Visher & Visher, 1988, 1989). Visher and Visher (1995) suggest that an initial goal is to strengthen the boundary around the couple so they can function well together and form a strong marital attachment bond. The family system must reshape, and there is often a homeostatic pull causing biological parents and their children to align against an "outside force"—that is, the new stepparent. Enactments (Minuchin, 1974) are often useful to have couples plan "dates" together without children, to negotiate household rules, or to discuss parenting issues.

The emotional intensity that may be present when everyone is seen conjointly may overwhelm therapists, and can lead to a premature push for quick changes. Therapists are advised to go slowly and to normalize the chaos and high level of emotions that may be expressed as a function of the family's anxiety. Once emotional reactivity is reduced, the same skills that are used with first-married couples can be used with remarried spouses to help build problem-solving and negotiating skills (Pasley, Dollahite, & Ihinger-Tallman, 1993).

Stepparents and disciplining. Problems related to disciplining children are often described as the most stressful aspect of being in a stepfamily. The parent needs to form a team with the new spouse, but can be torn when discipline differences arise.

Children often test limits and resent being told what to do by an outsider. Although stepparents are encouraged to defer taking on a parenting or disciplining role for the first few years of the marriage (Pasley & Dollahite, 1995), counselors should help stepparents learn to support their partner in their role (Pasley, Dollahite, & Ihinger-Tallman, 1993).

The stepparent role can be reframed as being akin to the role of a cabinet member to the president. Pasley, Dollahite, and Ihinger-Tallman (1993) suggest that a stepparent's role initially could be one of a monitor, similar to a babysitter, who monitors children's behavior and reports back to the parents for any disciplinary action. A role of monitor provides a foundation for the stepparent to gradually be assimilated into the preexisting biological parent-child subsystem. Stepparents can be coached to find methods to befriend each stepchild, preferably in ways that are less likely to become confrontational. At the same time, biological parents need to be encouraged to be active in disciplining their children. All this can alleviate some of the powerlessness that new stepparents often experience. Over time, once the stepparents and stepchildren have a positive, respectful relationship, stepparents may gradually assume a larger role in disciplining the children, with support from the partner.

Clarifying roles. Because roles are often unclear in stepfamilies, discussing roles is critical, especially in a residential stepmother family, according to Pasley, Dollahite, and Ihinger-Tallman (1993). Discussing expectations couples have for themselves and for the children promotes role clarity (Visher & Visher, 1990).

Second Guideline: Assessment of Stepfamily Strengths and Normalization of Common Stepfamily Pitfalls

Clinicians can explore the expectations of family members regarding the role of parents, as well as how each person perceives stepparent-stepchild relationships. Strengths that lead to increased stepfamily and child adjustment should be punctuated by the therapist; stepparents are often not clear when they are doing things "well," and focusing on these strengths can increase their frequency and heighten client confidence. Strengths that may be explored include ways that the family has successfully navigated conflict in the past, adjustments of the parents and children to current changes, fiscal management successes with stretched resources, and how families have successfully made numerous transitions prior to coming to counseling.

Exploration of Common Stressors

There are a myriad of common stressors that can be uncovered in order to explore how the family is coping, and to normalize their existence. These include the following issues.

Financial issues. Parents in stepfamilies often experience stress related to paying and receiving child support, household expenses, and the costs of raising children and stepchildren. These issues abound in stepfamilies.

Conflicting needs. Sometimes there is a conflict between the needs of adults and children. A new stepmother may need to spend time alone with her spouse, while his child may feel insecure and want to maintain the level of contact they had before the marriage. It is also important to examine the developmental needs of both individuals and of the stepfamily. For example, a newly formed stepfamily may emphasize togetherness at a time when adolescents are experiencing the need for increased autonomy (Pasley & Dollahite, 1995).

Loyalty conflicts. Children may feel that if they like a new stepparent they are being disloyal to their biological parent (Papernow, 1995). Children need to be given permission to love both parents, and the noncustodial parents should be held in good regard whenever possible.

Losses and other issues. Stepfamilies are families that are "born of loss" (Visher, 1994). Family members experience the loss of dreams, the loss of time (Papernow, 1995), a prior identity, and often the loss of daily contact between a biological parent and children (Visher & Visher, 1990). Often spouses have not completely mourned the emotional and psychological loss of the previous relationship (Pasley, Dollahite, & Ihinger-Tallman, 1993). Parents who do not have custody need to mourn the loss of both daily contact and of their parental role. These parents often feel a sense of alienation from their own children (Arendell, 1992), and many feel a simultaneous guilt about both biological and stepchildren. All of these experiences should be normalized and clients need to be able to openly express their feelings related to these losses.

Exploring common myths of stepfamilies. One task is to address the myth of instant love between stepparents and children (Bray, 1995). Because there are so few role models of healthy stepfamilies, some clients latch on to unrealistic media portrayals of stepfamilies, such as in the classic television show *The Brady Bunch,* making adherence to this family model impossible.

Unrealistic expectations. New stepfamilies are often idealistic and have unrealistic expectations (Visher & Visher, 1995), and need to be helped to understand the developmental stages of stepfamilies. It takes time to build trust and caring relationships. Client expectations are often rooted in their ideals of an intact nuclear family life, which may no longer be possible to achieve.

Limited resources. Often in stepfamilies there are just not enough resources to go around. When families merge to form a new stepfamily often there is stress related to how the resources are distributed. Single parents may have been able to give children more of the time, energy, and affection that now must be distributed among other new family members.

Alliances and coalitions. Visher and Visher (1995) report that there is more evidence of parent-child alliances in stepfamilies that function well, than in first-married families that are also well-functioning. These alliances should be allowed to continue to some extent so families do not get discouraged during attempts to strengthen stepfamily cohesion. By contrast, strong, rigid coalitions between a parent and child can be dysfunctional and leave the new stepparent feeling excluded. Clinicians must listen carefully and weigh the emotional and developmental needs of all family members.

Role ambiguity. There are few positive role models for stepparents and stepchildren in our society. Therefore, what one's role is and how one performs his or her role in a stepfamily is unclear and may cause anxiety, confusion, and hurt feelings if not discussed or "co-created."

Boundary issues. With nonbiological kin living in the same home, taboos against family member sexual contact are lessened. Boundaries between children and adults that are normally observed in nuclear families may be less respected in vulnerable stepfamilies.

Third Guideline: Focusing on Children's Needs

In addition to helping parents build a strong marital foundation, children need to be focused on as individuals, in addition to finding their role in the new family. Children should be included in counseling to assess their adjustment to the multiple transitions that have occurred in their lives, as well as how they are being affected by the conflict between the couple (see Sori, 2006c; Sori & Sprenkle, 2004). Dunn (2002) emphasizes the importance of gathering children's own perspectives of events in their lives. Children also can benefit from group therapy with peers, and schools often offer programs to facilitate the transitions of divorce and stepfamilies.

Acknowledging the child's losses. Parents often want to believe the myth of the "instant" stepfamily, where children are as excited as they are about their new life. However, children experience loss and should be able to express their feelings without fear of adult reprisal. Parents should be informed that changes are often experienced as losses—the loss of the familiar, the routine, and what is known and comfortable.

There are clear losses and ambiguous losses (see Boss, 1999). Clear losses may include obvious changes such as moving from the family home, changing schools, or no longer being the only child. Ambiguous losses are just as real, but are less recognized and more difficult to articulate. Ambiguous losses occur when children lose the closeness of a relationship with a noncustodial parent, when they lose contact with the noncustodial parent's extended family, or when a parent has new people in the family who garner time and attention. They also may lose a sense of identity when a parent remarries and takes a different surname. For children of divorce or stepfamilies, "one parent is always missing" from their daily lives, at special occasions (such as vacations or birthdays), and at holiday celebrations (see Papernow, 1995).

Transitions. Children in remarried families have often experienced a series of transitions in the reconfiguration of their families (Bray, 1995), often going from an intact two-parent family, through a separation and divorce, to a single-parent family where a child may visit the noncustodial parent, to a stepfamily that may include new stepsiblings. The blending of two families may be disorienting and introduce another series of losses. For example, a previously available mother may spend more time and energy on her relationship with her new spouse (Pappernow, 1995). All too often this may be followed by a second separation and subsequent divorce (see Bray, 1995).

The quality of the child's relationship with the nonresidential parent. Children need to have open access to the alternate parent. However, in addition to physical distance, other factors can decrease closeness between a child and a noncustodial parent. To prevent further loss, counselors should assess this relationship and advocate for changes as appropriate, perhaps including the nonresidential parent in counseling with the child. Some therapists may want to include former spouses in order to build a strong parenting team that consists of both biological parents as well as the stepparent(s) (Pasley, Dollahite, & Ihinger-Tallman, 1993). Bray (1995) suggests it may be important to involve nonresidential parents in therapy to hear their views about a child's problems, as well as to explore their relationship with the child. This may be especially pertinent during adolescence, to facilitate healthy identity development in a teen. However, sensitivity should be used not to see former spouses together while excluding a new stepparent, as this may undermine the goal of strengthening the new spouses' relationship.

Loyalty conflicts. When discussing the loyalty conflicts children often experience following a divorce and remarriage, Bray (1995) points out that younger children have fewer resources to cope with such conflicts, and may express their distress by acting out, withdrawing, becoming depressed, or by disrupting relationships with parents or a stepparent. All of these can be reframed as expressions of a loyalty conflict to help parents understand their child's behavior. However, many loyalty conflicts are covert and require careful assessment in order to intervene and educate parents "to reduce negative attributions about the children's behavior" (Bray, 1995, p. 68).

Children's fears. Children often have many fears. They may fear that "the stepparent is going to replace their nonresidential parent, what might happen to them if their custodial parent died or left, or what the stepparent can do with and for them" (Bray, 1995, p. 66). Bray suggests normalizing these fears and exploring any unrealistic expectations that may impede a child's adjustment. Fears can be accompanied by feelings of jealousy and concerns over favoritism.

Bibliotherapy. Papernow (1995) suggests the use of children's books to help children give voice to and to normalize their experiences. See Wark, Johnson, and Abrahamson (2003) for a list of books that includes divorce and stepfamilies. Sori and Hecker (2003a) have compiled an excellent handout with suggestions to use to coach parents in how to help children adjust.

Fourth Guideline: Aid Stepfamilies in Resolving Conflicts

Therapists often make the mistake of focusing initially on building cohesion, attempting to increase intimacy prematurely, before the family is sufficiently flexible to accommodate to the multitude of changes in the rules and structure of the family (Pasley, Dollahite, & Ihinger-Tallman, 1993). Once the family has stabilized and members feel more positive about their lives together, attention can be turned toward increasing intimacy. Helping families resolve conflict is a foundational skill that will allow other areas of family development to follow.

Stepfamilies often have great difficulty resolving conflicts. Children can be helped to constructively express their negative feelings toward a stepparent or stepsibling, and stepparents can be encouraged to empathize and show warmth and flexibility in their role as stepparent. It is also important to normalize these conflicts between children and stepparents in order to decrease unrealistic expectations and ensuing disillusionments (Pasley & Ihinger-Tallman, 1992).

In order to decrease conflict, one of the first targets of intervention with stepfamilies should be increasing flexibility. Family members often have set ideas of how a family should act based on their first-marriage experiences, and counselors can help them expand their ideas about how families should be, and explore unspoken wants and wishes regarding family life.

Fifth Guideline: Building a New Family Identity

Finally, counselors can assist families to build a new identity unique to the stepfamily. The following suggestions may be utilized to accomplish this goal. While it takes a good deal of time to merge two cultures into a new stepfamily that has aspects of the old identities blended with a distinct new identity, there is much that clinicians can do to foster identity development.

Special time assignment. Encouraging adults to have special time with each child individually diminishes feelings of favoritism and jealousy (Pasley, Dollahite, & Ihinger-Tallman, 1993). Papernow (1995) encourages all family members to plan one-on-one activities (called "compartmentalizing," p. 14) to begin bridging family structures divided along biological lines. This can begin to foster attachment between the stepparent and stepchild; and time with a child's biological parent reassures the child that they have not "lost" that connection.

Rituals. Pasley, Dollahite, and Ihinger-Tallman (1993) discuss the importance of rituals to help families establish and maintain an identity. They define a ritual as "more elaborate and/or meaningful shared experiences than routines" (p. 90). When stepfamilies form they are merging two family histories and identities. Aiding new stepfamilies to develop their own new rituals can help to foster the identity formation of the new family. However, this often means letting go of meaningful rituals from the past that connected family members to noncustodial parents or extended family. Thus, creating new rituals can also represent loss. Clinicians need to balance helping families continue with some past rituals that were especially meaningful, while designing rituals that are unique to the new stepfamily.

Routines. Routines are repeated daily events that shape our everyday lives. They can include getting ready for school and work, doing homework or chores, and preparing for bed. Routines help people, especially children, feel secure, and should be encouraged. Having families explore and create functional daily routines and tackle and change problematic routines together can be a way for families to create their lives together on a small, but important, scale.

PLAYFUL TECHNIQUES FOR COUNSELING CHILDREN OF DIVORCE AND STEPFAMILIES

In addition to these suggestions for counseling children and parents going through marital reconfigurations, there are numerous individual and family play interventions that are especially useful for these populations. Play is how children best express themselves, how they work through problems and transitions and make sense of the world. Often children in divorce or stepfamily situations benefit from individual or group sessions that provide them with a neutral place to process the changes and emotions they have experienced.

Also, when children and parents play together they often share a mutual joy that strengthens relationships. We will highlight a few techniques that can be used with children in individual sessions, in children's groups, as well as in family counseling, and refer readers to additional sources of information.

Of utmost importance is helping children find safe ways to express their feelings and experiences during transitions such as parental separation, divorce, living with a single parent, visiting a noncustodial parent, and a remarriage. However, children may find it difficult to do this verbally, or may be afraid of upsetting or overwhelming an already stressed parent. Seeing a child alone and using feeling charts or therapeutic books (see later) can be helpful to uncover and normalize the emotions these children commonly experience. Other methods to uncover feelings include asking children to draw a picture of their family (perhaps before, during, and after a divorce and/or remarriage). Children and parents might be asked to draw their family together, allowing clinicians to observe who is included (and omitted) in the picture, the family structure and boundaries, and the dynamics in the relationship as family members work together (see Sori, 1995). The picture can be a springboard to discuss changes, losses, and family issues.

Children also can be asked to draw a picture of a person in the rain (Beck & Biank, 1997). This projective technique indicates the degree to which a child feels vulnerable or protected from the fallout of a divorce. "Some children will draw huge raindrops, while others will draw a child unprotected by a raincoat or umbrella, often standing in a deluge of rain while lightning bolts fill the sky, sometimes pointing directly at the child's head" (Beck & Biank, 1997, p. 74). This can be useful to assess children who are unable or unwilling to talk about their experiences.

An excellent tool to help children express their somatic feelings and concerns is to depict them in a body drawing. Sori and Biank (2003a) suggest utilizing a diagram of a body and having children use different colors to represent various feelings, drawing them in different sections of the body where they experience those feelings (p. 16). Selekman (2000) has an intervention called the "imaginary feelings X-ray machine." Children lie on large sheets of paper while a family member outlines their body. The children are then asked to illustrate what their feelings would look like if an imaginary x-ray machine could be used to take pictures of the inside of their body. For example, in a family session one child whose father was in and out of the home drew large question marks in her head, stomach, hands, and knees. The question she wrote was "Is my daddy going to go away and never come back?" The counselor used this drawing to help the parents realize the tremendous insecurity the child felt, to encourage them to address her fears, and to recognize their need to provide stability in her life.

Having two dollhouses—one to represent each of the coparent's homes—is an excellent method to have children enact what occurs in each home. They can use doll figures to depict a "typical day" (Gil, 1994) in each home, as well as what occurs during transitions between homes (Beck & Biank, 1997). Therapists can readily discern the emotional climate between children and each parent, and between the ex-spouses. Relationship dynamics among stepfamily members are also illuminated. This is useful to assess how nurturing parents are, the child's general emotional state, the quality of the coparenting relationship, the boundaries in each home and between homes, and any specific areas of difficulty or conflict that need to be addressed.

Families also may do a mural series drawing. Using newspaper end rolls that are taped to the wall, the family is asked to draw various scenes with or without captions, to depict different phases or transitions as the family has reconfigured. Often the facial expressions, placement of figures, and activities family members are engaged in offer vital clues as to the family structure (Sori, 1995), and what children and parents have experienced over the course of the transitions. Selekman (2000), coming from a solution-oriented perspective, suggests a variation of the mural drawing, where families draw on a long sheet of paper "what they will be doing when they are defeating the problem" (p. 11). This offers family members a concrete picture of the solution, of what people will be doing when things are better.

The sandtray is a tremendous tool to help children as well as adults process unconscious feelings about transitions and losses (see Gil, 1994; Gil & Sobol, 2000), and also can strengthen parent-child relationships (McWey & Ruble, 2003). Children may be asked to do individual sandtrays, using miniatures to illustrate "their world in the sand" before, during, and after a divorce and remarriage. The objects chosen and the scenes depicted offer a rich metaphor of their experiences. Some children depict chaos and scenes that look like war zones; others may have a more barren terrain. Noting the use of objects to depict boundaries (e.g., fences, walls, or trees) is especially helpful in assessing children in stepfamilies. It is also useful to ask families to do conjoint sandtrays of their worlds. This allows the therapist to assess the involvement of family members, their boundaries and organization, as well as the emotional climate, and can be helpful in building stepfamily identity. Families can also be asked to depict their ideal world in the sand, when their problem is solved.

As mentioned earlier, there are numerous bibliotherapy resources to use for children from both divorced and stepfamilies (see Wark et al., 2003). Our favorites include *Dinosaurs Divorce: A Guide for Changing Families* (Brown & Brown, 1988); *Double-Dip Feelings: Stories to Help Children Understand Emotions* (Cain, 1990); *At Daddy's on Saturdays* (Girard, 1987); and *Divorce Workbook: A Guide for Kids and Families* (Ives, Fasler, & Lash, 1994). Therapeutic books are excellent tools to normalize children's feelings and situations, open communication between children and parents, as well as to educate parents about children's common experiences and how they can help.

Because "a picture is worth a thousand words," popular movies can help parents understand their child's experience more than any advice from a therapist. *The Quiet Room* is a moving film that offers a window in the life of a child who ceases to talk in response to her parents' conflict and decision to divorce. Viewers "hear" her anguished thoughts as she endures the hostility in her home. Although it is a comedy, *Mrs. Doubtfire* realistically depicts the devastation of a father whose access to his children is unfairly limited, as well as the pain his children endure. Finally, *Stepmom* portrays the difficulty that a new stepmother experiences as she attempts to help her husband parent his children while constantly being degraded by his ex-wife, with little support from her husband. The negative effects of split-loyalty conflicts on children are realistically depicted in this moving film. These videos can be useful to poignantly illustrate to parents how to help their children adjust.

There are numerous family play activities (Gil, 1994; Gil & Sobol, 2000) that are useful assessing family dynamics, as well as how to intervene according to one's theoretical orientation (e.g., assess structure, roles, to increase boundaries, strengthen dyadic relationships, or to increase the level of enjoyment among family members) (see Dermer, Olund, & Sori, 2006). We especially recommend the family puppet interview and the family aquarium (see Sori, 2006a; Gil & Sobol, 2000). The family play genogram (Gil, 2003) can be very helpful with stepfamilies who are seeking to establish their own identity. Other interventions include "Feeling Faces" (Biank & Sori, 2003a), "Spin Me a Yarn" (Sori & Biank, 2003b), and "A Child's Impossible and Scariest Tasks" (Biank & Sori, 2003b) to open communication and help children and adults discuss and understand one another's experiences.

Finally, filial therapy (see Sori, 2006b), in which parents are trained to do nondirective play therapy with each child, is an excellent method to promote attachment, improve parent-child relationships, and reduce child behavior and emotional problems. This is effective in helping children who are anxious from a divorce or remarriage to remain connected to each parent, as well as to help foster bonds between a child and a stepparent. Many other useful techniques can be found in Bailey (2000) and Sori, Hecker (2003b) that can be used with this population.

DIVORCE VIGNETTE: "MOLLY'S FOLLIES"

Maggie and Robert had been married since Molly was 4 years old, and Robert had adopted Molly when she was 5. Maggie had never been married to Molly's biological father and his whereabouts were unknown. Essentially, Robert was the only father Molly had ever known. She had longed for a father, and was delighted when Maggie married Robert and they "became a family."

Seven years later, when Molly was 11, Robert abruptly left the family. Maggie felt blindsided when she learned of his affair and his subsequent abandonment. She was extremely angry that Robert just walked out without warning. Although he had adopted Molly, he wanted no visitation or contact with her and had moved away. This devastated Molly.

Molly changed schools due to economic hardships following the divorce. The new school suggested Molly attend counseling because she had been sporadically refusing to go to her new school. Maggie called for counseling for both her anger and to address Molly's school problems that started when Robert left.

The therapist viewed the initial postdivorce tasks for Molly and Maggie as (a) to accept the reality of the divorce and begin to restructure their family, and (b) to deal with the feelings of abandonment and the loss of Robert as a husband and parent. Robert had been the primary disciplinarian and Maggie was overwhelmed with her sudden status as a single parent. She was struggling with getting Molly to attend school. Maggie would wake Molly up, give her breakfast, and while Molly was dressing Maggie would leave for work. Several days a week Molly would wait until Maggie left and then get undressed, and lie on the sofa, hugging her pillow and blanket while watching TV until shortly before Mom was due home from work. At that time she would get dressed again and be sitting at the kitchen table appearing to do her homework when Mom came through the door. The school eventually reached Mom to inquire about the multiple absences, and "Molly's follies" were revealed!

The therapist hypothesized that Molly's behavior might be a way to distract Maggie from her pain. In the first session the therapist asked Molly to do a series drawing that: (a) depicted her family before Maggie's marriage to Robert, (b) after they married, and (c) after Robert abandoned them. The first scene showed Molly and Mom standing together with smiles on their faces, and the caption read, "Once there was a mother and daughter, and they were very happy." The second scene showed Robert standing between Molly and Maggie, with a black dog, and the caption said, "And she married a nice man and they were very happy, and he bought her a dog!" In the third scene Molly and Maggie were standing together, and their smiles had clearly been turned into black frowns. The caption read, "But the man did something very, very bad, and he left them." There was a final picture that showed Molly and Maggie sitting on a couch, with the caption, "And then they went to counseling and they lived happily ever after."

The first issue the therapist addressed was increasing Mom's parental structuring in order to get Molly back in school. Mom's anger and sense of loss were crippling her ability to parent effectively. It became clear that Maggie was upset by the many losses and transitions that she felt alone in tackling.

At the therapist's urging, Molly and Maggie performed an enactment in which they talked together about the necessity of Molly attending school. With the support of the therapist, Maggie was able to ensure that Molly attended school regularly. In addition to helping Maggie get Molly in school and adjust to the changes, the therapist worked with Maggie to restructure rules, roles, and routines for their new family configuration.

In another session the therapist asked Molly and Maggie to do a sandtray using miniatures. On one side they were asked to depict their world when Robert was with them. On the other side of the sandtray they were asked to make their current world. The side with Robert was full of fun things to do, like beaches and a playground and people laughing and playing, and a beautiful home. The other world was rather barren looking, and had looming monsters and dangerous animals hidden in the sand. The figures had no safety fences, barriers, or weapons with which to defend themselves. In processing this activity Maggie and Molly began talking about the losses that they had incurred and how much their lives had changed after the divorce.

In an individual session with Molly she drew a picture of what divorce feels like. She disclosed that she felt responsible for Robert leaving. Later, Maggie, using the book *Dinosaurs Divorce* (Brown & Brown, 1988), was able to address the sadness that was underneath Molly's anger, her self-blame, and magical thinking that Robert would rescue her from her plight.

Individual sessions with Maggie addressed her anger at Robert, her sadness about the many losses for her and Molly, and her unwanted single-parent status. Maggie was encouraged to reach out to friends and family for support.

Near the end of therapy the therapist had Molly and Maggie construct a sandtray of their new ideal world—without Robert. They worked together harmoniously and created a warm and inviting world that had a lovely home surrounded by a white fence, lush plants, a pond with a bridge, and was full of life and laughter. Afterward, they talked together about steps they could take to build this new life.

In the final session Maggie reported that while she was still sad, she felt stronger and more confident in her ability to handle her feelings and in her role as a single parent. She also believed she could now aid Molly in expressing her feelings and adapting to the divorce. Molly reported that she now liked her new school and was making friends. Her final picture showed Maggie and Molly in a boat on a calm sea, with Maggie rowing them toward an island with a beautiful rainbow highlighting the sun-filled sky.

STEPFAMILY VIGNETTE: "RACE IS NOT AN ISSUE"

Mary and Tyron initiated counseling to help them manage Mary's son's behavior. Jason, age 14, was Mary's son from her first marriage, and had been getting into some trouble at his private school. Recently he had been suspended from the bus after tripping a boy and getting into a fight. Mary and Tyron had been married about a year and were expecting their first child. Although Jason visited his biological father once a month, his paternal grandparents had cut off from him because his Caucasian mother married Tyron, an African American. Tyron was an emergency room physician, and Mary was a nurse. On the intake form the clients were asked to write in their race. Both Mary and Tyron wrote "Human" in the space on their forms.

After joining with all three family members, the therapist glanced through the intake forms, and commented on their unique answer to the race question. Mary quickly said, "Race is not an issue for us. That's not why we're here. We're here because of Jason's trouble at school, and to help him adjust to our new family." She then moved on to explain her concerns over Jason's behavior on the bus. The couple was willing to discuss their excitement in the forthcoming birth of a new child. Jason also shared their anticipation of this event.

Mary explained that Jason and she had been very close before she met and married Tyron. They often did things together, and Jason had been "the man of the house." That changed when she remarried, although Jason was still good about helping his mother with chores. The therapist also learned that although Jason and Tyron were polite and got along, they were distant and shared little. The therapist asked Tyron and Jason to do an enactment in which they planned an activity together. Tyron agreed to take Jason to a baseball game. They went to the game as planned and had a good time at the game. The therapist encouraged Tyron to continue to develop his relationship with Jason.

In one session the family constructed a play genogram (Gil, 2003), where the therapist drew three generations of both Mary's and Tyron's family. Each person selected a miniature to represent their thoughts and feelings about each person on the genogram. In processing this activity Jason and Mary learned a lot about the family customs and relationships in Tyron's family, and vice versa. This led to a discussion among the three of them of what holiday traditions were most important to them that they wanted to keep, and to explore some new rituals that they could incorporate into their family. For example, Jason loved opening presents Christmas Eve, and it was important to Mary that they go to a candlelight service at their church. Tyron, who was an excellent cook, wanted to add some of his family's favorite foods to the holiday menu. Mary and Jason were delighted when he offered to teach them to make some of his favorite recipes. They decided on a new tradition—cutting down their own tree and trimming it together the Sunday after Thanksgiving. This was an important activity in building a new shared family identity.

In addition, Jason was able to share his sadness and anger at his paternal grandparents for cutting off from him. His mom explained that they had once been robbed at gunpoint by a black man and, unfortunately, generalized their fear and anxiety to all black men. This helped Jason better understand his grandparents, and opened the door for the family to discuss the "nonissue" issue of race. Mary and Tyron talked about stares and sotto voce comments they were forced to endure from both blacks and whites, even in their church. Jason then admitted that the fight on the bus had occurred after the boy made a derogatory comment about his biracial family. The therapist helped them explore their strengths as a couple and family, and highlighted their commitment and resiliency in shrugging off such negative comments.

Jason and Mary were seen together in a session where they did sandtrays. First, they built their world in the sand as it was before Mom remarried. Next, they built their current world. In discussing the differences in the trays the therapist remarked at how many things now competed with Jason for Mom's time and attention—not only Tyron, but new relationships with his family members, and his soon-to-be-born sibling. Jason was able to share his feelings about all the changes and his new role as a brother, and to talk about what things are better, like moving to a much larger home, going to a new private school (which he loved), seeing Mom happier, getting to take wonderful vacations, and developing a new relationship with Tyron.

In one couples session, Tyron and Mary were asked to do an enactment together. First they talked about how their lives would change once the baby was born, and how they would carve out time to be alone and to "date." The therapist gave them a handout (see Sori & Hecker, 2003a) that listed suggestions for stepfamilies. After reading this they discussed Tyron's role as a stepfather, which was for now to support Mary's parenting and focus on building a relationship with Jason. They also explored how Jason might react to the new baby, and how they could make his transition from only child to big brother easier. In another session Jason and Tyron did an enactment where they planned another activity. This time Tyron was going to teach Jason how to help put the new crib together and then they would build some new shelves for Jason's room, to hold the model airplanes he and Tyron were making.

Each week Jason felt better, and the excitement grew with Mary's approaching due date. One day Tyron called the therapist from the hospital to share the news that their baby girl had arrived safely, and to ask if they could bring her to a session. When they came in two weeks later for a final session they brought a camera and asked if someone would take their picture together with the therapist. They then asked her to take a picture of their new family, with Jason grinning as he held his baby sister. They thanked the therapist for helping them to talk about race, and for helping them to feel like a real family.

CONCLUSION

Although children are most certainly affected by divorce, each child is affected differently. Counselors are wise to aid parents in adjusting to divorce, as parental adjustment is directly linked to children's adjustment. Conflict can be as toxic, or even more toxic, to children than divorce itself. Thus, it is important that child and family therapists work fervently to reduce conflict between divorcing parents as well as in stepfamilies. In helping families through the transition of divorce, counselors need a good working knowledge of the legal system that families must navigate both before, during, and often after divorce.

While it is helpful to work with stepfamilies both with structural family therapy and play therapy techniques, it is important to remember that therapy with stepfamilies differs from therapy with first-married families in some important ways. Initially, stepfamily therapy must focus on the marital dyad so that the couple can form a strong marital attachment from which to parent. Counselors also can normalize the myriad of common stepfamily stressors that occur for many families. The counselor aids the couple in building a strong marital base. However, children often suffer silently, and their needs must not be overlooked. Children also may be focused on concomitantly to the couple counseling, or after the couple has secured a strong foundation for their relationship. Losses, transitions, and loyalty conflicts are common themes for children in divorce and stepfamilies. Learning how to resolve conflict together is another important task for stepfamilies. Finally, the stepfamily must build a new family identity.

Although working with families with the complexity of divorce or stepfamily issues can be difficult, counselors need to be on the front line of both healing these families, as well as advocating for a nonadversarial form of family transition within the legal system.

REFERENCES

Amato, P. R. (1994). Life-span adjustment of children to their parents' divorces. *Future of Children, 25,* 1031–1042.

Amato, P. R., & Keith, B. (1991). Parental divorce and the well-being of children: A meta-analysis. *Psychological Bulletin, 110,* 26–46.

American Psychological Association (1994). Guidelines for child custody evaluations in divorce proceedings. *American Psychologist, 49*(7), 677–680.

Arendell, T. (1992). After divorce: investigations into father absence. *Gender and Society, 6*(4), 562–586.

Bailey, C. E. (Ed.) (2000). *Children in therapy: Using the family as a resource.* New York: W. W. Norton & Co.

Beck, P., & Biank, N. (1997). Enhancing therapeutic intervention during divorce. *Journal of Analytic Social Work, 4*(3), 63–81.

Biank, N., & Sori, C. F. (2003a). A child's impossible and scariest tasks. In C. F. Sori, L. L. Hecker, & Associates, *The therapist's notebook for children and adolescents: Homework, handouts, and activities for use in psychotherapy* (pp. 18–24). Binghamton, NY: Haworth.

Biank, N., & Sori, C. F. (2003b). Feeling faces prevent scary places. In C. F. Sori, L. L. Hecker, & Associates, *The therapist's notebook for children and adolescents: Homework, handouts, and activities for use in psychotherapy* (pp. 92–95). Binghamton, NY: Haworth.

Boss, P. (1999). *Ambiguous loss.* Cambridge, MA: Harvard University Press.

Bray, J. H. (1995). Children in stepfamilies: Assessment and treatment issues. In D. K. Huntley (Ed.), *Understanding stepfamilies: Implications for assessment and treatment* (pp. 59–72). Alexandria, VA: American Counseling Association.

Brown, M., & Brown, L. K. (1988). *Dinosaurs divorce: A guide for changing families.* New York: Little Brown and Company.

Cain, B. (1990). *Double-dip feelings: Stories to help children understand emotion.* Washington, DC: American Psychological Association.

Dermer, S., Olund, D., & Sori, C. F. (2006). Involving children in family counseling and involving parents in children's counseling: Theoretical and practical guidelines, chap. 7 in this volume.

Dunn, J. (2002). The adjustment of children in stepfamilies: Lessons from community studies. *Child and Adolescent Mental Health, 7*(4), 154–161.

Ehrlich, J. (2001). Losing perspective: A danger in working with high-conflict divorces. *American Journal of Family Law, 4,* 307–310.

Gil, E. (1994). *Play in family therapy.* New York: Guilford.

Gil, E., & Sobol, B. (2000). Engaging families in therapeutic play. In C. E. Bailey (Ed.), *Children in therapy: Using the family as a resource* (pp. 341–392). New York: W. W. Norton.

Gil, E. (2003). Play genograms. In C. F. Sori, L. L. Hecker, & Associates, *The therapist's notebook for children and adolescents: Homework, handouts, and activities for use in psychotherapy* (pp. 49–56). Binghamton, NY: Haworth.

Girard, L. W. (1987). *At daddy's on Saturdays.* Morton Grove, IL: Albert Whitman and Company.

Glick, P. C. (1984). Marriage, divorce, and living arrangements: prospective changes. *Journal of Family Issues, 5*(1), 7–26.

Glick, P. (1989). Remarried families, stepfamilies, and stepchildren: A brief demographic profile. *Family Relations, 38*(1), 24–27.

Glick, P., & Lin, S. L., (1986). Recent changes in divorce and remarriage. *Journal of Marriage and Family, 48,* 737–747.

Hecker, L., & Sori, C. F. (2003). The parent's guide to good divorce behavior. In C. F. Sori, L. Hecker, & Associates, *The therapist's notebook for children and adolescents: Homework, handouts, and activities for use in psychotherapy* (pp. 323–329). Binghamton, NY: Haworth.

Hodges, W. F. (1986). *Interventions for children of divorce: Custody, access and psychotherapy.* New York: Wiley & Sons.

Hodges, W. (1991). *Interventions for children of divorce: Custody, access and psychotherapy.* New York: Wiley & Sons.

Ives, S. B., Fasler, D., & Lash, M. (1994). *Divorce workbook: A guide for kids and families.* Burlington, VT: Waterfront Books.

Kelly, J. (1993). Current research on children's postdivorce adjustment. *Family and conciliation courts review, 31,* 29–40.

Kelly, J. (2000). Children's adjustment in conflicted marriage and divorce: A decade review of research. *Journal of the American Academy of Child and Adolescent Psychiatry, 39,* 963–973.

Lyon, M., Surrey, E., & Timms, J. (1998). *Effective support services for children and young people when parental relationships break down: A child-centred approach.* London, England: Calouste Gulbenkian Foundation.

Martin, T. C., & Bumpass, L. L. (1989) Recent trends in marital disruption. *Demography, 26,* 37–51.

Mayes, G., Gillies, J., Wilson, G., & McDonald, R. (2000). An evaluation of the Parental Information Programme. Scotland: Scottish Executive Central Research Unit. Retrieved August 23, 2005, from http://www.scotland.gov.uk/cru/kd01/blue/parent-00.htm.

McClanahan, S. S. (1999). Family structure and the reproduction of poverty. *American Journal of Sociology, 90,* 873–901.

McIntosh, J. (2000). Child-inclusive divorce mediation: Report on a qualitative research study. *Mediation Quarterly, 18*(1), 55–69.

McWey, L., & Ruble, N. (2003). Family sandplay: Strengthening the parent-child bond. In C. F. Sori, L. L. Hecker, & Associates, *The therapist's notebook for children and adolescents: Homework, handouts, and activities for use in psychotherapy* (pp. 79–82). Binghamton, NY: Haworth.

Minuchin, S. (1974). *Families and family therapy.* Cambridge, MA: Harvard University Press.

Papernow, P. L. (1995). What's going on here? Separating (and weaving together) step and clinical issues in remarried families. In D. K. Huntley (Ed.), *Understanding stepfamilies: Implications for assessment and treatment* (pp. 3–24). Alexandria, VA: American Counseling Association.

Pasley, K., & Ihinger-Tallman, M. (1992). Remarriage and stepparenting: What the literature has added to our understanding of this family form. *Family Science Review, 5*(3/4), 153–174.

Pasley, K., & Dollahite, D. C. (1995). The nine Rs of stepparenting adolescents: Research-based recommendations for clinicians. In D. K. Huntley (Ed.), *Understanding stepfamilies: Implications for assessment and treatment* (pp. 87–98). Alexandria, VA: American Counseling Association.

Pasley, K., Dollahite, D. C., & Ihinger-Tallman, M. (1993). Bridging the gap: Clinical applications of research findings on the spouse and stepparent roles in remarriage. *Family Relations, 42,* 315–322.

Pruett, K. D., & Pruett, M. K. (1999). "Only God decides": Young children's perception of divorce and the legal system. *Journal of the American Academy of Child & Adolescent Psychiatry, 38*(12), 1544–1550.

Selekman, M. D. (2000). Solution-oriented brief family therapy with children. In C. E. Bailey (Ed.), *Children in therapy: Using the family as a resource* (pp. 1–19). New York: Norton.

Sori, C. F. (1995). The "art" of restructuring. *Journal of Family Psychotherapy* 6(2), 13–31.

Sori, C. F. (2006a). Family play therapy: An interview with Eliana Gil, chap. 4 in this volume.

Sori, C. F. (2006b). Filial therapy: An interview with Rise VanFleet, chap. 5 in this volume.

Sori, C. F. (2006c). On counseling children and families: Recommendations from the experts, chap. 1 in this volume.

Sori, C. F., & Biank, N. (2003a). Deflating fear. In C. F. Sori, L. L. Hecker, & Associates, *The therapist's notebook for children and adolescents: Homework, handouts, and activities for use in psychotherapy* (pp. 9–17). Binghamton, NY: Haworth.

Sori, C. F., & Biank, N. (2003b). Spin me a yarn: Breaking the ice and warming the heart. In C. F. Sori, L. L. Hecker, & Associates, *The therapist's notebook for children and adolescents: Homework, handouts, and activities for use in psychotherapy* (pp. 83–91). Binghamton, NY: Haworth.

Sori, C. F., & Hecker, L. L. (2006). Ethical and legal considerations when counseling children and families, chap. 8 in this volume.

Sori, C. F., & Hecker, L. L. (2003a). The ten commandments for stepfamilies. In C. F. Sori, L. L. Hecker, & Associates, *The therapist's notebook for children and adolescents: Homework, handouts, and activities for use in psychotherapy* (pp. 330–335). Binghamton, NY: Haworth.

Sori, C. F., Hecker, L. L., & Associates. (2003b). *The therapist's notebook for children and adolescents: Homework, handouts, and activities for use in psychotherapy.* Binghamton, NY: Haworth.

Sori, C. F., & Sprenkle, D. H. (2004). Training family therapists to work with children and families: A modified Delphi study. *Journal of Marital and Family Therapy, 30*(4), 479–495.

Strategic Partners (1999). Child Inclusive Practice in Family and Child Counseling and Family and Child Mediation. Report for Family and Community Services, Commonwealth of Australia. Retrieved August 25, 2005 from http://www.facs.gov.au/internet/facsinternet.nsf/family/frsp-tace_chap2.htm.

Visher, J. S., & Visher, E. B. (1989). Parenting coalitions after remarriage: Dynamic and therapeutic guidelines. *Family Relations, 38,* 65–70.

Visher, E. B., & Visher, J. S. (1988) *Old loyalties, new ties: Therapeutic strategies with stepfamilies*. New York: Brunner/Mazel.

Visher, E. B., & Visher, J. S. (1990). Dynamics of successful stepfamilies. *Journal of Divorce and Remarriage, 14*(1), 3–11.

Visher, E. B., & Visher, J. S. (1995). Avoiding the mind fields of stepfamily therapy. In D. K. Huntley (Ed.), *Understanding stepfamilies: Implications for assessment and treatment* (pp. 25–34). Alexandria, VA: American Counseling Association.

Visher, J. (1994). Stepfamilies: A work in progress. *The American Journal of Family Therapy, 22*(4), 337–344.

Wallerstein, J. S. (1983). Children of divorce: Stress and developmental tasks. In N. Garmezy and M. Rutter (Eds.), *Stress, coping and development in children* (pp. 265–302). New York: McGraw-Hill.

Wallerstein, J. S., & Kelly, J. B. (1980). *Surviving the breakup*. New York: Basic Books.

Wark, L., Johnson, J., & Abrahamson, L. (2003). Using children's books in family therapy. In C. F. Sori, L. L. Hecker, & Associates, *The therapist's notebook for children and adolescents: Homework, handouts, and activities for use in psychotherapy* (pp. 302–322). Binghamton, NY: Haworth.

Wolchik, S. A., Sandler, I. N., Millsap, R. E., Plummer, B. A., Greene, S. M., Anderson, E. R., et al. (2002). Six-year follow-up of preventive interventions for children of divorce. *Journal of the American Medical Association, 288*(15), 1874–1881.

Zill, N., & Schoenborn, C. A. (1990). Developmental, learning, and emotional problems: Health of our nation's children, United States, 1988. Advance Data, *National Center for Health Statistics, 120*, 9.

CHAPTER 10

Treating Children and Families with ADHD

CRAIG A. EVERETT, PH.D., AND SANDRA VOLGY EVERETT, PH.D.

INTRODUCTION

Attention deficit hyperactivity disorder (ADHD) is a psychiatric condition that affects children, not only during their formative school years but potentially throughout their adult lives. Beyond its biochemical, neurological, and genetic origins, it can create a complex web of symptomatology affecting a child's self-worth and self-esteem, cognitive development and intellectual achievement, peer and sibling attachments, and family dynamics.

These factors for the child may be exacerbated by the genetic component inherent in the disorder which means that a sibling, a parent, and other extended family members may also present with ADHD, diagnosed or otherwise. This factor can dramatize the individual's symptoms as they become mirrored in the reactivity of other family members and circularly connected to the presence of ADHD symptoms in other closely connected individuals within the household. The symptomatology and reactive dynamics may spread over three or four generations. In fact, the dysfunctional dynamics of an entire intergenerational family system may be focused solely around the ADHD symptoms of a child and can become embedded in the reciprocal dynamics of sibling, parent-child, and intergenerational subsystems.

Many clinicians who work solely with children and with this disorder often fail to recognize or examine the broader dynamics of the ADHD child's experience within her or his ongoing and historical family life experiences. In this chapter, we will present an overview of the etiology and diagnostic issues, and then examine treatment from the view of family systems therapy and a treatment team approach.

ETIOLOGY AND DIAGNOSIS OF ADHD

Etiology

While the etiology is based on a range of possible biochemical and neurological factors still being researched (Barkley, 1997), it is believed that between 75% and 80% of the incidence is transmitted genetically. This means that one day specific genetic markers may be identified for the ADHD disorder (see Levy & Hay, 2001, for a collection of 12 articles on genetic theories and studies).

Nongenetic causes usually involve prenatal or early infancy factors such as maternal use of alcohol or drugs during pregnancy, prenatal anomalies, birth complications, deprivation of oxygen at birth, and so on. Later factors could include head trauma; food, environmental and chemical sensitivities; and overuse of television and video games (Hallowell & Ratey, 2005). There has been very little literature regarding cultural factors affecting the diagnosis and treatment of ADHD. One report has discussed the need for the therapist to recognize the cultural and family milieu of the symptomatic child (Pitts & Wallace, 2003).

The chapter will discuss primarily clinical and psychoeducational methods of diagnosing ADHD. As a note, there is ongoing neurological research to identify other methods of evaluation. For example, new neuroimaging technology that include the qEEG (quantitative electroencephalogram) and the Spect scan (single proton emission computerized tomography) are being researched. For a further discussion, see Hallowell and Ratey (2005) and Pliszka (2005).

The present *DSM-IV* (American Psychiatric Association, 1994) has identified four possible diagnostic subtypes: *Predominantly Inattentive Type*, *Predominantly Hyperactive-Impulsive Type*, *Combined Type* (combination of the two above), and *Not otherwise specified.* The *DSM-IV* also has identified lists of specific *Hyperactive, Impulsive,* and *Inattentive* symptoms from which it suggested that a certain number of these symptoms (criteria) must be identified in the child before she or he can be placed in one of the subtypes.

What this means diagnostically for the therapist is that, once the basic symptom criteria are identified, a differentiation should be made as to whether the child is basically *Inattentive* (typically more prevalent with females) or *Hyperactive/Impulsive* (more prevalent with males). Some therapists simply transcribe the *DSM-IV* criteria list into a working checklist and utilize this as they interview children and parents. Many children will meet the criteria of the *Combined Type* (in our experience more males than females) because most *Hyperactive/Impulsive* children will also display inattentiveness and many primarily *Inattentive Type* children will display some mild hyperactivity or restlessness.

The *DSM-IV* also identified certain criteria, such as age at onset (7 years), duration (6 months), settings, and developmental comparisons. Some of these criteria, particularly the need to identify a specific age of onset, have become controversial and challenged in the field. (See the *DSM-IV* to review the specific criteria and Everett & Everett [1999] for a discussion of the use of the diagnostic criteria and the controversies surrounding them.)

The Differential Diagnosis of ADHD and Other Psychiatric Disorders in Children

The diagnosis of ADHD can be difficult, even for experienced child clinicians. In younger and less verbal children, the symptoms are often identified initially by parents and teachers. The therapist must be experienced enough to differentiate the concerns and agenda of parents and teachers (often issues of behavioral disruption), from the presence of clear underlying symptoms, and must be able to differentiate these from other possible clinical disorders.

The most prominent areas for differential diagnostic work for children include *Anxiety Disorders*, *Oppositional Defiant Disorder*, and *Bipolar Disorder*. For the clinician to differentiate these, it is helpful to observe the child in play and individual therapy sessions, as well as in family interactive sessions. The child may also need to be observed in the classroom setting, and the therapist may need to consult with teachers, as well as parents, for ongoing treatment needs.

Of these three areas of other childhood disorders, the work of differential diagnosis is probably the most difficult with bipolar disorders. In fact, many child therapists and even child psychiatrists are reluctant to use the bipolar diagnosis on children (Hallowell & Ratey, 2005). However, in our practices, we have seen many children (as well as adults) who had been diagnosed improperly due to confusion between these two disorders (see Everett & Everett [1999] for case examples). A helpful work for readers in this differential diagnosis of ADHD and bipolar disorder in children is Popper (1989).

Recognizing the Presence of Other Psychiatric Disorders Comorbid with ADHD in Children

The field also recognizes that ADHD in children can also coexist (comorbidity) with a rather broad range of other psychiatric disorders. The presence of these coexisting disorders can begin in childhood and continue into adolescence and adulthood. These other disorders may include any of the following:

1. Conduct disorder
2. Oppositional defiant disorder
3. Depression
4. Dysthymia
5. Bipolar disorders
6. Anxiety disorders
7. Substance abuse/addiction
8. Alcohol abuse/addiction
9. Learning disabilities
10. Sensory integration disorder

Many inexperienced therapists, or ones with a minimal of diagnostic training, are often prone to settle on a diagnostic view based on either the first symptoms that are presented, or the more persistent or prominent symptoms. For example, a 10-year-old child who displays dysthymic symptoms would most likely be treated for depression and possibly medicated for that condition if it persists. However, if the therapist looked at the child's history more carefully and identified a pattern of behavioral and/or school problems, the presence of ADHD might be detected. Clinically, many ADHD children who present with comorbid affective symptoms can be treated initially for the ADHD and the affective symptoms may disappear.

The greatest error that we observe in inadequate diagnosis occurs with children being diagnosed as a conduct disorder. Because of the drama associated behaviorally with this disorder, particularly with adolescent children, there is often no attempt by the therapist to look at the broader picture of possible inattentiveness, impulsivity, and hyperactivity. Again, these conduct difficulties, when they coexist with ADHD, can often be treated more successfully by identifying accurately the presence of ADHD.

DEVELOPING A MULTIDISCIPLINARY TREATMENT TEAM

Even though we believe strongly that family therapy should be a major component of treatment for ADHD children, we have found that the most effective assessment and treatment strategies need to involve a treatment team. This involves much more than simply using other specialists for consultation. A treatment team can share observations and data, and communicate regarding options for a treatment strategies to benefit the child and the family. The specialists that we have identified on our treatment team for ADHD children include the following:

1. Child psychiatrist or pediatrician
2. Psychometrist
3. Educational consultant
4. Attorney

A physician is an important ally on the team if medication becomes part of the treatment plan. While we work with many pediatricians in terms of the need for medication and consult with them regarding the medication's effectiveness, we prefer child psychiatrists on the team due to their specialization with these medications. They are more likely to be knowledgeable of not only ADHD, but also differential diagnostic issues of other childhood disorders and to recognize comorbid disorders. They are also capable of recognizing broader medical and developmental concerns. Finally, to be effective on the team, they must value and support working with other mental health professionals.

For children with ADHD, the milieu in which the greatest problematic symptoms occur involves not only the family but the school setting. Most ADHD children that you will treat will also display serious levels of personal discouragement, poor self-esteem, and low self-confidence. These emotional issues are reinforced daily for ADHD children. The fact that ADHD symptoms contribute *both* to behavioral problems as well as cognitive deficiencies in the child's school experience requires considerable focus on, not only the academic experience but also the child's emotional experience in the home and at school. (See Rief [2003] for a review of school-related issues.) Often the therapist can be helpful in the role of an advocate for the ADHD child by educating school staff about ADHD and consulting with teachers and school psychologists.

There is no specific "test for ADHD." Many pediatricians and school counselors utilize a variety of self-report questionnaires and checklists. However, these are often self-reports by busy and inattentive parents and teachers; or they are completed by older children who cannot recognize their deficiencies. While we occasionally use certain checklists in our practices, these are not good substitutes for thorough psychoeducational testing. We refer the child to a colleague on our team, a psychologist who specializes in testing (psychometrist). The primary tests that we request are the basic Wechsler "IQ Test" (WISC-IV, *Wechsler Intelligence Scale for Children)* and a basic test for cognitive processing and achievement, the *Woodcock–Johnson Psycho-Educational Battery (WJ-III).* The subscales of both of these tests identify certain cognitive patterns that become "red flags" for ADHD. In fact, many students who test positively for ADHD also have results that can indicate additional learning deficits, such as cognitive processing problems (e.g., as in processing speed or working memory) and specific learning disabilities. (See Everett and Everett [1999] for a further discussion of the use of testing for ADHD children.)

An additional member of our team is an educational consultant. This person provides a service which is different from that of a specific subject tutor. This is someone who can look at the broader picture of a student's learning difficulties and focus on issues of organization, time management, preparation of assignments, consideration of testing skills, management of larger projects, and overall achievement. This consultant may do as much, or more, than the therapist to help in creating success in the academic setting to improve self-esteem and self-confidence. For older children we often identify this person as a "coach." The most effective consultants with whom we have worked have been former or retired special education teachers. There are also individuals trained in school psychology who work in private settings and can be helpful in this consultant role. They often can be found through a school psychologist or a psychometrist.

The reader may be surprised to find an attorney on our team. The need for such a team member becomes necessary when ADHD children are in need of legal assistance, particularly when schools are reluctant or refusing to provide special services. ADHD is identified as a specific disability in the Federal Disability Act. This is referred to as a "504 Plan," which designates this portion of the Disability Act. This means that these children are entitled to special services as disabled individuals so that their disabling symptoms do not unduly penalize their academic functioning and success.

These potential services in the schools are referred to as *accommodations* and for children these may range from preferential seating (near the front of a classroom), to additional time to complete tests and assignments, to alternate testing (oral vs. written), to the provision of written notes and outlines from the teacher to the student. Most school districts understand their legal responsibilities to provide accommodations, but many are reluctant to do so based on staff time and availability, and whether a student is "in danger of failing." All public schools are mandated to provide these services to ADHD students who have been professionally diagnosed.

Often the therapist for the child and family must also become an advocate with the schools to obtain these services. When this is unsuccessful the parents may need to consult an attorney. (See Everett and Everett [1999] for sample advocacy letters to the school and list of potential accommodations for grade school aged children.)

MEDICAL INTERVENTIONS FOR ADHD CHILDREN

Most children, even with mild ADHD symptoms, may benefit from the adjunctive use of stimulant medications. While we cannot pursue the issues and controversies of the use of medication at length, our experiences show that medication is the single most helpful treatment with the *Predominantly Hyperactive and Impulsive* children. Symptom reduction is often dramatic with symptoms of hyperactivity, restlessness, impulsivity, and mood lability. However, the medications can also effectively improve concentration, attention, focus, and short-term memory. Most of the research in the field identifies that the use of stimulant medications in conjunction with therapy is the most effective treatment (Barkley, 1997). The effectiveness of these stimulants for children has been estimated by Quinn (1997) at 75–85% and by Barkley (1990) at 60–80%.

The most commonly prescribed medications in our practices include Adderall, Concerta, and Ritalin. These medications come in both short-acting (3.5 to 4 hours) and long-acting (sustained release, 8–12 hours). The most common side effects concerning children are appetite suppression and sleep disturbance (if the medications are taken too late in the day). Although there are controversies regarding the potential overuse of these medications in both the professional field and media, it has been our experience, based on nearly 30 years of clinical practice each, that these medications, when prescribed properly, quickly reduce problematic symptoms and improve personal, social, and academic functioning.

WORKING WITH ADHD CHILDREN AND THEIR FAMILIES

It is helpful to conceptualize clinical work with ADHD children from a family systems perspective (see Nichols & Everett [1987] and Everett & Everett [1999]). This involves understanding certain key family dynamics and recognizing that the points of intervention may not always involve just the symptomatic child.

Conceptualizing the Family System

It is important to recognize the central clinical concepts that define the functioning of a family system. Family systems operate with the principles of *circularity* and *reciprocity*. Events or behaviors or symptoms that occur for members of a family system do so in a circular manner—a symptom experienced by a child (e.g., hyperactivity) is experienced and shared by every member of the family. Similarly, the hyperactivity of the child causes a reciprocal response (usually negative) by all of the individual members of the family.

Family systems attempt to maintain a certain level of *balance* (homeostasis) in order to avert crises or chaos. This balance may include dysfunctional symptoms which are actually incorporated into the daily functioning of the system. Most notably for ADHD families is the use of another family dynamic—*scapegoating* (Ackerman, 1958; Bell & Vogel, 1961). This family dynamic involves the process whereby all members of the family, including extended family members, identify a selected family member—the hyperactive child—as "bad," disruptive, the "cause of the family's unhappiness." The family system will stabilize its overall level of functioning by labeling and scapegoating the ADHD child. There are many other systemic concepts that we have discussed elsewhere: the role of subsystem and intergenerational boundaries, the transmission of ADHD dynamics across multiple family generations, the role of intense and persistent vertical loyalties, and the roles of dependency, immaturity, personal failure, and guilt across generations (Everett & Everett, 1999).

The Range of Systemic Intervention Strategies

One of the benefits of the family system perspective is that it allows the therapist to take a broad look at the entire nuclear and intergenerational family and determine the role of the ADHD child within the system, as well as the most effective points of intervention. Traditional individually oriented therapies for children tend to focus on individual or play therapy for the child combined with occasional meetings with the child's parents. Other approaches offer primarily behavioral therapies (Adesman, 2003; Williams, Chacko, Gabiano, & Pelham, 2001). Group therapy also may be offered to older ADHD children (usually over 10 years). These approaches fail to recognize and utilize the powerful influence of the child's family milieu and interactive roles within the family. These broader dynamics can define both the dysfunctional elements for the child and the family, and the potential therapeutic resources for change.

In our work with ADHD children, we consider at least 10 possible points of intervention, each with associated clinical goals and strategies (Everett & Everett, 1999, p. 166):

1. The ADHD child individually (in an interview)
2. The ADHD child individually (in play therapy)
3. The ADHD child and parents (in an interview)
4. The ADHD child and parents (in joint play therapy)
5. The parents
6. The ADHD child and the siblings (in an interview)
7. The ADHD child and the siblings (in play therapy)
8. The nuclear family system
9. The marital subsystem of the parents
10. The intergenerational family system (e.g., including grandparents of the ADHD child)

The experienced family therapist will be able to conceptualize clinical goals for any of these points of intervention. For example, seeing a young ADHD child individually in play therapy will reveal elements of the child's maturity, interactive skills, and attention to dialogue with the therapist. To interview the same child with her or his parents will reveal immediately the parent-child dynamics and many aspects of the parents' management and disciplinary skills. To see the ADHD child with her or his siblings, without the parents present, will reveal important aspects of sibling interaction and bonding, as well as issues of respect, resentment, and scapegoating. To interview the same child with the entire nuclear family will reveal broader dynamics of parent-child dynamics and roles, the boundaries between the parental and sibling subsystems, the potential rigidity of the scapegoating, and the ADHD child's management of their own symptomatic and personal interactions within the family (e.g., manipulation or victimization).

As the reader will note, these issues are crucial to treatment and change for both the ADHD child and the family, but these occur at the clinical level *in addition to the actual cluster of specific ADHD symptoms.* A therapist who only sees the ADHD child individually in play therapy will be deprived of utilizing these rich and powerful resources in the therapy process.

A MODEL OF ASSESSMENT AND INTERVENTIONS FOR ADHD CHILDREN AND THEIR FAMILIES

In our practices, we have identified a model and sequence of interviews and interventions to facilitate three basic clinical goals:

1. Collect historical and family data to make an accurate ADHD diagnosis. Due to the complexity of these cases and the potential for intergenerational transmission, we view the use of a genogram as essential to the collection and organization of these families' data.
2. Recognize and evaluate the broader parent-child and family dynamics to identify points of intervention based on circularity, reciprocity, balance, and scapegoating.
3. Work directly with all relevant aspects of the family system to create effective change for the child and the family (Everett & Everett, 1999).

The following clinical model identifies the specific members and subsystems of the family with whom we are working and the goals of each. The sessions involved in each step of the model may range from one interview to four or five.

The parents. The initial interview for a symptomatic child involves the parents (both parents are expected to attend). The goals are (1) to identify relevant historical data about the child and the family regarding the origin and duration of the symptoms; and (2) to identify family dynamics and roles, interactional patterns, and the parents' views of the dynamics and symptoms.

The child or the parents. The initial sessions with children under the age of 4 years should occur in a play session with their parents present, rather than individually. This often provides a "safer" first experience for a young child in our offices and provides an immediate view of the parent-child dynamics and the parenting skills of the parents.

With older children, between 4 and 9 years, we will see them in a free play situation to view their attentiveness to the environment and toys, their abilities to sustain attention, their relative anxiety in a new physical setting, and their interactional style and skills with only the therapist present. Older children 10 and 11 years may be seen in play or in an individual interview. These sessions may be utilized partially for assessment purposes or for treatment purposes.

The parents—I. The next session involves providing feedback for the parents. However, in the broader treatment plan, this session is pivotal in that it creates an alliance between the therapist and the parents by supporting their concerns about their child and by giving them accurate feedback about the prognosis and treatment needs. The goals of this session are presented to the parents in the first meeting and they are advised at that time that after we get to know the child, we will share our observations and recommendations with them.

This session is conducted without the child present (we include ADHD adolescents in this feedback session). In this session we offer observations, identify the strengths and areas of concern regarding the child, and we relate symptoms that we observed to those identified by the parents and those identified historically. If there are sufficient symptoms present for a preliminary diagnosis of ADHD, we will spend the rest of the session offering psychoeducational information on ADHD in general, and we often recommend reading materials and other resources for the parents. For children over the age of 6 years, particularly those that are struggling in school, we will recommend psychoeducational testing. For the children who display clear symptoms of hyperactivity and/or inattention, we will begin to discuss the details and expectations of a recommendation for medications. However, we do not usually make the specific medical referral until we have had more time to work with the child.

It is often in this session that other family members with undiagnosed ADHD may be identified. Sometimes it is another child; often it is one of the parents. This phenomenon is quite common and the therapist needs to recognize the complicating overlay of new ADHD issues and dynamics that will be present throughout the family system.

We conclude this parent feedback session with the development of a treatment plan. We explain our goals to the parents and the specifics of why we may want to see their child individually or in sessions with the siblings or family.

The parents—II. In most cases of working with ADHD children, we actually begin therapy with the parents before we spend focused time on the symptomatic child. The reason for this is that the roles of the parents, their understanding and acceptance of the ADHD diagnosis, and their recognition of the associated family dynamics are crucial to all further treatment of the child. The therapist who fails to involve the parents in this early treatment process will find that her or his interventions may be sabotaged continually by the parents—sometimes inadvertently and sometimes intentionally.

Here we will discuss the impact of the ADHD child's symptoms on the entire family. Often we must deal with both parents who feel like a "failure" in their parenting because of their inability to improve or control their child's behaviors or functioning at home or at school. We also find high levels of conflict that have existed, perhaps for some years, between the parents over parenting strategies. By the time an ADHD child has reached the age of 8 to 10 years, and has several years of school dysfunctional history, some parents' marriages may be failing.

In these sessions we discuss the possibility of other comorbid symptoms, such as those described earlier. We will provide child management training as needed and attempt to alleviate family stress as quickly as possible through behavioral or structural interventions. We also will assess the relative parenting strengths and skills of each parent, their roles and relationships with the other children, their communication skills, and the relative strengths or conflicts in their relationships.

After specific interventions have been suggested in terms of parenting roles, discipline, behavioral management, and sibling issues, we will begin to work directly with the symptomatic child. The goals in working with the child include addressing emotional, behavioral, and interactional issues. Because young children are not very insight oriented, the role of play therapy is important in observing the child and teaching behavioral and cognitive changes. The therapist will encourage the child to become involved with selected play items and use this to reinforce the quality of play and enhance self-esteem, behavioral self-management, and self-reflection.

The therapist needs to be flexible in moving between individual play, parent-child play, and family sessions. We devote only a few sessions to the child individually because we believe that the more effective clinical interventions are going to involve the broader system of parents and siblings.

The child and parents in play therapy. These sessions need to be timed to occur after some progress has been made with the parents in their prior sessions—that is, in terms of accepting the ADHD diagnosis and understanding the struggles of the child instead of responding punitively or through scapegoating. It can become a significant therapeutic experience for an ADHD child to play successfully with one's parents without being the target of blame, criticism, anger, or resentment.

The therapist's goals here are to model effective parenting styles, reinforce the parents' management and communication skills with the child, and facilitate increased levels of humor, positive interaction, and playfulness between the parents and the child.

The siblings in therapy. In families where there are high levels of sibling conflict and animosity, we will schedule one or two sibling sessions. These are intended to observe the interactional patterns and roles among the siblings as a subsystem, and for the symptomatic child within the sibling group. In many cases the therapist will observe that the scapegoating of the ADHD child continues independently among the siblings. Certain siblings can be caustic, critical, and cruel toward the ADHD sibling. However, in some systems, the sibling group may be more accepting of the ADHD sibling and these siblings may present age-appropriate interaction and play. When this occurs, the therapist can assume that the dysfunctional family dynamics may be less rigid and ingrained.

In the sibling group session, the therapist will model appropriate behaviors as was modeled with the parents and the child, except they will be directed at sibling levels of communication and interaction. Often successful sibling group sessions can be used as an effective intervention resource to challenge patterns of scapegoating in the full family sessions. However, the therapist should not be surprised if, in the presence of the parents, a sibling takes on a parent's critical and blaming role toward the ADHD child.

The nuclear family therapy. These sessions can provide the basis for positive change within the family. However, they should be scheduled only after some progress has been seen in the attitudes and behaviors of the parent, and some progress has been made in the symptomatic child's response to the parenting changes. If these nuclear family sessions are conducted prematurely before a foundation of change has been created, the ongoing conflict and chaos within the family will simply be reenacted for the therapist. Such sessions can be not only unmanageable but move the therapy process backward.

The goals of these family sessions include blocking and extinguishing the scapegoating dynamics, supporting and empowering the positive changes for the parents in management skills for all of the children and in their specific relationship with the ADHD child, marking the parental boundaries to further empower their management roles, and repairing and enhancing the marital satisfaction and stability.

CASE EXAMPLE

To illustrate this model, we will use the case of a previously diagnosed ADHD boy, 8 years old. He was referred by his pediatrician, who said that he had medicated the boy for ADHD but "it did not seem to help him in school." In the initial session with the parents the boy's and family's medical history was unremarkable, and his hyperactive symptoms were present as early as 3 years of age. Both parents were frustrated due to complaints by his teacher that he was "not doing his work well" and may be "falling behind the other students." The child was seen initially in the playroom and, at the request of his parents, was not given his Adderall that morning. This play session confirmed the ADHD (predominantly impulsive and hyperactive). In unstructured play with the therapist, he was full of energy, moved from one toy or activity to another, and could not contain himself in wandering around the rest of the office. He did discuss his unhappiness in school, except for recess. One play session was sufficient to complete this initial assessment.

Before the parents' feedback session, the therapist talked briefly with the boy's teacher by phone. She explained that while at times he was distracted easily, she was primarily concerned that he was not able to remember his math tables and displayed difficulty when reading aloud. In the parents' session some of the boy's school work was reviewed, along with the feedback from the teacher. The therapist explained the possibility that there could be other cognitive deficits, in addition to the inattention, by saying, "Sometimes the ADHD symptoms, particularly the hyperactivity, mask these other difficulties—and some of these do not necessarily respond to the stimulant medications."

The therapist recommended two immediate interventions: (1) referral for psychoeducational testing to determine the child's cognitive strengths and weaknesses; and (2) referral to a child psychiatrist for a medication consultation. The therapist suspected that the Adderall may be prescribed by the pediatrician at too low of a dose.

Because many of the hyperactive and impulsive symptoms had been improved with the medications, it was felt that therapy should proceed concurrently with the other interventions. (In cases where the child has not been evaluated for medication, it is often best to postpone other therapy interventions until some progress is made with reducing symptoms.) One additional session was held with the parents to review basic child management issues for the hyperactivity and impulsivity. This session also focused on helping the parents understand the inattentive, and possibly cognitive, deficits that were also present. This involved issues of structure at home, time management, expectations, communication, homework assistance, and so on. While the parents were somewhat skeptical and frustrated, they were responsive. One additional play session was scheduled for the boy, not specifically for assessment, but to assist the therapist in connecting with him and to gain further data on his relationship with his older sister (10 years) and the family in general.

The next session was for the entire family. The goal was to observe the parents' roles with the children, as well as the sibling interaction. Here the family dynamics became clear: the parents were split, with the mother being the rescuer and mediator and the father being closer to the daughter and a bully toward the ADHD child. The son was being scapegoated by the father and both parents were allowing the daughter to demean her brother. She even commented on how "bad" he was doing in school. Two more family sessions were conducted to deal with setting boundaries for the parents and helping them learn about coparenting roles, to block the scapegoating, and to return the daughter to a sibling role with her brother. These were followed by one couple session to support their work on uniting their parenting and reinforce their new roles with both children.

The testing results reported an above average intelligence for the child. However, they also indicated clear deficits for the ADHD child in areas of "working memory" and "processing speed" (these are in an assessment area called cognitive processing). Because these do not always respond to stimulant medications, the frustration of the pediatrician and the parents for the "failure" of the medications to help the child in his school performance was explained. In addition, the child psychiatrist was concerned that the Adderall was leading to some mild appetite suppression for the child, so he changed the medication to Concerta. He also felt that the Adderall had been underdosed. The testing data did not indicate that the child needed tutoring in any specific areas so the parents were referred to an educational consultant to help the child learn to work with the cognitive deficits in areas of study habits, preparation for and taking of tests, and managing academic projects. The therapist was asked at a later date to assist the school psychologist in developing a list of accommodations to help the student perform better in the classroom.

The outcome of the case included the child performing better in school due to assistance from the educational consultant; a more therapeutic level of his medications and improved self-esteem; and improvement in family interaction as the scapegoating stopped and the parents were able to maintain better boundaries for themselves and the children.

Special circumstances and participants. In working with *postdivorced and blended families,* the vulnerability of the ADHD child is heightened many-fold. The ADHD symptoms are exacerbated by increased levels of parental conflict, physical separation, and loss of the family's familiar structure. These can be devastating to the ADHD child who struggles through most of her or his childhood to maintain consistency and predictability. The experience of parental divorce can lead to more dramatic levels of behavioral distress and acting out, as well as school failure. The divorcing parent must also struggle to deal with the stress and conflict of a divorce while trying to maintain structure and parental consistency for all of the children. The ADHD child's former levels of attention and management may be lost in this experience for the parent and the child.

In these clinical situations, the therapist must develop reasonable strategies to include stepparents, remarried partners, step- and half-siblings. These interventions can follow the model sessions above. For example, sibling sessions may be held at first for biological siblings and then be expanded to include stepsiblings. Similarly, parent-child sessions may begin with the divorced biological parents, or with the remarried parent and spouse, and then be expanded to include the additional parents. The parents may need separate sessions for support and parenting education. Due to the disruptive role of the ADHD symptoms throughout a blended family system, the therapist must not overlook the role of other family members as either potentially sabotaging the therapy process or as offering a positive resource.

In the broader intergenerational family system, we have observed that the roles of *grandparents* may either be detrimental to the therapy goals or can be important resources. We believe that grandparents, even if they do not live in the immediate geographical area, need to be included in the overall therapy process. If they do not live nearby, we may have parents send the grandparents reading materials or checklists to help them understand the disorder. We also may include them in either personal telephonic interviews with the therapist or as a conference call with the entire family present. Many parents make a specific decision to be secretive about their participation in therapy, and choose not to reveal this to their parents.

Some grandparents, for example, may not believe in coddling or medicating a child with an ADHD diagnosis. They may be quite critical of the parents in not being able to manage or control the child. They may say, "We didn't raise you that way." This reinforces not only the parents' mismanagement of the child, but also increases the parents' frustration, stress, and sense of failure. By contrast, some grandparents have a more objective, supportive, and nurturing role with the ADHD child and can remain somewhat removed from the high levels of frustration experienced by the parents. These grandparents can become important resources for family interventions. We have benefited from the inclusion of grandparents in many intergenerational family sessions through their roles in helping us to therapeutically block and extinguish the scapegoating of the ADHD child by the parents and all of the siblings.

CONCLUSIONS

The diagnosis and treatment of ADHD in children involves a clinical awareness of a complex range of neurological, biochemical, genetic, behavioral, cognitive, emotional, and family dynamics—all coexisting simultaneously in the life experience of a young child within the context of the family. The therapist can benefit from the resources of an interdisciplinary team, and he or she also must be knowledgeable about the symptomatology, differential diagnoses, comorbid conditions, and the nature of the symptomatic child's experience within family, school, and social systems.

We believe that family therapy, enhanced by additional resources as needed, is the treatment of choice (see also Orr, Miller, & Polson, 2005). The therapist utilizing the broad resources of systemic family therapy can effect change at both an individual level and at a broader family interaction level. For positive outcomes to be lasting, interventions must target all levels of the individual's and family's dynamics.

REFERENCES

Ackerman, N. A. (1958). *The psychodynamics of family life*. New York: Grunne & Stratton.

Adesman, A. (2003). Effective treatment of Attention-Deficit/Hyperactivity Disorder: Behavior therapy and medication management, *Primary Psychiatry, 10*(4), 55–60.

American Psychiatric Association (1994). *Diagnostic and Statistical Manual* (4th ed.). Washington, DC: Author.

Barkley, R. A. (1997). *ADHD and the nature of self-control*. New York: Guilford.

Barkley, R. A. (1990). *Attention-deficit hyperactivity disorder: A handbook for diagnosis and treatment*. New York: Guilford.

Bell, N., & Vogel, E. (Eds.). (1961). *A modern introduction to the family* (rev. ed.). Glencoe, IL: Free Press.

Everett, C. A., & Everett, S. V. (1999). *Family therapy for ADHD: Treating children, adolescents, and adults*. New York: Guilford.

Hallowell, E. M., & Ratey, J. J. (2005). *Delivered from distraction: Getting the most out of life with attention deficit disorder*. New York: Balantine Books.

Levy, F., & Hay, D. (2001). *Attention, genes and ADHD*. Philadelphia: Taylor & Francis.

Nichols, W. C., & Everett, C. A. (1987). *Systemic family therapy: An integrative approach*. New York: Guilford.

Orr, J. M., Miller, R. B., & Polson, D. M. (2005). Toward a standard of care for child ADHD: Implications for marriage and family therapists. *Journal of Marital and Family Therapy, 31*(3), 191–205.

Pitts, G., & Wallace, P. A. (2003). Cultural awareness in the diagnosis of Attention-Deficit/Hyperactivity Disorder, *Primary Psychiatry, 10*(4), 84–88.

Pliszka, S. R. (2005). Recent developments in the neuroimaging of ADHD. *The ADHD Report, 13*(2), 1–5.

Popper, C. W. (1989). Diagnosing bipolar vs. ADHD. *Newsletter of the American Academy of Child and Adolescent Psychiatry. Summer*, 5–6.

Quinn, P. (1997). *Attention deficit disorder: Diagnosis and treatment from infancy to adulthood*. New York: Brunner/Mazel.

Rief, S. F. (2003). Educating the child with Attention-Deficit/Hyperactivity Disorder. *Primary Psychiatry, 10*(4), 61–65.

Williams, A., Chacko, A., Gabiano, G. A., & Pelham, W. E. (2001). Behavioral treatment for children with Attention-Deficit/Hyperactivity Disorder. *Primary Psychiatry, 8*(1), 67–72.

CHAPTER 11

Counseling Children and Families Experiencing Serious Illness

CATHERINE FORD SORI, PH.D., AND NANCEE M. BIANK, MSW

> Illness has, in effect, metastasized in this family, usurping and altering the normal functions and relations of family life. Says Peter Steinglass, "It can be like a terrorist, who has appeared on the doorstep, barged inside the home and demanded everything the family has."
>
> **—McDaniel, Hepworth, & Doherty (1993)**

When one family member is diagnosed with a serious illness, it takes over not only the life of the patient but drains the resources and energy from other family members as well. Some families respond to this crisis by seizing the opportunity for "emotional as well as physical healing. For others, the illness ravages everything in its path" (McDaniel, Hepworth, & Doherty, 1993, p. 21). Families are faced with the enormous task of needing to make treatment decisions, deal with the health care system, and manage the illness, while still maintaining some degree of normal family life in order to meet the individual needs of family members. To navigate this course successfully, families need to be flexible and cohesive to draw on their strengths and resources, as they must adapt to meet the unique demands of each stage of the illness.

This chapter discusses a myriad of issues that families face at various stages of an illness, and general ways that individual family members are affected when either a parent or child is ill. Next, the chapter explores specific concerns families face when a child is seriously ill, and finally, clinicians are introduced to family-centered interventions to strengthen family communication, adaptability, and cohesion as they cope with the ravaging effects of the illness.

COHESION AND ADAPTABILITY ACROSS STAGES OF ILLNESS

The concepts of adaptability and cohesion are important characteristics that have been related to how well families adjust to the demands of a serious illness in a child or parent. These demands change over the course of an illness, and Kazak (1989) points out that a family's ability to adapt must be viewed over time. Families that lack flexibility often get stuck when either the demands of the illness change, or the developmental needs of the patient change. For example, the mother of an adolescent with diabetes may have trouble allowing the adolescent to assume responsibility for testing his or her own blood sugar levels, making dietary adjustments, and taking required medication without parental supervision.

Family cohesion is characterized by emotional bonds and closeness among family members. Cohesion can be beneficial as children feel supported and that their family can function in the face of an illness to care for the needs of everyone. However, in families that are too cohesive parents may become overprotective and not allow children to develop autonomy (Kazak, 1989). Minuchin, Rosman, and Baker (1978) found that enmeshed psychosomatic families were characterized as being overprotective, rigid, and lacking in good conflict resolution skills. On the other hand, in families that are too distant and lack emotional closeness, patients might feel isolated in their experience. This can be especially difficult for children who have no one to share their fears with or turn to for answers to their questions about what is happening.

The ability to adapt and reorganize to the different stages of an illness is paramount when families face a long-term serious illness (Rait & Lederberg, 1990; Rolland, 1994). At the *time of diagnosis* of a serious illness in a parent or child, the family is often thrown into chaos and a crisis mode (see Loscalzo & Brintzenhofeszoc, 1998; Pearse, 1977; Rait & Lederberg, 1990). Families need to quickly gather resources and information in order to make informed treatment decisions, and begin to plan how to adjust to the realities of how the illness will change their lives (Rolland, 1994). This requires that families pull together and be able to quickly adapt and reorganize. In the face of this crisis some semblance of normal family life must also be maintained (Loscalzo & Brintzenhofeszoc, 1998; Pearse, 1977; Rait & Lederberg, 1990).

Families need flexibility to restructure roles and rules to ensure that the necessary tasks get done, and the needs of all family members are met (Rolland, 1994). One focus of treatment at this stage should be on helping the family to stabilize and begin the process of reorganization. Children still need to do homework, laundry needs to get done, and meals need to be cooked. The first thing families must do is to re-establish a sense of some stability. Counselors might also help family members express and process their emotions (Sherman & Simonton, 2001), and to normalize reactions such as fear, shock, anxiety, nightmares, and denial. Differences in how people cope with difficult emotions should also be uncovered and normalized. Another focus of treatment in the diagnostic stage is to help adults decide what information should be shared with children, and how to talk to their children in a manner that is developmentally appropriate. This is often very difficult for parents, who want to shield their children from the realities of a life-threatening illness.

In the treatment or *chronic stage* of an illness families often have reached some type of equilibrium and have adjusted to the new realities of family life (see Rolland, 1994). Counselors need to assess how families have restructured to adapt to the shifts in roles that occur at this stage of the illness (Loscalzo & Brintzenhofeszoc, 1998; Sherman & Simonton, 2001). For example, a father whose role was breadwinner and is now called on to also assume most of the cooking and cleaning may experience role overload. Adolescents may be asked to give up some outside activities to help out more at home, and may miss out on important school or social activities. An ill mother who is not able to care for her young children may feel robbed of her role identity and guilty for burdening her older children and spouse.

Families that are not able to adapt to the changing demands of the chronic stage may experience problems. For example, the mother of an ill child who devoted the majority of her time and energy into managing a child's initial crisis cannot maintain that pace over the long haul of the chronic stage (Rolland, 1994). The family must be flexible in order to protect her from caregiver stress. This may mean that other family members take over some of the caregiving or household tasks, or that extended family or friends come in to help out. Families who are more enmeshed or rigid may need encouragement to allow outside helpers to come in. It is also important to assess how the family has organized around the illness, to ensure that individual needs are being met. For example, caring for a chronically ill child may not leave much time, energy, or financial resources to devote to other children or for the couple's relationship. Counselors should acknowledge the efforts of family members to assume new roles while heralding family strengths and promoting adaptability.

At the *end of treatment* or remission for an illness such as cancer, families may experience ambivalent feelings (Loscalzo & Brintzenhofeszoc, 1998). On the one hand, there is great relief because treatment is over and the patient is doing well. But, on the other hand, there may be some anxiety and uncertainty (Sherman & Simonton, 2001). Many describe the feeling as waiting for the other shoe to drop. There is no longer the safety net of frequent doctor visits or ongoing treatment. Once again, the family experiences disequilibrium because the roles and structure that were necessary for the treatment stage are no longer appropriate (Rolland, 1994). Energies should be increasingly focused outward as families no longer need to organize around the illness in the same manner (Sherman & Simonton, 2001). However, to some comes the realization that "normal" family life will never exist again in quite the same way. For example, during the remission of a child's illness, parents often remain hypervigilant and overly protective, afraid the child might catch something, or that they might miss signs or symptoms that the illness has returned. This could interfere with the child's need to develop more autonomy and independence. Therapy at this stage may focus more on individual needs and family growth, and dealing with anxiety about any possible relapse (Sherman & Simonton, 2001).

If a *relapse* occurs in a disease such as cancer, the family is often thrust into a state of shock, increased anxiety, fear, hopelessness, grief, great uncertainty, and despair (see Christ, 1991; Pearse, 1977). Often adults ruminate on past treatment decisions that have failed (Loscalzo & Brintzenhofeszoc, 1998). Families need to pull together to reinitiate treatment and gear up for what is to come, and this will be more difficult for families who are less cohesive and adaptable. Families often have less outside support at this stage as friends and even family may distance themselves. Often insurance benefits are depleted and the family may be in a financial crisis. These families need much support and encouragement as they once again muster their waning resources to reorganize and make treatment decisions.

In the *terminal phase* of an illness there can be denial, anger, and anticipatory grief (see Rolland, 1994). Family members must confront the issue of mortality and the impending loss of a loved one. Families that are more disengaged may lack the cohesiveness and open communication skills necessary to manage the crisis of an impending loss. Families are often depleted physically, emotionally, and financially. Caregivers need support, regular breaks to avoid burnout, and encouragement to care for their own individual needs. Ideally, both the ill person and family members can be helped to accept the inevitable, and to reflect on the meaning of life. Although a time of great sadness, this can also be an opportunity to resolve past conflicts, and for families to openly share their love and how they appreciate one another. (See Biank & Sori [2006] for a more detailed discussion on the impact of death on family members.)

During this phase, children need to be kept informed and prepared for an impending death, and to be included in planning the funeral, if they wish (see Biank & Sori, 2006). Children will have many questions about death, dying, and their future. Too often, however, parents avoid talking with their children about these difficult issues (Barnes, Kroll, Burke, Lee, Jones, & Stein, 2000).

Rolland (1994) points out that the transitions between stages of an illness can be difficult, as unfinished business from a previous stage can impede adjustment. During transitions families must reevaluate their ability to cope and readjust to the changing demands of an illness. In all these stages, it is important that children be kept informed by being given accurate, age-appropriate information in order for them to feel the adults in their lives are trustworthy. The challenge is for parents to balance truthfulness with hopefulness, in order to optimize coping (Biank & Sori, in press-a).

THE IMPACT OF AN ILLNESS ON A FAMILY

Life-cycle stages. Families are impacted by an illness differently according to their stage in the family life cycle (Rait & Lederberg, 1990; Rolland, 1994). For example, when a parent with young children is seriously ill, the parents need to manage the anxieties that come with having a life-threatening illness. Special attention also needs to be paid to the needs of the young children: How to tell them about a diagnosis, answer their questions age appropriately, and help them express their concerns. If it is a young child who is diagnosed, the parents will need extra support because their illness experience is out of sync with their life-cycle stage, and is out of the frame of reference of their friends (see Rolland, 1994). This may leave them feeling especially isolated.

Beliefs, shared meanings, and past experiences of illness. A family's belief system can shape its attitude, flexibility, and adaptation to an illness (Rait & Lederberg, 1990). It is important to assess each person's belief about the cause of an illness. Some blame the patient for poor lifestyle choices. One parent may blame a child's genetic illness on the other parent. Parents may feel culpable for not being able to protect their child from getting sick. Children may feel responsible for the illness of a family member. For example, one boy believed he caused his brother's leukemia. His brother was diagnosed a week after a wrestling match where his brother's leg was accidentally bruised.

Illnesses can have different meanings to each person in the family, and this may stem from family of origin beliefs (Rolland, 1994). For example, in a family that has lost several members to cancer, this diagnosis can be wrought with terror and an expected negative outcome (Sherman & Simonton, 2001). Some families may talk openly about certain illnesses, and others may be private or secretive. Some illnesses, such as AIDS, have a stigma attached, and the family may be less comfortable discussing the illness. The family's cultural background is an important factor in assessing meaning and how openly families communicate about an illness.

It is also important to explore how each parent's original family organized around an illness. What happened when someone got sick? How did the family talk about the illness? What were they not permitted to discuss? One spouse may have come from a family where everyone rallied around the ill person, while the family of the other spouse didn't talk about it. How did these families care for dying family members? Were they able to talk openly about death? What were the children told and how were they prepared? Did they participate in the funeral rituals? How did family members grieve? These differences need to be identified, discussed, and normalized.

Family communication. Sometimes family members will attempt to protect one another by being overly optimistic, or by avoiding sharing any difficult emotions (Sherman & Simonton, 2001). Too often, this leaves individuals with little choice but to attempt to cope and make sense of the illness and the changes in isolation, just at a time when more cohesion would be helpful (Rait & Lederberg, 1990; Sherman & Simonton, 2001).

Counselors can help by normalizing the disruption illness can have on family life. Ideally family members should be encouraged to openly communicate about how each is impacted by the illness and changes in the family roles and structure. Families can be gently persuaded to share their experiences, and to develop pockets of normalcy, where they are not focused on illness-related demands. This may mean scheduling a family night every Friday, with board games and popcorn. Couples, too, need to set aside time for intimacy, to talk, but not about problems or the illness; to touch, relax, laugh, and enjoy one another.

Often parents want to protect children from the reality of a life-threatening illness. It is strongly suggested that parents share information in an age-appropriate and timely manner; otherwise, children have a tendency to create their own reality, which often is worse than the truth. Many children do not ask questions or let their parents know how they are being affected, so counselors need to encourage parents to take the lead in discussing the illness.

Parents should share information objectively using concrete language that the children can comprehend. Children should be given honest, factual information that balances hope with reality. The tone should be matter-of-fact, and children should be encouraged to ask any questions they have. Children should be reassured that they will be kept up to date on what is happening. This builds trust and allows children to relax and let go of worry (Biank & Sori, 2003c). Children also benefit by having someone to talk to outside the immediate family, such as an aunt, grandparent, or school counselor.

Social support. Sometimes it is necessary to look outside the family for resources in order to maintain a balance for everyone (Rait & Lederberg, 1990). For example, both children and adults need to identify their "support team" (see Biank & Sori, in press-a) of people who are willing to offer emotional and practical help with specific tasks, such as grocery shopping, driving children to activities, or being a family liaison who passes information on to others. A closed family system will have a more difficult time allowing outsiders in to help, but needs to be encouraged to do so, especially when an illness is chronic and caretaking requires the pacing of a marathon (see Rolland, 1994).

Prior stressors. Families who have prior stressors, such as marital conflict, financial difficulties, job loss, child problems, or parental addiction or psychopathology, may have a more difficult time coping with the demands of an illness. Multicrisis families—those who live in poverty, are unemployed, lack access to health care, have other family members with an illness or disability, are going through a divorce, or are single-parent families with little outside support—are at special risk. These families may need supplementary assistance and possible referrals to outside agencies for additional sources of support. These may include referrals to psychiatrists, social workers, or collaboration with the family's clergy member. Clinicians should look for evidences of individual and family strengths and help to foster resilience in children, for example by helping them to build and utilize a support team (Biank & Sori, in press-a; Klimes-Dougan & Kendziora, 2000).

SPECIAL CONSIDERATIONS WHEN A CHILD IS ILL

Parental reactions to a child's serious illness. Parents are supposed to be able to protect their children from danger, and the diagnosis of a life-threatening or debilitating illness in a child can be devastating. On diagnosis, a parent's initial reaction is often shock or denial. Parents may feel emotionally distraught, and experience a deep sense of mourning and grief (Pearse, 1977). There is a sense of being overwhelmed as they try to learn about the illness, navigate medical and insurance systems, and make life and death treatment decisions. The family also must learn how to care for a sick child at home, while earning a living, taking care of other children, and sometimes ill parents as well. Many parents experience guilt for not recognizing symptoms earlier and for failing to protect their child (Pearse, 1977; Rolland, 1994). They question whether they took proper care of their child prior to the diagnosis, and may become overprotective and doubt their parenting skills. This may result in separation anxiety in the child and discipline problems. Numerous studies have found high levels of parental anxiety, depression, sleep problems, and posttraumatic stress disorder (PTSD) symptoms in parents of pediatric cancer patients, and these symptoms are prevalent and long-lasting (see Die-Trill & Stuber, 1998; Hill & Stuber, 1998).

It is important to note the reciprocal impact that is created: Just as parents are impacted by a sick child, both sick and well children are impacted by the emotional reactions of their parents. Many children feel guilty for worrying their parents, so they don't share their own fears, anxieties, or questions.

Couple's relationship. Having a child with a serious illness, such as cystic fibrosis or cancer, can seriously impact the marital relationship (Kazak &

Nachman, 1991; Rolland, 1994). Previous marital issues get put on hold, but often resurface when emotions are high, energy is depleted, or treatment ends. Roles can become skewed, with mothers often taking on the role of caregiver and fathers focusing on providing for the family. Often there is little time or emotional energy to focus on the couple's relationship apart from the illness. Partners can become isolated and tensions can build as mothers focus most of their attention on the ill child. This leaves the father and well siblings feeling excluded and isolated. As mentioned earlier, couples need to be encouraged to carve out time to connect in ways that are not related to the illness. Asking a relative to help out so a couple can have an intimate evening can be crucial in reducing stress and helping couples stay close.

Emotional impact of illness on a child or adolescent. Children diagnosed with a serious illness, such as pediatric cancer, often experience an array of emotions, including increased anxiety, depression, panic (Frager & Shapiro, 1998), regression, withdrawal from peers, separation anxiety, and attachment issues (e.g., clinging or distancing). Boys can be more adversely affected than girls. Ill children need to know what is happening to their bodies, but parents are often reluctant or unsure how to share a life-threatening diagnosis with their child. One girl who was HIV-positive was simply told that the treatments she was getting were because she was anemic. Counselors need to spend time with parents in helping them make decisions about what to share with a child about his or her diagnosis, as well as what to tell siblings.

Children whose appearance has been altered due to surgeries or from the side effects of medications are often dismayed at the physical changes, and that they look different than their peers. They also may be afraid that they will never regain their normal appearance or activity level. Some may experience not being recognized due to physical changes that are the result of treatment (such as hair loss, significant weight gain, or loss of limbs), and may even be mistaken for the opposite sex. Counselors and parents need to be sensitive to these emotions, especially among teens.

It should be noted that repeated hospitalizations, separations, and treatments often interfere with normal family relationships. For example, an ill child and a parent may move to a distant city for specialized treatment for an extended period of time, often a year or more. The social, academic, emotional, and physical development of all children is impacted due to the separation and isolation experienced by children who lose their normal context of family, school, peers, and community.

Adolescents. The illness experience may leave adolescents feeling more dependent, and paradoxically, also more mature as they have been forced to face adult issues, including their own mortality. Overprotective parents interfere with the adolescent's need for autonomy. Parents of adolescents coping with illnesses like diabetes, cancer, or cystic fibrosis may struggle with their teenager about managing their illness and related decision-making issues, including taking their medications or going for treatments, such as chemotherapy (Sawyer, Couper, Kennedy, & Martin, 2003). In an attempt to gain independence or control, or to deny the reality of a serious illness, adolescents are often noncompliant with medication regimes or dietary needs (see Die-Trill & Stuber, 1998). This may be an attempt to control something about their own body, when adolescents feel they have little or no control over what is happening to them. These issues can polarize parents and children, and can seriously impact adolescent development. For example, survivors of childhood cancer have been found to leave home later, marry later or they may never marry, have lower educational goals, and more employment problems (see Hill & Stuber, 1998). Clinicians need to help these families to balance the child's need for increased autonomy with the parents' need to ensure their child is complying with treatment and dietary regimens.

Sexual development. Some illnesses affect normal adolescent sexual development. For example, treatments for cancer can delay puberty and affect the development of sexual identity in an adolescent (Woolverton & Ostroff, 1998). Treatments can cause sterility and the loss of bodily hair, including pubic hair. Thus, sexual exploration is curtailed and the adolescent experiences a regressive pull back into the family.

Terminally ill children. Parents may not be able to accept a terminal diagnosis for their child themselves, let alone share the diagnosis with the child or other family members. Yet children who are dying are often aware of what is happening to their bodies. Some want to talk about it. Most need to be assured that they will not be alone, and that they will be loved and cared for. Many have questions about an afterlife, and some may want to talk to clergy. Counselors need to offer much support to parents in this predicament, and be open to exploring the child's spiritual and religious issues and questions (see Biank & Sori, in press-b).

Well siblings. Well siblings are often more adversely affected by the illness and the emotional reactions of their parents than the ill child. For example, many well siblings of children with cancer are impacted as much or even more than their ill sibling in areas such as fear, lowered self-esteem, and social isolation (Rait & Lederberg, 1990). Healthy siblings also have been found to experience symptoms of PTSD (see discussion in Hill & Stuber, 1998). However, other studies report siblings have a more positive outcome (see Rait & Lederberg, 1990; Rolland, 1994).

These children experience multiple losses, including the loss of parents' time and attention, and resources, such as time with their friends, and money for activities. They may experience a family identity crisis as they are no longer "normal" like their friends' families. Often they are farmed out to relatives while their sibling goes through lengthy treatment, and may be uninformed for long periods as to what is happening. Frequently, while given little information, children are asked to adapt to changes in the family structure, roles, rules, and activities. Many are called on to assume adult responsibilities, and may feel burdened and overwhelmed.

Well siblings can experience a wide range of emotions, such as confusion, anxiety, and worry that they or a parent will also get sick. They may also endure feelings of jealousy due to the increased attention given to the sick child, and simultaneously feel guilty for being jealous of the ill sibling, as well as for causing the illness (Rolland, 1994). Children who are egocentric experience magical thinking and may believe that they not only had the power to cause the illness, but they also have the power to cure it.

These children also have a fear of death: not only their sibling's, but their parents' and their own. Children frequently wonder, "If everyone dies, who will take care of me?" When not directly told about what is happening, and because there may be an air of secrecy in the family, children often listen at keyholes and pick up much misinformation. For example, one mother found one of her children crying disconsolately. Although reluctant to talk at first, the child finally confessed that she'd overheard her mother talking on the telephone, saying, "You mean we only have two weeks left?" The child assumed this meant her sibling would die in two weeks. However, the mother was talking to an insurance representative about filing medical papers! Too often, children are afraid to ask questions, discuss their feelings, or ask for support for fear of further burdening their parents. Many well children develop somatic complaints (Rolland, 1994) (often similar to the ill child) and experience sleep disturbances. Some go through a decline in school performance due to decreased concentration, a lack of structure at home, depression, or sleep deprivation. This can lead to school phobia and withdrawal from one's peers. For others, school can offer a "pocket of normalcy," where they can forget for a time about the illness.

Grandparents. The role of grandparents must be noted. They worry not just about their grandchild, but also about what their adult child is going through. Grandparents can be a tremendous source of emotional and practical support, or they may cause a further drain on the family by requiring emotional buttressing from their adult child, who is already overburdened. In addition, grandparents may contribute to divisiveness in the family by questioning or interfering with treatment decisions. In either case, it is sometimes helpful to include grandparents (or other extended family) at some point in counseling to assess their role, the impact of the illness on them, and their ability to support the family.

The role of the school in keeping a child on track developmentally. Next to the family, school and friends make up the majority of a child's social life (see Pearse, 1977). In school, kids learn to work together cooperatively, form friendships, discover how they are perceived by others, and recognize how their actions affect others. School is practice for the future. It teaches self-discipline, reinforces rewards for good work, and introduces children to external controls that the world imposes. Children benefit from both vertical (teacher, principal) relationships, as well as horizontal (classmates, teammates) relationships that are experienced in a school setting. School provides part of the foundation for a child's developing self-concept and self-esteem. A good school experience promotes healthy cognitive, social, psychological, and even physical development. Anything that interferes with school can seriously affect the child's entire life—present and future.

This points to the necessity of helping ill children maintain a connection to the school environment (see Pearse, 1977). When a child is absent for long periods of time, he or she loses connections to friends, and cognitive development can also suffer. Parents need to work with teachers in order to maintain these connections. In addition, parents need to be encouraged to help a child return to school as soon as he or she is medically able. Often, when children are reluctant to return to school it is because there were preexisting incidences of learning or school problems prior to the diagnosis. There could also be preexisting family problems that prevent timely school reentry, such as an overprotective parent who is afraid to allow the child to return to school. Ethnic factors may influence a child's reentry, and non-English-speaking parents may have increased difficulty. The child who has had many rich and satisfying social relationships and whose parents were involved with the school before diagnosis has much more to look forward to in returning to a normal school life.

Schools need to be aware of children's medical condition, and how it might impact the child in the classroom. For example, children who have undergone radiation or intrathecal chemotherapy often experience late side effects that can impair their cognitive functioning and lower their IQ. A second round of treatments can cause even more serious impairment. Cranial radiation affects nonverbal memory and causes subtle learning problems. Many children who've undergone treatment for brain tumors need special education classes due to a decline in IQ, memory, and attention problems. These deficits are not often identified on IQ tests, but commonly affect reading, spelling, and math. There is much research in this area, some of which is contradictory (Hill & Stuber, 1998; Kingma, Van Dommelen, Mooyaart, Wilmink, Deelman, & Kamps, 2002; Kramer, Crittenden, DeSantes, & Cowan, 1997; Steinhertz & Simone, 1998; Walch, Ahles, & Saykin, 1998). Because physicians may be reluctant to share this research with parents, parents are often unaware of the late effects of pediatric cancer treatment. Counselors need the skills to collaborate with physicians and teachers, to empower parents to seek information (McDaniel, Hepworth, & Doherty, 1992), and to advocate for testing and any special services their child might need.

For example, one family was referred to a family therapist who worked with illnesses by the social worker in a pediatric oncology unit at a hospital. The 6-year-old boy had been out of school for many months receiving treatment, had recently returned to first grade, but was having a terrible time learning. Every evening when his mother attempted to help him, he would end up crying hysterically, throwing his books, and sobbing, "I can't do it anymore! Something happened to me and I can't learn! I wish I'd died!" The family counselor consulted with the hospital social worker, and learned that this family had received no information about the possible late effects of cancer treatment in young children. First, the family counselor referred the parents back to the physician for this information, and then helped them to accept the implications of this in their son's life. The parents also were encouraged to contact their school superintendent and ask him to send a school counselor to a free seminar the therapist was offering, which explained the educational and social needs of children with cancer in the school. After this seminar, the school counselor called the mother, and apologized for not being sensitive to her son's predicament. She vowed to begin seeing him weekly and to refer him for testing. The boy did need special services, and once these began his school performance improved. The therapist also worked with the family to help them all begin to share their experiences and the changes they had endured since the son's diagnosis. The boy's older brother, who felt guilty for doing so well in school, also benefited from participating in a special group for children who have a sibling or parent with cancer.

STRENGTH-BASED FAMILY TREATMENT

Summary of factors associated with adaptive coping. Certain factors have been associated with adaptive coping in families experiencing the serious illness of a family member. These factors include:

- Family cohesion (Rolland, 1994; Sherman & Simonton, 2001)
- Open communication (Kazak & Nachman, 1991), and good problem-solving skills (Rolland, 1994)
- Adaptability that allows the family to shift roles, responsibilities, and family organization at different stages of the illness and based on the life-cycle stage of the family (Rolland, 1994; Sherman & Simonton, 2001)
- Permeable boundaries that allow for outside support for the family (see Kazak & Nachman, 1991)
- An ability to maintain hope and see positive benefits to the illness experience (Sherman & Simonton, 2001)
- The ability to put the illness in its place and maintain as much "normalcy" as possible (see McDaniel, Hepworth, & Doherty, 1992)
- Marital satisfaction (Kazak & Nachman, 1991)
- Few prior or concurrent stressors (e.g., marital conflict, financial instability, unemployment, family of origin conflicts) (Kazak & Nachman, 1991)

Goals of family treatment. From these factors the goals of family treatment can be derived. Sherman and Simonton (2001) state the four goals of family treatment are: (1) enhancing communication and emotional contact within the family; (2) addressing illness-related changes in family structure; (3) finding meaning in illness; and (4) managing mortality issues (p. 193). Families also need to be encouraged to seek and utilize outside support, and to learn to balance the demands of an illness with the needs of individual family members. Finally, it is important to explore hidden individual and family strengths and evidences of resiliency, both in the current and in past instances of family illness.

Creative Techniques

Family play (Gil, 1994) is especially useful in working with illness-related issues. It allows the clinician to get to know the child and family apart from the illness, and play is a developmentally appropriate method to engage children in a safe and nonthreatening manner. It will provide much information about individual and family functioning, and it decreases both children's and adult's defensiveness and resistance. Play exposes underlying and often unrecognized feelings and thoughts—as well as family issues—in a nonthreatening manner. Families become reenergized as they engage in enjoyable and expressive activities, which is often a relief from the tensions and worries that characterize these families. Playful activities provide family fun and enjoyment that lessen inhibitions and can lead to deeper levels of communication. Finally, family cohesion is strengthened as families experience a sense of working and playing together. Three illness-related goals are listed here, with suggestions for creative activities that promote family cohesion, adaptability, and emotional expression.

First, in order to promote family discussions about how the illness has changed the family, members may be asked to draw pictures of their family now, before the illness, and to draw themselves having fun in the future. These drawings may be done individually, each person can share, and the family can discuss each drawing. Families also can do a family mural drawing where they collectively create scenes of the family before and at different points in the illness experience. Clinicians can observe how the family organizes around this task, how they make decisions, their communication styles, level of enjoyment, and type of affect (see Gil, 1994).

Families also may create a "family book" that describes who they are and what their experiences have been. Each page could contain a sentence stem for the family to complete. For example:

- My family is important to me because …
- The illness has negatively changed my family in the following ways …
- The illness has changed my family in good ways, such as …

- Write a letter to the illness
- Draw a picture of the illness
- What we have learned about our family is …
- Good things about my family include …

Readers are referred to use the "Spin Me a Yarn" activity (Biank & Sori, 2003b) for a creative and fun activity that opens family communication and identifies individual and family strengths as well as concerns. As family members hold a piece of yarn and toss the ball to one another, they answer questions such as, "What has changed the most in my family since the illness?" "What is one thing that I miss the most?" "What is special about me and my family?" In the end they have created a web of yarn that connects them in their shared experiences.

The second goal is to help siblings share their unique experiences, especially when a child is ill. Enactments can be introduced, where siblings share what they like, envy, or resent about each other. They can be encouraged to make lists of the advantages and disadvantages the other has. What do well siblings think is the hardest thing about being sick? What do ill children think their well siblings would say is a benefit of being ill? How can they help each other?

A third important goal is to help children express their emotions in a healthy manner. They might be given a plain T-shirt and asked to decorate it with pictures of good family times. Clinicians should help children develop a language for feelings, and understand that we can experience two feelings at the same time. "Feeling Faces" (Biank & Sori, 2003a) is an activity in which children learn that we all have both inside feelings (that we keep to ourselves), as well as outside feelings that we show to others. They can draw examples of and discuss inside and outside feelings, while clinicians normalize this experience to both parents and children. For example, it is not uncommon for children to depict that inside they feel sad, scared, and worried, but outside they want to appear happy, happy, and happy.

"Pie Scapes" (Sori & Biank, in press) is a two-part activity for children and families. Using paper plates to depict pies, family members first draw proportionate slices to depict their daily activities. This allows everyone to share how much of their daily time is centered on managing the illness and treatment. Next, they use another paper plate "pie" to illustrate their thoughts and feelings. Families can also draw "pies" that represent how they were before the illness, which opens a discussion for how the illness has altered people, activities, thoughts, and feelings to varying degrees. In one family with an ill child, the boy indicated that much of his time was spent on illness-related activities, whereas before the diagnosis he had spent a good deal of time playing soccer and riding his bike. Before he became ill his feelings included a large "slice" of "having fun"; while currently his biggest slice was "worried." His mother's current pie also depicted a large slice of worry, while her husband's (the optimist) had no worry at all! This opened a discussion between the couple about their differences in coping with their son's life-threatening illness. The sister's "pie" showed anger, and she was able to express her anger at not getting as much attention as her younger brother. This helped her parents see the need to balance their time and energies between both children.

Family Sessions

Family sessions should help promote open sharing of individuals' illness experience, and offer an opportunity to ask questions and reflect on how the family has been impacted and how they are coping. Sherman and Simonton (2001) suggest using circular questions, such as "Who has been the most affected by the illness?" to open communication. An overarching goal is to help families "put illness in its place" (Gonzalez, Steinglass, & Reiss, 1989; McDaniel, Hepworth, & Doherty, 1992). This means that the illness does not permeate every aspect of the family's life. Time and attention are set aside for normal family activities, and for relationships within and outside the family, thus allowing for normal individual development. Family sculpts (see Dermer, Olund, & Sori, 2006; Sherman & Simonton, 2001) are useful to ascertain the degree to which the family has organized around the illness, and how family members are being impacted. Families also should be encouraged to resume family rituals, such as birthday or holiday celebrations (Sherman & Simonton, 2001). These help families maintain a sense of normalcy and hopefulness when facing an uncertain future. Additional ideas are detailed at the end of this chapter in Appendix A, "Family Sessions When There is Illness in a Family Member."

Brief Case Vignette

A social worker from a hospital pediatric oncology unit called to refer Jamaal and his family for counseling. Jamaal had been treated for acute lymphocytic leukemia (ALL) and was in remission and doing well at home. However, even though the doctor had given him a release to return to school two months previously, he had yet to return.

Jamaal Jackson was a 10-year-old African-American boy, and the youngest of three siblings. He lived with his mother, his 20-year-old brother, his 18-year-old sister, and his brother's girlfriend and their newborn baby. His parents had never married, but his father visited him frequently in his mother's home. The older two children had different fathers.

All the family except for Jamaal's father attended the first and most family sessions. Jamaal was a quiet boy who had gained significant weight due to the medications he'd taken to treat the cancer. In giving a history of the illness, Mom revealed how he had come to be diagnosed. The year before Jamaal had not felt well and had several bruises. She took him to a clinic, where the physician sent them immediately to a local hospital for tests. Ms. Jackson was told that she would be called as soon as the results of the tests were in. For a month she called the hospital, and was repeatedly told the results were not yet available. Finally she was able to get through to the referring physician, who called the hospital and learned that Jamaal's tests had been lost. He was retested and they learned that he had leukemia. Jamaal was immediately sent to a children's hospital in a nearby city to begin treatment, and remained there for several months.

Each of the family members shared what this experience had been like for them. The older siblings said they'd been worried about both their little "bro," as well as their mother. Because Mom worked day shift in the garment industry, the boys and other extended family members had taken turns visiting Jamaal daily. During this time, Jamaal's father would visit him once or twice a week, but never stayed very long. Everyone in this close-knit family was happy that Jamaal was in remission and doing better. However, when asked how he felt, Jamaal said he was tired most of the time and spent his days while Mom was at work napping on the couch and watching TV. When asked about friends before his illness, Mom said Jamaal had friends at school, but that "school was for school and home was for home"—so he had never had friends over to his house, and had seldom engaged in any extracurricular after-school activities.

When the counselor discussed the doctor's concern that Jamaal was not yet back in school, Mom seemed ambivalent. While she agreed that school was important, she seemed reluctant to push him to go. She preferred to chat about how close she was to her children, and how Jamaal had always been a homebody. Her bigger concern in coming to counseling was actually her daughter, who had dropped out of high school after Jamaal was diagnosed, and now seemed to want to party all the time. Formerly she had not been in any serious trouble, but recently she had been arrested for reckless driving and soon had to appear in court. Her older son was the "man of the house"—the one she leaned on and depended upon for both emotional support and to help run the home. She was worried that because he now had his own family, perhaps she shouldn't lean on him as much. Throughout this discussion, none of her children spoke. The therapist commented on how loving her children were, and how each of the older two had found ways to distract Mom so she didn't worry so much about Jamaal. They looked confused, but smiled vaguely. This opened the conversation about how the family was coping with all the recent events and changes, including the birth of the first grandchild.

The counselor met alone with Jamaal to get to know him better as an individual, and to see what his goals were. He said he really didn't care for school and didn't want to return, but wouldn't elaborate. In discussing what the hardest part of his illness had been, Jamaal said that he didn't understand why his father had not visited him in the hospital more often, and why he never got to go to his father's house.

In individual time with Mom, she disclosed that when she was pregnant with Jamaal she learned that his father was already married and had other children. While her two older children knew of this, it was a secret from Jamaal. The other family lived in the same community and, in fact, Jamaal had a half-brother a year younger who attended his school. Mom confessed that she was very worried that Jamaal would find out the secret about his half-brother, who was a grade behind him. In discussing the family secret, Mom said she knew she would have to tell Jamaal about his father's other family some day, but she just was reluctant to do so. The counselor wondered what role the secret might have on Jamaal's failure to return to school.

When seen individually, Jamaal did a fill-in-the-blank story about having cancer, and drew a picture of himself and his family before cancer, after his diagnosis, and now. He did the "feeling faces" activity, and shared his drawings with Mom and his siblings. These showed that inside he often felt worried, sad, and scared, but outside the faces he wore showed no real emotions. He was clearly keeping his feelings bottled up inside. This created an opportunity for everyone to talk about the masks that they wore and their underlying emotions.

In one individual session when the counselor was exploring with Jamaal what his school experience had been like before he was sick, and how he felt about returning, Jamaal blurted out that he knew "the secret," and why Mom was "afraid" for him to return. With his permission, this information was shared with his mother at the end of the session, and she agreed that it was time for them to talk. The counselor also talked with Mom about the importance for Jamaal to return to school, and how she might encourage him to develop outside friendships and participate in some extracurricular activities (with the doctor's permission), in order to keep him on track developmentally. Unfortunately, Mom never persuaded Jamaal's father to attend family sessions.

In the last session, Ms. Jackson shared that she and Jamaal had talked, and both seemed relieved to finally have the secret out in the open. As Jamaal asked questions about his father and his parent's relationship, he was quiet and seemed to just absorb the whole story. At the end of the session he finally agreed to go with Mom to meet the school counselor to plan his school reentry. They were even talking about Jamaal joining scouts!

In a follow-up phone conversation, Mom said that counseling had helped her to see she needed to let go a bit of all her children, and to focus on creating more of a life for herself apart from her children. She was thinking about taking an evening class, and even considering dating again.

This was a family in which there was a convergence of life-cycle and developmental issues that intersected with illness-related concerns. These included how the illness had impacted the older children at their stages of development, how their previous roles became more polarized as they both tried to distract Mom from her worries, and from how she had to handle the serious illness of her youngest child with little support from Jamaal's father. This rather enmeshed family had done well in pulling together in the crisis and treatment stages of Jamaal's illness, but was having difficulty being flexible enough in the recovery stage to allow Jamaal and his siblings more autonomy. They were also at a transitional stage in the family life cycle—launching children and becoming a grandparent. The issue of the family secret was brought to a head as Mom became aware that Jamaal knew, and that it was interfering with him returning to school. Mom realized that she had ambivalent feelings about him returning herself, and that she wanted to keep him safe and protected at home.

Counseling gave each person in the family an opportunity to share their experience of the illness, as well as recent changes in the family. It opened communication enough to give Jamaal permission to begin to express his hidden emotions about the illness, and the impact the secret was having on him. Above all, Mom was able to see the importance of helping Jamaal return to school, and allowing all of her children more space to develop autonomy. In doing so, she was also able to begin to develop her own personal life.

REFERENCES

Barnes, J., Kroll, L., Burke, O., Lee, J., Jones, A., & Stein, A. (2000). Qualitative interview study of communication between parents and children about maternal breast cancer. *BMJ, 321,* 479–482.

Biank, N., & Sori, C. F. (2003a). Feeling faces prevent scary places. In C. F. Sori, L. L. Hecker, & Associates, *The therapist's notebook for children and adolescents: Homework, handouts, and activities for use in psychotherapy* (pp. 3–8). Binghamton, NY: Haworth.

Biank, N., & Sori, C. F. (2003b). Spin me a yarn: Breaking the ice and warming the heart. In C. F. Sori, L. L. Hecker, & Associates, *The therapist's notebook for children and adolescents: Homework, handouts, and activities for use in psychotherapy* (pp. 83–91). Binghamton, NY: Haworth.

Biank, N., & Sori, C. F. (2003c). Tips for parents when there is illness in the family. In C. F. Sori, L. L. Hecker, & Associates, *The therapist's notebook for children and adolescents: Homework, handouts, and activities for use in psychotherapy* (pp. 150–156). Binghamton, NY: Haworth.

Biank, N., & Sori, C. F. (in press-a). Coping circles: Exploring children's ability to manage in times of stress. In C. Elias & L. Jameyfield (Eds.) *The therapist's notebook: Resources for working with children.* Binghamton, NY: Haworth.

Biank, N., & Sori, C. F. (in press-b). Integrating spirituality when working with children and families. In K. B. Helmeke & C. F. Sori (Eds.), *The therapist's notebook for integrating spirituality in counseling II: More homework, handouts, and activities for use in psychotherapy.* Binghamton, NY: Haworth.

Biank, N., & Sori, C. F. (2006). Helping children cope with the death of a family member, chap. 12 in this volume.

Christ, G. H. (1991). Principles of oncology social work. In A. L. Holleb, D. J. Fink, & G. P. Murphy (Eds.), *American Cancer Society textbook of clinical oncology* (pp. 594–605). Atlanta, GA: American Cancer Society.

Dermer, S., Olund, D., & Sori, C. F. (2006). Integrating play in family therapy theories, chap. 3 in this volume.

Die-Trill, M., & Stuber, M. L. (1998). Psychological problems of curative cancer treatment. In J. Holland (Ed.), *Psycho-Oncology* (pp. 897–906). New York: Oxford University Press.

Frager, G., & Shapiro, B. (1998). Pediatric palliative care and pain management. In J. Holland (Ed.), *Psycho-Oncology* (pp. 907–922). New York: Oxford University Press.

Gil, E. (1994). *Play in family therapy.* New York: Guilford.

Gonzalez, S., Steinglass, P., & Reiss, D. (1989). Putting the illness in its place: Discussion groups for families with chronic medical illnesses. *Family Process, 28,* 69–87.

Hill, J. M., & Stuber, M. L. (1998). Long-term adaptation, psychiatric sequelae, and PTSD. In J. Holland (Ed.), *Psycho-Oncology* (pp. 923–929). New York: Oxford University Press.

Kazak, A. E. (1989). Families of chronically ill children: A systems and social-ecological model of adaptation and challenge. *Journal of Consulting and Clinical Psychology, 57*(1), 25–30.

Kazak, A. E., & Nachman, G. S. (1991). Family research on childhood chronic illness: Pediatric oncology as an example. *Journal of Family Psychology, 4*(4), 462–483.

Kingma, A., Van Dommelen, R. I., Mooyaart, E. L., Wilmink, J. T., Deelman, B. G., & Kamps, W. A. (2002). No major cognitive impairment in young children with acute lymphoblastic leukemia using chemotherapy only: A prospective longitudinal study. *Journal of Pediatric Hemotology-Oncology, 24*(2), 106–113.

Klimes-Dougan, B., & Kendziora, K. T. (2000). Resilience in children. In C. E. Bailey (Ed.), *Children in therapy: Using the family as a resource* (pp. 407–427). New York: W. W. Norton & Company.

Kofron, E. E. (1993). The language of cancer. *The Family Therapy Networker, 17*(1), 35–43.

Kramer, J. H., Crittenden, M. R., DeSantes, K., & Cowan, M. J. (1997). Cognitive and adaptive behavior 1 and 3 years following bone marrow transplantation. *Bone Marrow Transplantation, 19,* 607–613.

Loscalzo, M., & Brintzenhofeszoc, K. (1998). Brief crisis counseling. In J. Holland (Ed.), *Psycho-Oncology* (pp. 662–675). New York: Oxford University Press.

McDaniel, S. H., Hepworth, J., & Doherty, W. J. (1992). *Medical family therapy: A biopsychosocial approach to families with health problems.* New York: Basic Books.

McDaniel, S. H., Hepworth, J., & Doherty, W. J. (1993). A new prescription for family health care. *Networker, (1),* 19–63.

Minuchin, S., Rosman, B., & Baker, L. (1978). *Psychosomatic families: Anorexia nervosa in context.* Cambridge, MA: Harvard University Press.

Pearse, M. (1977). The child with cancer: Impact on the family. *Journal of School Health,* 3, 174–179.

Rait, D., & Lederberg, M. (1990). The family of the cancer patient. In J. Holland & J. H. Rowland (Eds.), *Handbook of psychooncology: Psychological care of the patient with cancer.* New York: Oxford University Press.

Rolland, J. S. (1994). *Families, illness, & disability: An integrative treatment model.* New York: Basic Books.

Sawyer, M. G., Couper, J. J., Kennedy, J. D., & Martin, A. J. (2003). Chronic illness in adolescents. *The Medical Journal of Australia.* Retrieved November 2, 2003, from http://www.mja.com.au.

Sherman, A. C., & Simonton, S. (2001). Coping with cancer in the family. *The Family Journal: Counseling and Therapy for Couples and Families, 9*(2), 193–200.

Sori, C. F., & Biank, N. (in press). Pie scapes: Exploring children's thoughts and feelings. In C. Elias & L. Jameyfield (Eds.), *The therapist's notebook: Resources for working with children.* Binghamton, NY: Haworth.

Steinhertz, P. G., & Simone, J. S. (1998). Biology of childhood cancers. In J. Holland (Ed.), *Psycho-Oncology* (pp. 881–896). New York: Oxford University Press.

Walch, S. E., Ahles, T. A., & Saykin, A. J. (1998). Cognitive sequelae of treatment in children. In J. Holland (Ed.), *Psycho-Oncology* (pp. 940–945). New York: Oxford University Press.

Woolverton, K., & Ostroff, J. (1998). Psychosexual sequelae. In J. Holland (Ed.), *Psycho-Oncology* (pp. 930–939). New York: Oxford University Press.

APPENDIX A

FAMILY SESSIONS WHEN THERE IS ILLNESS IN A FAMILY MEMBER

(ADAPTED FROM THE WORKS OF ROLLAND [1994]; MCDANIEL, HEPWORTH, & DOHERTY [1992, 1993]; KOFRON, 1993; BIANK & SORI [2003A, 2003C, 2006, IN PRESS-A])

1. Encourage ill child and siblings to discuss how the illness has changed their lives. What are changes they don't like (e.g., additional chores, fewer vacations)? What's harder to do, and what is still possible? What are some positive changes (e.g., Mom is not working and is home more)?
2. Encourage children to discuss both what they like, and what they resent about each other. For example, a well sibling may like it that his brother is always a ready playmate, but resent that the sick child doesn't attend school and gets gifts from family and friends. The ill child appreciates his older brother's help with schoolwork, but resents that the well child can attend birthday parties, stay overnight with friends, and goes to the movies.
3. Encourage children to share their worries and concerns, and normalize these experiences. Facilitate this with verbal and nonverbal (art, play) activities that both teach about emotions ("inside and outside feelings") and facilitate their expression. Perhaps list any unanswered questions children have about the illness, treatment, and prognosis, and coach parents to answer their questions honestly and in an age-appropriate fashion. Families might fashion the illness out of clay, and then smash them! They might write a letter and/or draw a picture of the illness, or draw their "Impossible/Scariest Tasks" and what helps them do these things. This is fun and it helps children let go of fears and worries.
4. Encourage families to hold regular family meetings, where everyone can voice their complaints. Writing complaints down and then brainstorming together to come up with possible solutions promotes effective problem-solving skills, as well as family team-

work and unity, as everyone is free to share his or her ideas. (Kids are more likely to follow through if it was their idea in the first place!) Encourage the use of humor! Parents function as "Benevolent Dictators," promoting both justice and fairness. Discuss how vital everyone is in helping the family function.

5. Encourage children to plan a special surprise for their parents (e.g., candlelight dinner). Have parents and children discuss what fun activities they miss, and plan one special family time in the next week. Draw pictures of a future family outing or vacation.
6. Have children draw "Feeling Faces," and discuss how the family expresses emotions such as anger, fear, sadness, joy, appreciation. Have each person talk about who and what helps them to feel better if they are feeling down or stressed. Compile a list of positive ways to cope and how to soothe one's self. Have children and parents each list who is in their "Circle of Support."
7. Have each person share what is special about their family as a whole, and about each individual family member. What is one positive thing they have learned through this illness experience?

CHAPTER 12

Helping Children Cope with the Death of a Family Member

NANCEE M. BIANK, MSW, AND CATHERINE FORD SORI, PH.D.

> The grieving child is any child or adolescent who has experienced circumstances that alter what is known, what is safe, what defines life as they know it.
>
> **—Jennie D. Matthews (1999)**

Adults often struggle to understand death, and to confront their own fears about dying and the end of life. What then should children know of death? How can parents admit to the reality of death in the lives of their children? Parents' own anxiety often prevents them from discussing death with their children, as it is a parent's job to protect and avoid distressing the children who are part of themselves. Although children are exposed to death almost daily on television, cartoons, movies, and the news, talking honestly and openly about death is still a taboo subject in our society. Children's grasp of what death really means—that it is irreversible, inevitable, and universal—comes gradually, and is the result of both normal cognitive development as well as life experiences (Reilly, Hasazi, & Bond, 1983).

ASSESSING CHILDREN'S GRIEF

Webb (1993a) discusses the importance of examining three broad factors when assessing a bereaved child. These include individual factors, death-related factors, and systemic/contextual factors. When thinking about *individual factors* that affect bereaved children one must consider their age, stage of cognitive development, and temperamental factors. A 3-year-old will be unable to grasp the same concepts that a 10-year-old would understand. How children have adapted to changes and losses in the past (such as divorce, moves, loss of pets, or death of other family members) is also important to consider when assessing children. With each new loss, previous losses will be reactivated and may need to be revisited. All children who have experienced the death of a close family member should be assessed for depression and suicidality.

When a parent, sibling, or child dies, it is important to understand whether the death was sudden or expected, if the children were present at the death and had a chance to say goodbye, and if they participated in the funeral. The closer the relationship was the more difficult the loss. These *death-related factors* play a large role in how children adjust (Webb, 1993a).

Culturally, how a family experiences death can make a difference in how a child interprets the loss. Some families grieve silently while others wail. Some have strict religious rituals such as last rites, being buried before sundown, or sitting Shiva with family and friends. Therefore, it is important to understand both the nuclear and family of origin beliefs and practices about death and dying. These are all examples of *systemic/cultural factors* that will influence children's experience of a death (Webb, 1993a).

TYPE OF DEATH EXPERIENCE

There are variations in how children are impacted by a death, some of which are related to the type of death experienced by a loved one. This is an important consideration when assessing children and families who have experienced a loss. Webb (1993a) discusses several categories of death experiences and their implications.

Anticipated death. According to Webb (1993a), the period preceding an anticipated death can be very difficult for children. From the time they learn that the death will occur until the time that the person dies, children's lives are filled with tensions and wondering "what if." For example, "What if she dies before my dance recital? What if she's not here for my birthday to bake my special cake, or what if I'm alone with her when she dies—what do I do?" Even though they may have been told and they say they understand what death means, children often do not have a frame of reference to grasp the concept of death until it happens, and then it is as if they are hearing it for the first time. While they may have understood it on some level cognitively, they may not have integrated or internalized the information.

In addition, during the time preceding the death of a close family member, the adults may be preoccupied with caregiving and their own anticipatory grief, so children's needs may not have been met during this period. This loss of parental attention can leave children feeling abandoned, and they may experience anticipatory grief in isolation.

Families often experience many changes in the structure, roles, and emotional climate leading up to a death. Children often have to assume adult responsibilities, which may include housework, cooking, mothering younger children, and caregiving for the ill family member. Some may see school as a welcome respite, while others find it difficult to go to school and fit in with peers who are not facing such imminent loss. Many experience somatic complaints and a decline in school performance. Children may wonder who will be the next in the family to get sick and die. It is difficult for children and adolescents to face the coming death and how they will face the future. This period of anticipatory grief is often more intense than the grief felt after the death.

Sudden death. While children anticipating the death of a loved one struggle with many difficult issues and emotions, it is even more difficult when the death is sudden and unexpected, as in the case of a heart attack or accident (Webb, 1993a). Children may buffer themselves from the shock by using denial, and may act as if nothing has happened, refusing or unable to accept the reality and implications of the sudden, tragic loss. Adults and children alike often agonize over the perceived preventability of sudden deaths.

Traumatic death. Children often experience increased anxiety when the death is violent, such as a homicide, or traumatic, such as those from a natural disaster. They may feel the world is not a safe place and that disaster can strike again at any time. Children may also be more sensitive and afraid of pain. There are stigmas attached to some types of death, such as from AIDS, suicide, drugs, and even cancer (Webb, 1993a). These deaths may not be openly acknowledged or discussed, which can lead to a child feeling both shame and disenfranchised grief. All of these complicate the mourning process.

Deaths associated with disasters. At special risk are children who have been through a natural disaster, such as the recent experiences of thousands of children who lived in the southern United States that were devastated by Hurricane Katrina. Many of these children lost not only family members, but their homes, schools, playmates, pets, familiar toys and transitional objects, and their communities. In short, they have lost much of their context, most of what was familiar. These children must be carefully assessed for PTSD, depression, and even suicidality. One helpful resource is *After the Storm: A Guide to Help Children Cope with the Psychological Effects of a Hurricane* (La Greca, Sevin, & Sevin, 2005), which may be downloaded at http://www.psy.miami.edu/.

When losses are so severe and compounded, children and parents often need individual and/or group support, as well as family counseling to help them stabilize, restructure in a way that allows they to function, and come to terms with the meaning of so much loss. Counselors need to be comfortable addressing the many spiritual or religious issues that arise from such disasters with both children and adults (see Biank & Sori, in press-a).

In addition to these concrete losses, many children who go through natural disasters of such magnitude also experience ambiguous loss (Boss, 1999), when they have been separated from their family, have assumed the burden of looking for their loved ones, and are uncertain if they will ever be reunited. These children are left with the enormous uncertainty of what will happen to them, and who will take care of them if their parents or relatives are not found. Although it is outside the scope of this chapter to address the special needs of children who have experienced this degree of trauma, readers are referred to the works of La Greca, Silverman, Vernberg, and Roberts (2002), Gordon, Farberow, and Maida (1999), Webb (1991), Linesch (1993), Figley (1986), and Johnson (1998).

GRIEF AND THE FAMILY SYSTEM

Each member is uniquely affected when there is a death in the family. There is a reciprocal influence among how a death impacts individuals, how individual reactions influence family members, and how the family as a whole is altered. Unresolved past losses will prevent healthy grieving. For example, a new mother who never fully grieved the loss of her mother who died when she was pregnant now finds it difficult to grieve the death of her young child.

A family system can be affected by a death on many levels. Unresolved grief issues in adults may exacerbate the instability and chaos that initially occurs following a death. These issues can interfere with the necessary tasks of stabilization and then restructuring, which are necessary for families to function in order to provide a safe, stable environment during the grieving process. Problems that can arise include role reversals, in which children take care of a grieving parent, or a child becomes parentified and cares for grieving siblings because a parent is not emotionally available. Some children act out and become either family scapegoats, or try to be "perfect," both of which distract the family from their pain, but are potentially harmful to the child.

IMPACT OF LOSS ON A CHILD

Symptoms in grieving children. Bereaved children often experience a variety of physical symptoms in the aftermath of a loss. Matthews (1999) points out that a child's level of activity may initially be suppressed, or the opposite may occur and the child might appear rambunctious or overactive

(Klicker, 2000). Over a period of time, children who have lost a parent or sibling may experience changes in appetite and sleep habits, somatic complaints that may mimic those of the deceased, anxiety attacks, headaches, and frequent colds.

Emotionally, children may appear numb or confused, fearful, sad, angry or guilty (Matthews, 1999). The intensity of these emotions may feel so foreign and overwhelming that children may fear they are loosing their minds. It is not unusual for children to say they see or hear the deceased. This common experience actually helps them to finish unfinished business and continue the relationship with a dead parent or sibling. Children have a limited capacity to tolerate pain so they may grieve intensely for brief periods and then go outside to play to escape the pain. Grollman (1991a) points out that there is a thin line of demarcation between what are normal and abnormal grief reactions. The difference is not in symptoms alone, but in the degree of intensity and how prolonged these reactions are.

Younger children also lack the vocabulary to express intense emotions. Parents may not be emotionally available (Casini & Rogers, 1996), and unlike adults, children don't have easy access to outside sources of support. According to Matthews (1999), children may be apathetic and have little or no interest in peers or activities. Children often wonder if it was their fault, what the loss really means to them, and what will happen to them. They need special attention and support from parents or caregivers who can focus on their unique needs and experiences.

Behavioral changes that may occur include children acting out to seek attention or punishment (or to distract grieving adults), open defiance, or emotional withdrawal. Children may become distracted and more accident prone, and teens are at increased risk of substance abuse and sexual activity.

It is important to remember that loss changes a child's course academically, socially, personally, and economically. For instance, a family's finances may be drastically lower following the death of a parent, and children might have to move, change schools, and lose friends. Children may also no longer be able to participate in extracurricular activities or sports, which they previously enjoyed and which were part of their identity, as they attempt to adjust to the loss and a lowered standard of living. Academically, children's grades may suffer, due to all the losses which can interfere with concentration. They may become disruptive in the classroom or develop attendance problems (Matthews, 1999).

Loss erodes children's trust as they question an adult's ability to protect them from pain and suffering. At a time when the adults in the family are overwhelmed and distracted as they focus on their own grief and are unable to respond to their children's needs, children may feel they have no place to process their interpretation of the loss.

PARENTAL LOSS

The death of a parent is the most difficult for a child to experience. Their entire world is shaken as they struggle to make sense of the meaning of the loss. Children lose their innocence and trust because they no longer feel protected. Parents supply a foundation for their world and the death of a parent changes the definition of their existence. Children never really complete the mourning process until they are adults. They need to have two parents in order to grow and function well (Biank & Sori, in press-a). Therefore, it is helpful for children to access and share memories of their parents, be encouraged to keep the parent's love in their hearts so they can maintain the parent as an ongoing attachment figure (Batten & Oltjenbruns, 1999). At each developmental stage children need to revisit the loss, and make adjustments to their perceptions of the deceased parent and the meaning of the loss. For example, not having a mother at age 5 means there is no one to be room mother, and no one to make a Mother's Day present for at school. Not having a mom as an adolescent means there is no mother to discuss the facts of life and dating, or take you shopping for your first bra or first prom dress. It is often not until children are adults and have their own children that they are able to fully grieve the loss of a parent.

LOSS OF A SIBLING

Experiences before the death. Children who have experienced the death of a sibling often feel helpless in their grief. Depending on whether the death is from illness or is a sudden death, there may be unresolved emotional issues from circumstances in the family before the death (Casini & Rogers, 1996). When a brother or sister suffers from a chronic or life-threatening illness, well siblings often feel ignored. They may sense their parents are preoccupied or overwhelmed, and hesitate to ask for support or to have other needs met. There is a loss of attention from parents and extended family members, and children must adapt to changes in the family structure that were made as the family reorganized to meet the needs of caring for an ill child.

When a sibling is dying, well siblings may suffer from guilt over past behavior toward the dying sibling. They may be jealous and resent the attention that the sick brother or sister receives, and can even feel abandoned and that they are not valued by the family. Well children encounter a loss of normalcy, may have to give up activities because of a loss of resources, and may worry that things are forever changed. These children may also worry that they, too, will get sick, and can even experience the symptoms of the ill sibling. Some studies on childhood cancer have shown that siblings are often more impacted than the ill child (see Sori & Biank, 2006).

Sibling reactions to death. Surviving children are affected on two levels. Internally, they experience a deep personal loss that will alter the course of their life. Externally, they are affected by grieving parents (Kaplan & Joslin, 1993). Likewise, parents are also impacted by grieving children and family members, and may worry about how to help their surviving children. To avoid adding more distress to grieving parents, surviving children may put on a brave front and appear to be doing "just fine." Thus, parents may mistakenly believe that their child is coping well when he or she is not. By contrast, a parent may feel the child isn't showing appropriate grief, and misinterpret this to mean that the child isn't sad. Any of these reactions separate children and parents from sharing their grief and taking comfort from one another.

The death of a sibling is difficult for the remaining children due to the nature of the sibling relationship (Rando, 1988). The sibling subsystem is one in which children learn to get along with others, and where they have shared many experiences. A child may have lost his or her playmate, confidant, rival, or best friend. They struggle with fear and anxiety due to their close identification and similarity, and often fear they too will die (Kaplan & Joslin, 1993). For example, one adult client whose sibling was killed in childhood 30 years ago in a tragic car accident, never lost her terror of the highway, and was never able to drive, due to her anxiety.

The sudden death of a sibling can be devastating for all family members, but may leave the surviving children wondering about how their role will change within the family. They often experience survivor guilt, wondering why they are alive when a brother or sister is not (see Rando, 1988). Surviving siblings sometimes attempt to step into the role of the dead child in order to compensate for the grief in the family as well as filling the gap in the family structure (see Rando). For example, a young girl whose deceased brother was a local football hero became interested in football, and changed the way she dressed by exclusively wearing football jerseys and sports caps to emulate him and evoke his presence in the house. If this role assumption becomes permanent, the child will not grieve and can lose his or her own identity.

Siblings often experience separation anxiety in reaction to their parents' anxiety that something might happen to them as well. At the same time, they may feel resentful because parents may idolize the dead sibling, and a surviving sibling may feel unable to live up to the image of a deceased "saint" (Rando, 1988). Parents may be so consumed with grief that they are unavailable for the surviving children. Younger children who use magical thinking may feel guilty, and even believe that their hostile thoughts or wishes actually caused the death. They can be overwhelmed with sadness because of the loss of a very close, irreplaceable relationship.

Tasks in understanding death. Children are limited in their ability to understand the concept of death by their level of cognitive development, as well as their life experience (Reilly, Hasazi, & Bond, 1983). Doka (1995) discusses the concepts that children must come to understand in order to comprehend what death means. First, children must grasp that *death is universal:* everything that is living dies. Young children may wonder if some can escape death, or if it is avoidable. They also may wonder about the predictability of death; when they or a surviving parent might die.

Second, young children cannot grasp the concept that *death is irreversible* (Doka, 1995). Children might wonder how long their sister will be dead, or when she'll be alive again. Elisabeth Kübler-Ross used to tell the story of her young daughter who did not seem sad after the death of her beloved dog. When Kübler-Ross asked her why she wasn't sad, the girl replied that because they had buried the dog in the yard, she knew he'd come up with the flowers in the spring! Parents need to explain to children in simple, concrete terms; that when a person dies they no longer eat, sleep, breathe, walk, talk, or feel pain (Biank & Sori, in press-a). It is good to prepare children before a death by using teachable moments, such as seeing a dead bird and noticing how different it is than a living bird. It is not flying, singing, hopping from branch to branch, or pecking at seeds, and it never will again.

It is important not to assume that young children understand the concept that a body ceases to function on death. Children may silently wonder if their mother will get hungry or cold in the casket, how she'll go to the bathroom, or what people do when they are dead.

Hardest of all might be the task of helping a child understand why people die, or what causes death. Children who are egocentric may believe that Daddy died because they were bad or wished he was dead. When two events happen contiguously, children often assume one event caused the other. For example, a father commented, "Son, you'll be the death of me if you keep leaving your toys on the floor" and then died in a car accident two days later. His young son believed he had caused his father's death.

One way that children can be helped to understand death is if concrete language is used to explain what happens when someone dies. There is a natural tendency for parents to want to soften the blow and protect children from the harsh realities that death brings, but in the long run that can be more detrimental to their well-being. Grollman (1991b) cautions not to tell children something that they will later need to unlearn. "Distortions of reality create lasting harm. It is far healthier to share with children the quest for wisdom than to appease their curiosity with fairy tales in the guise of fact" (p. 5). Young children think concretely, and abstract language is confusing and often misleading. Therefore, it is imperative to use concrete (not metaphorical) terms when explaining death (Biank & Sori, in press-a; Lewis & Lippman, 2004). For example, parents should avoid saying that Grandpa is sleeping or Aunt Mary went on a journey to her final resting place, because the child may fear going to sleep or going on a trip. If a mother states she "lost" her husband, children may wonder why the adults aren't searching for him! This could also create the fear that if the child got lost that no one would come to find him. Using the term "passed away" is too vague for children to comprehend, and encourages them to use their imagination in a harmful way to fill in the gaps (Seibert, Drolet, & Fetro, 1993). Telling a child that Mom is "in heaven" can be confusing, and young children may wonder why Mom abandoned them. Children who do not yet understand the irreversibility of death may contemplate suicide to be with the deceased. When talking to children, always be objective and use factual words, such as Mother is "dead" or Grandpa "died."

As children mature they are gradually able to understand these concepts. Seibert, Drolet, and Fetro (1993) believe children go through stages in understanding death. In the first stage they cannot grasp the finality of death, and believe death is like sleeping or when someone is away on a trip. In the second stage, children understand that death is final, yet believe they can somehow outwit or avoid it. By stage three, children have grasped that death is both final (irreversible) and unavoidable (universal). By the time children are bordering on Piaget's formal operational stage, by about age 9 or 10, they are able to have a realistic perception of death, and can connect concrete elements (e.g., the body no longer functions) with the abstract (religious beliefs about life after death) (Biank & Sori, in press-a).

Addressing spiritual or religious issues. Children also wonder about the continuation of life after death. They question where the spirit goes when the body dies, and what it is like in heaven. Parents need to answer these questions according to their belief systems. However, it is imperative that children first be helped to understand the reality of physical death before spiritual or religious issues are discussed. The family's religious and cultural background will influence a child's understanding about the nature of death, life after death, and rituals. A child absorbs (and often misinterprets) these beliefs and customs, and will fill in the gap when something is unclear or vague.

Adults need to be aware that the child may wish to be with a dead parent, or may be angry at God for taking his or her mommy up to heaven. Children may wonder how God could be loving when he did something that made them so sad. They may feel they are being punished for being bad, or that if they would have prayed harder they could have saved Mommy. Young children may even believe that their prayers may bring Mommy back to life. All of these possibilities need to be explored and addressed, and care needs to be taken to help parents navigate these sensitive issues within their own belief system (see Biank & Sori, in press-a).

Factors that inhibit grieving. Rando (1988) points out several factors that could interfere with children's ability to grieve. If parents are unable to grieve themselves or to allow their children to express their feelings, this interferes with a child's ability to grieve. Other factors that influence the grief process include not having a secure environment or a loving adult to turn to for support. Some children may fear their parent's vulnerability and therefore try to protect them by not sharing their own sad or angry feelings. Confusion about the death, self-blame, or ambivalence toward the deceased also complicates the normal grieving process. Fogarty (2000) points out that unaddressed magical thinking (such as that the child somehow caused the death) can lead to serious psychopathology as the child matures into adulthood.

For example, Maria, a woman in her mid-50s, had experienced severe pain in both legs since she was a child. She had visited the most renowned doctors and hospitals in the country, and had undergone countless expensive diagnostic tests. No one could identify the source of her debilitating pain. She was referred for counseling by her most recent physician. In the first session, as the family therapist started a genogram, Maria's tragic story emerged.

Maria came from a large Mexican-American family. One day when she was about 10 her mother sent her to the store on her bicycle, and asked her to take her younger sister, Rosa, who rode on the back of her bike. As she turned a corner a car jumped the curb and struck them. Maria awoke in the emergency room with two broken legs, with several doctors and nurses in attendance. Her sister lay silently across the room. Maria kept protesting to the doctors that she was fine, and that they needed to check Rosa, who had been in her care. She was told her sister was fine and was asleep.

Maria spent a week in the hospital. Every time she asked where her sister was she was told Rosa was one floor above her and doing fine. Finally her mother and their priest brought her home from the hospital. As they parked in the driveway the priest asked if she noticed all the cars, and explained that her sister had died at the scene of the accident, had been buried that very morning, and the cars belonged to the mourners who had returned to their house from the cemetery. She was told not to cry. In shock, she stumbled into the house where all conversation ceased. She spent several days alone in her room feeling numb.

Her family blamed her and was forever changed. Maria carried the blame, guilt, responsibility, trauma, and emotional scarring with her throughout her life. Her pain was manifested in somatic symptoms that were located at the site where she had been physically injured (see Griffith & Griffith, 1994; Minuchin, Rosman, & Baker, 1978, for treating psychosomatic issues.)

It is imperative that children be able to share their feelings and memories of their loved one with others in the family.

Predicting more positive outcomes. The impact of the loss will be reduced if adequate information is shared by people who are close to the child before the death. For instance, a parent or other significant person who sits with the child and prepares the child using age-appropriate language can give the child confidence to be able to say goodbye to a loved one. This will create a foundation for their grieving process. In the case of the death of a parent, the quality of the relationship with the remaining parent is crucial in helping the child navigate the future. If a parent is distracted or unavailable, children can feel abandoned and left to their own discretion as to how to make sense of the loss. In the event a surviving parent is unavailable, resilient children often find an outside person, such as an extended family member or teacher, to offer them support and encouragement. In addition, having a community of support for the family helps both parents and children to cope and move forward (Biank & Sori, in press-b).

Four things parents need to offer their children. Grieving children need information, reassurance, the opportunity to express their feelings and concerns, and to be involved with the dying person, according to Monroe (1995). A parent needs to make sure that each child understands how the person died, what death means, and that it was not their fault. Although parents may share this information, it is also their attitude that makes a difference in how children interpret the meaning of what is said. For instance, if parents are too consumed with their own grief and answer questions abruptly or refuse to answer them, the child learns the parent is unapproachable and death is not a topic to be discussed. Children naturally want to protect their parents from additional grief, so they often hide their true feelings. It also helps children to be included in conversations both prior to and after the death, so that they feel involved and a valued member of the family. This includes being a part of planning the funeral, where children might choose a song or hymn to be played, pictures to be displayed, or write a poem or letter to be read or enclosed in the casket. After the death it is up to family to set the pace for conversations and rituals in remembering the loved one at special occasions, anniversaries, and in everyday conversations.

Playful activities. Many who work with bereaved children find play activities are helpful in allowing children to express their emotions and work through their grief. Modalities using art, puppets, music, and pictures are all extremely helpful in giving children and families a common venue. Play is the language of children and it is how they make sense out of incomprehensible events in their world. For example, one 5-year-old girl who discovered her adolescent brother's body following a heart attack after a sporting event, repeatedly used a dollhouse to reenact finding her older brother's body, calling the ambulance, and his body being taken away to the hospital. She directed the therapist to use doll figures and play with her as she enacted all these events in great detail. (See Gill, 1991, for ideas that can be adapted to help children traumatized from a death experience.)

One activity that is useful in helping children process how a death has impacted their lives is to have them share their "impossible and scariest tasks" (Biank & Sori, 2003). A turtle puppet is used to introduce children and families to the idea that some things make you want to hide like a turtle, but there are things that also help the turtle come out of his shell. The bumblebee puppet—that shouldn't be able to fly because of his great body mass—illustrates overcoming a great obstacle to do what is impossible. Children can then write or draw their own illness or death-related experiences. The puppets can be used to help them express their feelings related to these events, which can then be validated by parents and the therapist. For example, one child's scariest task was having to say goodbye to his father who was on life support.

What helped him come out of his shell was knowing that he had the support of his mother and grandparents, who stayed close to his side. Another child's impossible task was going to sleep at night without her mother being there to sing their special song. What helped her was when her father found a tape of her mother singing, and he played it for her each night when he tucked her in bed.

Some families benefit from bringing in photographs and mementos to create a memory box or "treasure chest" (Schutten, Foraker-Koons, & Sori, in press). This helps reinforce the concept of keeping the memory of the loved one in the child's heart and head. When families share memories and stories of the deceased, connections are strengthened as people come together to share their grief. This also allows counselors to normalize and validate differences in family's grief reactions.

Excell (1991) suggests that bereaved children draw pictures of themselves before the death, at the point of the death, and currently. She also has children create three different drawings. The first is what causes death (e.g., murder, cancer, car accidents), second is to draw what death looks like (e.g., a monster or angel of death), and third is what happens after death (e.g., the funeral service or graveside gathering).

One way to "externalize the problem" (White & Epston, 1990), which is the death or the cause of death, is to have families write a letter to death or to the illness. Children also may draw a picture of what they think the cause of death (e.g., cancer, a hurricane) looks like. Additional ideas may be found in Biank and Sori (in press-a), Smith and Pennells (1995), and Webb (1993b).

BRIEF VIGNETTE

Jill's biological father, Tom, called a local cancer support center to inquire about services for Jill, her half-sister, and himself. Jill was 10 and her mother was dying of a brain tumor. She lived with her mother, her stepfather Bill, and her half-sister Amy. Amy's father was from a relationship that Jill's mother had between the two marriages, and Jill's stepfather was in the process of adopting Amy. Jill's maternal grandmother had come from out of state to help care for her dying daughter. Tom also was remarried, and lived in a neighboring state with his wife, their newborn son, and his wife's two sons from her first marriage. Jill visited her father and his family on a regular basis, and they often included her half-sister Amy in these visits.

Jill had experienced several changes in her family structure even before her mother became ill. First she lived with both biological parents until the divorce when she was 4. She and her mother lived alone for several months before a boyfriend (Amy's father) moved in, and within a year Amy was born. This relationship was short-lived, and for a year the family household included Jill, Mom, and Amy. When Jill was 8 her mother remarried, and was diagnosed with cancer soon thereafter. Despite all the chemotherapy and radiation treatments that left Mom violently ill and very weak, the cancer spread relentlessly.

During this period Jill assumed more and more responsibilities, such as cooking, cleaning, sometimes holding Mom's head when she vomited and was too weak to make it out of bed, and cleaning up after her. Her stepfather worked long hours to help cover some of the medical bills, as the family had limited health care insurance. By the time she was 10 and her mother was in the terminal stage of the illness, Jill had assumed most of the parenting responsibilities for her 6-year-old sister. She fed her dinner, cleaned up, made sure she did her homework and took a bath, and got her to bed. In the mornings she was up at 6:00 a.m. to fix Amy's cereal, help her dress, and be sure she had her backpack and made it on time for the bus.

Jill was a resilient child. Despite the tremendous loss of her mother's time and attention due to the illness, Jill was able to survive and do well in school academically and socially. Having the ongoing love and support of her father during those difficult years helped Jill to believe in herself and in her future.

Tom came in for a couple of individual sessions to discuss how to help Jill, and brought Jill and Amy for a few family sessions. Both children joined a group for children who have a parent or sibling with cancer, and Tom joined the corresponding parent group. Individual sessions with Tom focused on the importance of preparing the children for her impending death, and how to talk to them using language and explanations that they would understand. Also discussed was how children need to be able to say goodbye to a parent. The family sessions focused on the changes in the household the children had experienced since their mother had become ill, what cancer was (and what it was not), and any magical thoughts the children had (e.g., that they caused the illness). With prompting, Tom clarified that cancer was not contagious, that nothing the children did caused the disease, and that nothing they could do would cure it. Tom told the children that the doctors were doing all that they could for their mother, and that there was one more medicine they wanted to try. However, they didn't know if the medicine would help. Mom's body was getting sicker and weaker, and they had to give her lots of medicine so she wasn't in so much pain. That was why she slept so much and could not do things like play or read to them like she used to.

Jill did well in the children's group where she learned about cancer, and was able to share her feelings and talk about changes in her family. Amy participated quietly and stayed close to Jill's side.

After only a few weeks of counseling Tom called the center to report that his ex-wife had died the previous day. He told the counselor the following:

> Yesterday I was out of town and got the call that Mary was dying. I caught the first plane home and went right to the house to pick up Jill and Amy, to take them home with me. It was about midnight and we were driving home when I suddenly remembered what you'd said about preparing the kids. So I pulled into a parking lot, turned around, and asked the kids if they knew what was happening to their mother. They shook their heads no, so I told them that the medicine had not worked and that there was nothing more the doctors could do for their mommy. Her body was just too sick and too weak to go on working much longer. She couldn't wake up, eat, or drink anymore, and it was hard for her to breath. Then I said that the doctors think her body is just wearing out and that she will soon die. They began sobbing, and I did, too. I climbed into the backseat and just held them both while we cried together. Later we drove home and they slept for several hours. But I also remembered what you said about how important it is for them to say goodbye. So I got them up very early and drove them back to Mary's. I told them again that Mommy would probably not be able to live much longer and would soon die, that they could go in and talk to her, and while she couldn't talk, she would hear them. I told them they could say goodbye if they wanted to. I asked if they had any questions and if they understood. Jill said she did, and that she wanted to go in and talk to her mother. Amy just stood quietly, holding Jill's hand, sucking her thumb.
>
> When Jill went into her mother's room she climbed up on the hospital bed and lay on top of her mother. Sobbing, she told her mother that she loved her so much, but that it was OK for her to die now because she had been so sick and had hurt so much. She then said, "But please, Mommy, please ask Jesus into your heart so you can go to heaven and Amy and I will know that we will see you again! Amy's here and she loves you too. We both will always love you, Mommy! You'll always be in our hearts."

Tom then tearfully continued:

> After a while I took both kids back to my house, and Mary died later that morning. I explained, just like we talked about, what

it meant that their mommy was dead—that she wouldn't talk to them anymore, that they wouldn't see her after the funeral, that she wouldn't eat or sleep or play anymore, but that they'd always keep her love and memory in their hearts. I think Jill understands, but am not sure Amy gets it. But Jill's stepdad said he's willing to come in for counseling with Amy now. Coming here has really helped us so much. The kids loved coming here, and want to come in to see you soon …

Later that day a huge bouquet of flowers arrived at the center—with handwritten thank-you notes from Jill, Amy, and Tom.

Several days after the funeral, the entire extended family of nine came in for a session: Tom, his wife, and their three children, Jill and Amy, Bill (Mary's husband), and Mary's mother, Betty. Betty would soon be moving back to her home, so it was important to include her in this session. There were two primary goals for this meeting. First, each person had an opportunity to share memories of Mary and express what the loss meant to them. Jill talked about many happy memories of her mommy playing Barbies with her, and reading to her and Amy. Amy said she'd miss Mommy's macaroni and cheese, and her hugs. Bill expressed his anger at losing his wife so soon after they'd married, and for all the dreams they'd had that would now never happen.

The second goal was to have all the adults begin to discuss how to maintain as much stability as possible in the lives of Jill and Amy. With Grandma leaving soon they would lose the daily presence of another loving figure in their lives, so they discussed when she could come for another visit and how they would keep in telephone contact. This was also a tremendous loss for Betty, who had lost her only daughter, and had her own grief issues. Betty was given the name of a cancer organization close to her home where she might be able to attend a bereavement group.

Tom, his wife, and Bill all discussed how important it was for Jill and Amy to be together as much as possible. Jill had been a surrogate mother to Amy, so it would be another loss to both of them if she abruptly moved away to live with her father's family. It was also pointed out that Jill might need help in letting go of her role as a parentified child. Together they worked out a schedule for the summer where the two children would remain together and alternate where they stayed.

Bill, who was clearly very angry, was encouraged to come in for both individual and family sessions. Amy, who was only 6, seemed somewhat dazed and did not seem to understand what death really meant. She would need extra support. In the fall Jill would go to live with her father permanently, so Amy would lose not only her mother and grandmother but also daily contact with her sister, on whom she depended for so much. Jill would experience the same secondary losses but also would have to change schools and loosen the connections with her friends and her scout troop.

In a follow-up couples session, Tom and his wife discussed the implications that Mary's death would have on their family, and how it would be when the children visited, and when Jill moved in with them in the fall. Luckily, Tom's wife was a loving and understanding mother who was dedicated to doing all she could to help Jill and Amy. They were encouraged to schedule regular times as a couple to talk about issues as they arose, so feelings wouldn't be bottled up, as well as to schedule "date nights" when they could be alone without children. The couple also explored how to help Jill adjust to all the secondary losses, including the loss of her role as a parent figure to Amy. They agreed to call if they felt they needed another appointment.

About a month later Tom called in rather urgently and requested a family session as soon as possible. Mary had been cremated and Jill had possession of the urn. They were concerned because Jill talked to the urn, and made everyone line up and say goodnight to her "mom" each night before bed. Jill would put the urn by her bed at night and pray and talk to her mother.

When the therapist met alone with Jill and broached the subject of her mother's ashes, Jill shared the following:

> I know that it's just my mother's ashes in the urn, and that she's dead. But her spirit is in heaven, and it just makes me feel better having it to talk to. It makes me feel like she hears me and that I'm closer to her. I don't think I'll need it much longer though. Bill said we would have this ceremony, where we will all go to Pigeons Point. My mom used to love climbing way up to the top where you can see the hills for miles and miles. Then we will all say a prayer and open the urn and let her ashes blow in the wind. I'm not ready to do that yet, but I will be soon. I'll let them know when.

With Jill's permission, this information was shared with her father and stepmother. The counselor suggested that they let Jill bring a few of her mom's personal articles (such as a scarf or nightgown) to their home. Having a transitional object might help her let go of the urn and sleep better. A month later they had their celebration.

Jill made an easy transition to Dad's house and thrived in her new home. Bill, however, did not follow through with counseling for himself or for Amy. Tom and his wife became a huge source of support for Amy, who continued regular visits in their home.

REFERENCES

Batten, M., & Oltjenbruns, K. A. (1999). Adolescent sibling bereavement as a catalyst for spiritual development: A model for understanding. *Death Studies, 23*(6), 529–547.

Biank, N., & Sori, C. F. (in press-a). Integrating spirituality when working with children and families experiencing loss of a parent. In K. B. Helmeke & C. F. Sori (Eds.), *The therapist's notebook for integrating spirituality in counseling II: More homework, handouts, and activities for use in psychotherapy*. Binghamton, NY: Haworth.

Biank, N., & Sori, C. F. (in press-b). Coping circles: Exploring children's ability to manage in times of stress. In C. Elias & L. Jameyfield (Eds.), *The therapist's notebook: Resources for working with children*. Binghamton, NY: Haworth.

Biank, N. & Sori, C. F. (2003). A child's impossible and scariest task. In C. F. Sori, L. L. Hecker, & Associates, *The therapist's notebook for children and adolescents: Homework, handouts, and activities for use in psychotherapy* (pp. 18–24). Binghamton, NY: Haworth.

Boss, P. (1999). *Ambiguous loss: Learning to live with unresolved grief*. Cambridge, MA: Harvard University Press.

Casini, K. K., & Rogers, J. L. (1996). *Death and the classroom: A teacher's guide to assist grieving students*. Cincinnati, OH: Griefwork of Cincinnati.

Doka, K. J. (1995). *Children mourning: Mourning children*. Washington, DC: Hospice Foundation of America.

Excell, J. A. (1991). A child's perception of death. In D. Papadatou & C. Papadatos (Eds.), *Children and death*. New York: Hemisphere Publishing Corporation.

Figley, C. R. (Ed.). (1986). *Trauma and its wake: Tramatic stress theory, research, and intervention* (vol. II). *(Psychological Stress Series, No. 8)*. Levittown, PA: Brunner/Mazel.

Fogarty, J. A. (2000). *The magical thoughts of grieving children: Treating children with complicated mourning and advice for parents*. Amityville, NY: Baywood Publishing Co.

Gil, E. (1991). *The healing power of play: Therapy with abused children*. New York: Guilford.

Gordon, N. S., Farberow, N. L., & Maida, C. A. (1999). *Children and disasters*. New York: Brunner/Mazel.

Griffith, J. L., & Griffith, M. E. (1994). *The body speaks: Therapeutic dialogues for mind-body problems*. New York: Basic Books.

Grollman, E. A. (1991a). *Talking about death: A dialogue between parent and child* (3rd ed.). Boston: Beacon Press.

Grollman, E. A. (1991b). Explaining death to children and to ourselves. In D. Papadatou & C. Papadatos (Eds.), *Children and death* (pp. 3–8). New York: Hemisphere Publishing Corporation, a member of the Taylor & Francis Group.

Johnson, F. (1998). *Trauma in the lives of children: Crisis and stress management techniques for teachers, counselors, and students service professionals* (2nd ed.). Alameda, CA: Hunter House.

Kaplan, C. P., & Joslin, H. (1993). Accidental sibling death: Case of Peter, age 6. In N. B. Webb (Ed.), *Helping bereaved children: A handbook for practitioners* (pp. 118–136). New York: Guilford Press.

Klicker, R. L. (2000). *A student dies, a school mourns: Dealing with death and loss in the school community*. Ann Arbor, MI: Accelerated Development.

La Greca, A. M., Sevin, S. W., & Sevin, E. L. (2005). *After the storm: A guide to help children cope with the psychological effects of a hurricane*. Coral Gables, FL: 7-Dippity, Inc. Retrieved on September 1, 2005, from University of Miami, College of Arts and Sciences Web site: http://www.psy.miami.edu/.

La Greca, A. M., Silverman, W. S., Vernberg, E. M., & Roberts, M. C. (Eds.) (2002). *Helping children cope with disasters and terrorism*. Washington, DC: American Psychological Association.

Lewis, P. G., & Lippman, J. G. (2004). *Helping children cope with the death of a parent: A guide for the first year.* Westport, CT: Praeger.

Linesch, D. (1993). *Art therapy with children in crisis: Overcoming resistance through nonverbal expression*. New York: Brunner/Mazel.

Matthews, J. D. (1999). The grieving child in the school environment. In J. D. Davidson & K. J. Doka (Ed.), *Living with grief: At work, at school, at worship* (pp. 95–113). Levittown, PA: Brunner/Mazel.

Minuchin, S., Rosman, B., & Baker, L. (1978). *Psychosomatic families: Anorexia nervosa in context*. Cambridge, MA: Harvard University Press.

Monroe, B. (1995). It is impossible not to communicate—Helping the grieving family. In S. C. Smith & S. M. Pennells (Eds.), *Interventions with bereaved children*. (pp. 87–106). Bristol, PA: Jessica Kingsley.

Rando, T. A. (1988). *How to go on living when someone you love dies*. New York: Bantam Books.

Reilly, T. P., Hasazi, J. E., & Bond, L. A. (1983). Children's conceptions of death and personal mortality. *Journal of Pediatric Psychology, 8*(1), 21–31.

Schutten, B., Foraker-Koons, K., & Sori, C. F. (in press). Treasure chest. In C. Elias & L. Jameyfield (Eds.), *The therapist's notebook: Resources for working with children*. Binghamton, NY: Haworth.

Seibert, D., Drolet, J. C., & Fetro, J. V. (1993). *Are you sad too? Helping children deal with loss and death*. Santa Cruz, CA: ETR Associates.

Smith, S. C., & Pennells, S. M. (1995). *Interventions with bereaved children*. Bristol, PA: Jessica Kingsley.

Sori, C. F., & Biank, N. M. (2006). Counseling children and families experiencing serious illness, chap. 11 in this volume.

Webb, N. B. (1991). (Ed.) *Play therapy with children in crisis: A casebook for practitioners*. New York: Guilford.

Webb, N. B. (1993a). Assessment of the bereaved child. In N. B. Webb (Ed.), *Helping bereaved children: A handbook for practitioners* (pp. 19–42). New York: Guilford.

Webb, N. B. (Ed.). (1993b). *Helping bereaved children: A handbook for practitioners*. New York: Guilford.

White, M., & Epston, D. (1990). *Narrative means to therapeutic ends*. New York: W. W. Norton.

Index

B

C

D

E

F

M

N

O

P

Q

R

S

T

Y

www.ingramcontent.com/pod-product-compliance
Ingram Content Group Australia Pty Ltd
76 Discovery Rd, Dandenong South VIC 3175, AU
AUHW011837030125
405075AU00010B/104

9 781138 872790